Andrew Phipps & Robert Schwandl

METROS & TRAMS IN JAPAN

Hokkaido

● **Sapporo**

Hakodate

Tohoku

Band 2 - Nord- & Zentraljapan
Vol. 2 - North & Central Japan

Sendai ●

H o n s h u

Takaoka   ● **Toyama**   *Kanto*   ● **Utsunomiya**
Kanazawa   **Nagano**   **Saitama**
    Tokyo
● **Fukui**   *Chubu*   **Yokohama**   Band 1 | Vol. 1
    Chiba   Tokyo Region

Band 3 - West- & Südjapan   **Nagoya**
Vol. 3 - West & South Japan   **Shizuoka**
    Kansai   **Kyoto**
Chugoku   **Kobe**   **Toyohashi**
Okayama   **Osaka**
Hiroshima   **Takamatsu**

Kitakyushu   **Matsuyama**
    Kochi
Fukuoka   *Shikoku*
Kumamoto
Nagasaki   *Kyushu*   **Naha**
    Okinawa
Kagoshima

Berlin 2017

Andrew Phipps & Robert Schwandl

METROS & TRAMS IN JAPAN

Band 2: Nord- & Zentraljapan
Vol. 2: North & Central Japan

Unser Dank für ihre Hilfe geht an | Our sincere thanks are due to:

Anthony Robins, Bernhard Kußmagk, Felix Thoma and Oliver Mayer.

Robert Schwandl Verlag
Hektorstraße 3
D-10711 Berlin

Tel. 030 - 3759 1284 (0049 - 30 - 3759 1284)
Fax 030 - 3759 1285 (0049 - 30 - 3759 1285)

www.robert-schwandl.de
books@robert-schwandl.de

1. Auflage, 2017

Text & Fotos ohne Vermerk | Text & Photos without credits © Andrew Phipps
Fotos mit Vermerk RS | Photos marked RS © Robert Schwandl
Netzpläne | Network Maps © Robert Schwandl

Druck: Ruksaldruck, Berlin

ISBN 978-3-936573-52-7

Der erste Band (Region Tokyo) ist 2016 erschienen, der dritte (West- und Südjapan) erscheint voraussichtlich 2018/19.
The first volume (Tokyo Region) was published in 2016, the third (West & South) is expected in 2018/19.

Sendai Subway

Echitetsu, Fukui

Tosaden, Kochi

VORWORT

Sie haben nun Band 2 unserer Trilogie über Japans städtischen Schienenverkehr in Ihren Händen. In Band 1 konzentrierten wir uns auf die Metropolregion Tokyo mit ihrem riesigen Netz an intensiv genutzten U-Bahn- und S-Bahn-Linien. Der vorliegende Band enthält hingegen eine Mischung aus großen städtischen Zentren (Sapporo, Sendai und Nagoya) mit modernen U-Bahn- und S-Bahn-Netzen und mittelgroßen Provinzstädten mit Straßenbahnen und/oder besonderen Vorortbahnen. Einige der kleineren Unternehmen, die in diesem Buch beschrieben werden, haben mit Fahrgastrückgang und Investitionsdefizit zu kämpfen, was einen interessanten Gegensatz zu den allgemein besser dastehenden Betrieben in Band 1 darstellt.

In diesem Band reisen wir durch Nord- und Zentraljapan. Wir starten auf der nördlichen Insel Hokkaido, wo wir Sapporo und Hakodate besuchen, bevor wir mit dem *Hokkaido/Tohoku Shinkansen* nach Sendai in der Region Tohoku im Norden der Hauptinsel Honshu fahren. Dann lassen wir Tokyo links liegen (siehe Band 1), steigen in Omiya um und machen eine Rundfahrt durch die Region Chubu in Zentraljapan (*Hokuriku Shinkansen* nach Kanazawa, *Limited Express „Shirasagi"* von Kanazawa nach Nagoya und dann *Tokaido Shinkansen* nach Shizuoka). Wir legen einen Zwischenstopp ein in Städten mit Straßenbahnen bzw. Lokalbahnen sowohl am Japanischen Meer als auch am Pazifik und besuchen Nagoya, das Zentrum von Japans drittgrößter Metropolregion.

Als Abschluss machen wir zwei kleine Abstecher – auf Japans viertgrößte Insel Shikoku sowie zur tropischen Insel Okinawa im äußersten Süden des Landes. Diese Regionen gehören eigentlich in Band 3 (Westen und Süden), doch aus Platzgründen und um das Kansai-Ballungsgebiet mit Osaka, Kobe und Kyoto nicht auf zwei Bände aufteilen zu müssen, haben wir sie hier mit hineingenommen.

Wir hoffen, dass die Informationen, Fotos und detaillierten Netzkarten sowohl für erstmalige als auch für wiederkehrende Besucher Japans hilfreich sind. Wir haben so sorgfältig wie möglich recherchiert. Aber teilen Sie uns bitte mit, wenn Sie irgendwelche Fehler bemerken.

Die englischsprachige Zeitschrift „Bullet-In" der *Japanese Railway Society* (www.japaneserailwaysociety.com) hält Sie stets am Laufenden über aktuelle Entwicklungen.

London, im Februar 2017
Andrew Phipps

Inhalt | *Contents*

■ **Intro** 4

▨ **SAPPORO** 16

▨ **HAKODATE** 36

■ **SENDAI** 40

■ **UTSUNOMIYA** 51

▨ **NAGANO** 52

■ **TOYAMA** 56

■ **TAKAOKA** 66

▨ **KANAZAWA** 72

▨ **FUKUI** 76

▨ **NAGOYA** 82

▨ **TOYOHASHI** 114

■ **SHIZUOKA** 118

▨ **TAKAMATSU** 122

▨ **KOCHI** 126

▨ **MATSUYAMA** 130

■ **NAHA** 138

Quellen und Verweise
Sources & References 142

FOREWORD

Welcome to Volume 2 of our trilogy covering Japan's urban rail systems. In Volume 1 we concentrated on the Tokyo metropolitan region with its vast network of intensively-used metros and suburban railways. This volume contains a varied mix of large urban centres (Sapporo, Sendai and Nagoya) with modern metro and suburban rail systems together with medium-sized provincial cities served by tramways and/or local railways. Some of the smaller undertakings described in this book have struggled with declining ridership and limited resources for investment, providing an interesting contrast with the generally busier and more prosperous concerns covered in Volume 1.

Our primary focus is northern and central Japan which we traverse in a broadly north-to-south direction. Thus, our journey commences on the northern island of Hokkaido where we visit Sapporo and Hakodate before heading south on the Hokkaido/Tohoku Shinkansen to Sendai in the northern Tohoku region on the main island of Honshu. By-passing Tokyo (see Volume 1), we change trains at Omiya and then take a tour around the Chubu region of central Japan (Hokuriku Shinkansen to Kanazawa, Limited-Express 'Shirasagi' from Kanazawa to Nagoya, and Tokaido Shinkansen to Shizuoka) stopping off at cities with tramways and/or local railways along both the Sea of Japan and Pacific coasts and visiting the major city of Nagoya, the centre of Japan's third largest metropolitan area.

In addition, we have taken the geographical liberty of including two out-of-sequence side trips in this volume - to Shikoku, Japan's fourth largest island, and to the tropical island of Okinawa in the far south of the country. These are effectively tasters for Volume 3 (West & South) which we have covered here for space reasons, and to avoid splitting the major Kansai conurbation (Osaka, Kobe, Kyoto) over two volumes.

We hope the information, photos and detailed network maps in this book will assist first-time and returning visitors who wish to explore Japan's fascinating urban transport scene. As always, we have attempted to ensure that the information in this book is accurate but please let us know if you notice any errors.

For those wishing to keep up to date with Japanese railway developments, the English-language journal 'Bullet-In' published by the Japanese Railway Society (www.japaneserailwaysociety.com) contains a regular news update and other articles.

London, February 2017
Andrew Phipps

Takaoka - Sakashitamachi – Manyosen MLRV #1006 (Niigata Transys, 2009) ▶ Takaoka-Eki

EINFÜHRUNG

In Band 1 (Region Tokyo) gaben wir eine allgemeine Einführung in die japanischen Schnellbahnen mit besonderem Augenmerk auf U-Bahnen und wechselseitigen Betrieb mit Vorortbahnen. In diesem Kapitel betrachten wir Allgemeines über japanische Straßenbahnen und Lokalbahnen (JR, privat oder halböffentlich), da solche in vielen Städten dieses Bandes sowie des kommenden Bandes 3 (West- und Südjapan) vorhanden sind.

Straßenbahnen

Für diejenigen, die Japan mit moderner Verkehrstechnik wie den Hochgeschwindigkeitszügen Shinkansen, Einschienen- oder Maglev-Bahnen assoziieren, können japanische Straßenbahnen eine Überraschung sein. Auch wenn es mittlerweile allmähliche Anzeichen für eine Modernisierung gibt, litten japanische Straßenbahnen jahrelang an mangelnden Investitionen und viele Betriebe hinterlassen auch heute noch einen veralteten Eindruck hinsichtlich Fahrzeugpark und Infrastruktur. Für viele Bahnfreunde ist natürlich gerade diese Mischung aus Tradition und Moderne das, was die japanische Nahverkehrslandschaft so faszinierend macht.

Viele japanische Städte hatten Anfang des 20. Jahrhunderts Straßenbahnen und am Ende des Zweiten Weltkriegs 1945 gab es noch 58 Betriebe. Jedoch kamen Straßenbahnen in der Nachkriegszeit während des schnellen Wirtschaftswachstums und Anstiegs der Zahl von Privatautos aus der Mode und viele Netze wurden stillgelegt. Zuerst traf es die kleineren Städte, doch Ende der 1970er Jahre waren auch die meisten Straßenbahnen in den größeren Städten verschwunden und durch U-Bahnen und/oder Busse ersetzt worden: Kawasaki 1969; Osaka 1969; Kobe 1971; Tokyo 1972; Yokohama 1972; Nagoya 1974; Sendai 1976; Kyoto 1978; und Fukuoka 1979. Einzelne Strecken überlebten in Tokyo, Osaka, Kyoto und Sapporo, jedoch findet man

INTRODUCTION

We gave a general introduction to Japanese urban railways in Volume 1 (Tokyo Region), paying particular attention to metro systems and reciprocal through-running services. Here we take a closer look at Japanese tramways and local railways (JR, private and third-sector), which feature in many of the cities covered in this volume and in forthcoming Volume 3 (West & South Japan).

Tramways

Japanese tramways may come as something of a surprise to those who associate Japan with modern transport technology such as Shinkansen high-speed trains, monorails and maglev guided-transit systems. Although there are now gradual signs of modernisation, Japanese tramways have suffered from a lack of investment over many years and many systems still have a very old-fashioned feel, with much ageing rolling stock and infrastructure still in evidence. Of course, for many enthusiasts, it is this very mix of the traditional and modern that makes the Japanese transport scene so fascinating.

Many Japanese cities had tramways in the early 20th century and there were still 58 systems in operation at the end of World War II in 1945. However, in the post-war period of rapid economic growth and rising car ownership tramways were viewed as out-of-date and many systems were abandoned. Closures initially affected mainly smaller undertakings but by the end of the 1970s most tramways in the largest cities had closed and been replaced by new metro systems and/or buses, with the last trams running on the main networks as follows: Kawasaki, 1969; Osaka, 1969; Kobe, 1971; Tokyo, 1972; Yokohama, 1972; Nagoya, 1974; Sendai, 1976; Kyoto, 1978; and Fukuoka, 1979. Residual lines remain in operation in Tokyo,

Straßenbahnen heute am ehesten in mittelgroßen Städten. Die letzten wesentlichen Netzstilllegungen gab es in Kitakyushu (2000) und Gifu (2005), so dass heute insgesamt nur noch 21 Betriebe existieren.

Nach dem Zweiten Weltkrieg wurden in Japan nur zwei völlig neue Straßenbahnen eröffnet, in Takaoka (1948) und die Portram in Toyama (2006). Aber auch in Städten, in denen eine vollständige Schließung abgewendet werden konnte, haben die Betreiber oft versucht, Verluste zu reduzieren, indem sie unwirtschaftliche Linien kürzten und sich auf Hauptlinien konzentrierten (z. B. Hakodate, Kagoshima). In der Tat ist es überraschend, dass angesichts sinkender Fahrgastzahlen und mangelnder staatlicher Zuschüsse doch so viele Betriebe überlebt haben.

Die Einstellung gegenüber Straßenbahnen hat sich in den letzten Jahren jedoch etwas gebessert, da man erkannt hat, dass sie dazu beitragen können, die Abhängigkeit vom Auto zu verringern, die Stadtzentren zu revitalisieren und den Mobilitätsbedürfnissen einer alternden Bevölkerung gerecht zu werden. Mancherorts unterstützte die Zentralregierung oder die Kommune finanziell den Kauf neuer Niederflurwagen (Toyama, Hankai Tramway in Osaka), Netzerweiterungen in Stadtzentren (Sapporo, Toyama) und Umstrukturierungsprogramme zur Rettung von ums Überleben kämpfenden Privatbahnen (Takaoka und Fukui). Eine Finanzierung aus öffentlichen Mitteln spielte auch eine wesentliche Rolle bei der Umsetzung von Japans erster moderner Stadtbahn (Portram in Toyama), wodurch ein größeres Interesse an potenziellen neuen Straßenbahnen geweckt wurde. Zahlreiche Stadtbahn-Machbarkeitsstudien, auf offizielle oder private Initiative, wurden im ganzen Land durchgeführt, darunter Osaka (Sakai), Yokohama und Hamamatsu, doch bislang wurde erst der Bau einer einzigen Linie beschlossen, nämlich in Utsunomiya, wo bis 2019 eine 14,6 km lange Strecke errichtet werden soll.

Trotz dieser Anzeichen eines Wandels haben Straßenbahnfreunde wohl noch genügend Möglichkeiten, die alten japanischen Straßenbahnen zu besuchen. Die Größe der

Osaka, Kyoto and Sapporo but most surviving networks are in medium-sized cities. The last major network closures occurred in Kitakyushu (2000) and Gifu (2005) leaving a total of 21 systems operating today.

Only two completely new tramways have opened in Japan since World War II, Takaoka (1948) and Toyama's Portram (2006), and there have been very few extensions to existing networks; on the contrary, even where complete closure has been avoided, operators have often sought to reduce losses by pruning uneconomic lines and concentrating services on limited core networks (e.g. Hakodate, Kagoshima). In fact, it is surprising that so many systems have survived given declining ridership and, until recently, the lack of government subsidy or support for tramways.

Attitudes to trams have, however, become somewhat more positive in recent years with the recognition that they can help to reduce car dependency, revitalise city centres and cater for the mobility needs of an ageing population. There have been small-scale examples of central government and/or local authority support for tramways including the purchase or part-funding of new low-floor cars (Toyama, Osaka – Hankai Tramway), city centre network extensions (Sapporo, Toyama) and financial restructuring packages to rescue and revitalise struggling privately-owned lines (Takaoka and Fukui). Public-sector funding was also a key ingredient in the development and implementation of Japan's first modern light rail scheme (Portram, Toyama) which has fuelled greater interest in the potential for new tramway projects. Numerous official and unofficial light rail feasibility studies have been undertaken around the country, including Osaka (Sakai), Yokohama and Hamamatsu, though to date the only scheme authorised for construction is a 14.6 km line in Utsunomiya which is scheduled to open in 2019.

However, despite these signs of progress, enthusiasts wishing to sample old-style Japanese trams still have plenty of opportunities to do so. The remaining 21 net-

Kochi - Sambashidori-Itchome – Tosaden #209 (Hitachi, 1952) ▶ Norden | *north* & #1001 (Alna Koki, 1981) ▶ Süden | *south*

Hakodate - Goryokaku-mae – #8002 (Niigata, 1962
- umgebaut von | re-bodied by Alna Koki) ▶ Hakodate Dock-mae

Kochi - Kagamigawa-bashi – Tosaden #615
(eigene Werkstatt | company workshop, 1959) ▶ Gomen-Machi

verbleibenden 21 Netze reicht von 4,7 km (Okayama) bis 34,9 km (Hiroshima), wobei es sich meist um relativ kurze Strecken zwischen den Innenstädten und den inneren Vororten handelt, dazu kommen einzelne längere Strecken wie die Arakawa Line durch die Vororte Tokyos (12,2 km) oder die Miyajima Line, eine Überlandbahn in Hiroshima (16,1 km). Die Netze sind in der Regel in sich abgeschlossen, nur in Fukui und Hiroshima verkehren Interurban-Fahrzeuge auch auf dem städtischen Netz und seit 2016 gibt es wechselseitigen Betrieb zwischen der Straßenbahn von Fukui und der Echizen Railway. Einen ungewöhnlichen Mischverkehr findet man in Kyoto, wo die Hama-Otsu-Straßenbahn von Keihan auf die Tozai Line der Municipal Subway übergeht, auch wenn die eingesetzten 4-Wagen-Züge eher U-Bahn- als Straßenbahnwagen gleichen. Die japanischen Straßenbahnen sind überwiegend in Privatbesitz (13 Unternehmen, die teilweise auch Eisenbahnen betreiben), aber es gibt auch fünf traditionelle städtische Verkehrsbetriebe (Sapporo, Hakodate, Tokyo [Toei], Kumamoto und Kagoshima) sowie einen neu gegründeten (Tosaden in Kochi), außerdem zwei gemischt staatlich-private Unternehmen (Manyosen in Takaoka; Portram in Toyama).

Während einige Straßenbahnen ganz oder überwiegend auf Strecken mit eigenem Gleiskörper verkehren und Hochbahnsteige aufweisen (z. B. Tokyos Arakawa und Setagaya Line), herrschen die straßenbündigen Netze vor, wobei die Gleise meist in Fahrbahnmitte liegen und durch weiße Linien abgetrennt sind. Es sei hier daran erinnert, dass in

works range in size from Okayama (4.7 km) to Hiroshima (34.9 km), mostly comprising relatively short routes linking city centres with inner suburbs, plus some longer routes such as Tokyo's suburban Arakawa Line (12.2 km) and Hiroshima's interurban-style Miyajima Line (16.1 km). Most networks are self-contained but interurban cars run through to the urban networks in Fukui and Hiroshima and, since 2016, reciprocal through-running has been introduced between the Fukui tramway and the third-sector Echizen Railway. An unusual arrangement occurs in Kyoto where there is through running between Keihan's Hama-Otsu tramway and the Municipal Subway Tozai Line, albeit using 4-car metro-style units rather than tramcars. Japanese tramways are mainly privately-owned (13 companies, some also operating heavy rail lines) but there are also five traditional municipal undertakings (Sapporo, Hakodate, Tokyo [Toei], Kumamoto and Kagoshima), one newly-formed public-sector operator (Tosaden in Kochi) and two third-sector companies (Manyosen in Takaoka; Portram in Toyama).

Whilst a few tramways operate entirely or largely on segregated tracks and have high-level platforms (e.g. Tokyo's Arakawa and Setagaya Lines), most are predominantly street-running systems (traffic keeps to the left in Japan) with tracks laid in the centre of the carriageway, though generally separated from other traffic at least by white lines. On street-running sections, passengers usually board and alight from (very) narrow low-level islands, with shelters where space permits, but some-

Takaoka - Sakashitamachi

Zeichenerklärung | Legend
- in Info-Boxen | in information boxes
  - Ⓤ unterirdischer Abschnitt | underground section
  - ⭳ seitliche Stromschiene | third-rail power supply
  - ⭱ Oberleitung | overhead power supply
  - ⇔ wechselseitiger Betrieb | reciprocal through-running
  - pax/d (pax/a) Fahrgäste/Tag (Jahr) | passengers per day (year)
- in Bildunterschriften | in photo captions
  - > Blickrichtung | viewing direction
  - ▶ Fahrtziel bzw. Fahrtrichtung | train destination or direction
- auf Netzplänen | on maps
  - Ⓓ Betriebshof | depot

Toyohashi - Shiyakusho-mae – #3202 (Nippon Sharyo, 1955) ▶ Undo-Koen-mae, #781 (Nippon Sharyo, 1997) ▶ Ekimae (beide Wagen | both cars ex-Meitetsu)

Japan allgemein Linksverkehr herrscht. Auf den Straßenabschnitten wird meist von (sehr) schmalen Niedrigbahnsteigen, die bei genügend Platz über Unterstände verfügen, eingestiegen, manchmal aber auch direkt von der Fahrbahn. Mancherorts sind die Haltestellen nummeriert und hin und wieder gibt es elektronische Anzeiger. Betonklötze oder Gummireifen bieten oft rudimentären Schutz vor Autos. Auch straßenbündige Gleise weisen meist Vignol-Schienen auf, Rillenschienen sind hingegen eher auf Weichen und andere besondere Örtlichkeiten beschränkt. Die meisten Netze haben eine Spurweite von entweder 1067 mm oder 1435 mm, doch in Hakodate und auf Tokyos Arakawa und Setagaya Line findet man 1372 mm. Es gibt keine Wendeschleifen, Endstellen haben stets Stumpfgleise, so dass nur Zweirichtungsfahrzeuge eingesetzt werden können. In den letzten Jahren ist auf manchen Abschnitten ein Rasengleis verlegt worden. Elektrifizierung mit 600 V Gleichstrom über Oberleitung ist der Standard, lediglich die Keihan Hama-Otsu Line nutzt 1500 V DC.

Trotz der im Allgemeinen rückläufigen oder stagnierenden Fahrgastzahlen bieten die meisten Betreiber angemessene Takte, selten muss man tagsüber außerhalb der Hauptverkehrszeiten länger als 10-15 Minuten warten, in Spitzenzeiten nur 3 Minuten. Allerdings sind Ampelvorrangschaltungen unüblich, was zusammen mit dem zeitaufwändigen Kassieren des Fahrpreises (siehe unten) auf vielen Strecken zu Durchschnittsgeschwindigkeiten von nur 10-15 km/h führt, während in Europa bei Straßenbahnen 17-20 km/h normal scheint. In Hiroshima beispielsweise verbringen die Straßenbahnen durchschnittlich rund 34% ihrer Fahrzeit an Ampeln, 16% beim Ein- und Aussteigen und nur 50% bei der Fahrt selbst.

times directly from/to the carriageway. Some stops are numbered and some have car approaching indicators. Protection from road traffic can be rather rudimentary in the form of concrete blocks or rubber tyres. Most track is laid with Vignoles rail set in the road surface with grooved rail generally confined to points and other special situations. Most systems are either 1067 mm or 1435 mm gauge but 1372 mm gauge is used in Hakodate and on Tokyo's Arakawa and Setagaya Lines. There are no turning loops, termini have stub tracks and all cars are doubleended. A few examples of grassed rights-of-way have appeared in recent years. 600Vdc overhead electrification is standard apart from the Keihan Hama-Otsu Line which uses 1500Vdc.

Despite generally declining or static ridership most operators maintain reasonable service frequencies, rarely less than every 10-15 minutes during the midday off-peak period and in some cases up to every 3 minutes during the peaks. However, priority at traffic lights is unusual, and this combined with time-consuming fare collection arrangements (see below) contributes to slow running times on many lines with average speeds of only 10-15 km/h compared to 17-20 km/h for street-running in Europe. In Hiroshima, for example, trams spend an average of around 34% of journey time at traffic lights, 16% boarding and alighting and only 50% moving.

METROS & TRAMS IN JAPAN

Fukui

Matsuyama – Kassieren des Fahrpreises beim Aussteigen | *supervised fare collection on alighting*

In vielen Teilen der Welt wurden Straßenbahnfahrer von Aufgaben wie **Fahrkartenverkauf** und -kontrolle entlastet, um das Ein- und Aussteigen zu beschleunigen. In Japan hingegen sorgen die Fahrer weiterhin dafür, dass der korrekte Fahrpreis entrichtet wird. Auf Netzen mit Entfernungstarif steigen die Fahrgäste in der Mitte oder an der hinteren Tür ein und ziehen eine Marke mit einer Nummer (*seiri-ken*), die die aktuelle Tarifzone anzeigt. Eine elektronische Tafel im vorderen Bereich der Straßenbahn zeigt den entsprechenden Fahrpreis an. Die Fahrgäste steigen schließlich vorne aus und werfen dabei die *seiri-ken* und den Fahrpreis in eine durchsichtige Box, die vom Fahrer überwacht wird. Alle Straßenbahnen verfügen über Geldwechselautomaten. Auf einigen Netzen mit Einheitstarif (Tokyo, Okayama, Toyohashi) bezahlen die Fahrgäste beim Einsteigen vorne und steigen hinten aus. Da das Kassieren zu längeren Aufenthaltszeiten an den Haltestellen führen kann, setzen einige Betreiber an stark frequentierten Stationen Schaffner am Bahnsteig ein. Die zunehmende Verwendung von IC Cards hat dieses Problem auch gemildert. Fast alle Betreiber bieten Tageskarten an, die in der Regel auch beim Straßenbahnfahrer gekauft werden können.

*In many other parts of the world, tram drivers have been relieved of responsibility for **fare collection** to speed up boarding and alighting. However, in Japan drivers are still required to ensure that correct fares have been paid. On systems with stage (distance-related) fares, passengers board at the centre or rear doors and take a numbered ticket (seiri-ken) from an automatic dispenser indicating the fare stage at which they boarded. An electronic display sign at the front of the tram indicates the appropriate fare to be paid; passengers alight from the front of the tram depositing the seiri-ken and fare into the transparent farebox overseen by the driver. All trams have change-giving machines. On some systems with flat fares (Tokyo, Okayama, Toyohashi) passengers pay on entering at the front entrance and leave the tram via centre doors. Fare collection can lead to extended dwell times and some operators deploy roving conductors with mobile fareboxes to collect fares off-tram at busy stops. Increasing use of IC cards may go some way to reducing dwell time. Nearly all operators offer ride-at-will tickets which can usually be bought from tram drivers.*

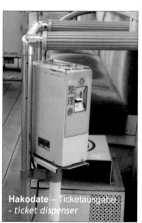

Hakodate – Ticketausgabe - *ticket dispenser*

Hakodate – Fahrpreisanzeige | *fare display*

Matsuyama - Zahlbox und Geldwechsler - *farebox & change machine*

Matsuyama - Sekijuji-Byoin-mae > Teppocho
- Iyotetsu #68 (Naniwa Koki, 1962) ► Matsuyama-shi Eki

Viele Straßenbahnliebhaber freuen sich, dass man in Japan immer noch Fahrzeuge im regulären Linienverkehr sehen kann, die anderswo längst als Museumswagen eingestuft würden; einige Flotten umfassen vorwiegend Triebwagen aus den 1950er und 1960er Jahren. Die mehr als 700 derzeit in Japan eingesetzten **Tramwagen** können grob in drei Hauptkategorien unterteilt werden:

1) **Triebwagen aus den 1950/60ern** [45% aller Fahrzeuge]: Während Niederflurwagen allmählich den Anteil älterer Fahrzeuge verringern, ist die typische japanische Straßenbahn immer noch ein hochfluriger Drehgestellwagen mit einer Länge von etwa 12-13 m mit zwei Türen pro Seite

*An attraction for many enthusiasts is that it is still possible to see many tramcars in regular service in Japan that would be regarded as museum cars elsewhere; some fleets still mainly comprise cars from the 1950s/60s. Broadly speaking, the 700+ **tramcars** operating in Japan today can be divided into three main categories:*

1) Cars from the 1950s/60s [45% of all cars]:
Whilst low-floor cars are gradually reducing the proportion of older cars in service, the predominant type of Japanese tram remains the high-floor bogie car, approximately 12-13 m in length, with two doors per side and a typical capacity of 80-100 passengers, 25-30 of whom can

Fahrscheine
Viele Betriebe in diesem Band geben eigene Wertkarten (IC Cards) und/oder Tageskarten aus. Es ist anzumerken, dass nicht alle IC Cards gleich sind, was die landesweiten Nutzungsmöglichkeiten betrifft, denn manche sind nur im lokalen Bereich verwendbar. Die folgenden zehn größeren IC Cards sind jedoch miteinander kompatibel: Kitaca (*JR Hokkaido*), Suica (*JR East*), PASMO (Region Tokyo), Manaca (Region Nagoya), TOICA (*JR Central*), PiTaPa (Region Kansai), ICOCA (*JR West*), Hayakaken (*Fukuoka Subway*), Nimoca (*Nishitetsu*, Fukuoka) und SUGOCA (*JR Kyushu*). Mit IC Cards zahlt man bequem, bekommt aber in der Regel keinen Rabatt auf normale Fahrpreise, abgesehen von ein paar Yen in der Region Tokyo.

Tageskarten sind meist vom ersten bis zum letzten Zug gültig, nicht für 24 Stunden! Sie sind in der Regel an Fahrkartenautomaten und/oder am Schalter in den Bahnhöfen der jeweiligen Betreiber erhältlich. Tageskarten für Straßenbahnen bekommt man meist auch beim Fahrer.

Tickets
Many of the operators in this volume issue stored-fare cards (IC cards) and/or ride-at-will tickets. It should be noted that not all IC cards are equal in terms of inter-availability and some can only be used in the local area of issue. However, the following ten 'major IC cards' are compatible with each other and can be used interchangeably - Kitaca (JR Hokkaido), Suica (JR East), PASMO (Tokyo region), manaca (Nagoya region), TOICA (JR Central), PiTaPa (Kansai region), ICOCA (JR West), Hayakaken (Fukuoka Subway), nimoca (Nishitetsu, Fukuoka), and SUGOCA (JR Kyushu). IC cards provide a convenient means of payment but generally without any discount over regular fares, apart from a few yen reduction in the Tokyo area.

Ride-at-will tickets are mostly valid from first to last trains, not for 24-hour periods, and are usually available from ticket machines and/or ticket offices at the stations of the relevant operators. Tram ride-at-will tickets are usually sold by drivers.

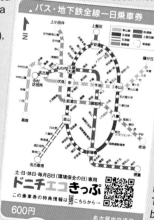

Sapporo - Nishi-Hatchome – #211 (Sapporo Sogo Tekko, 1958) ► Nishi-Yon-Chome

und einer typischen Kapazität von 80-100 Fahrgästen, von denen 25-30 auf Längsbänken Platz nehmen können. Viele der noch im Einsatz befindlichen Fahrzeuge wurden in den 1950er und 1960er Jahren neu beschafft, aber selbst damals waren sie bereits technisch veraltet, z. B. mit traditionellen Walzenfahrschaltern von Dick Kerr/Mitsubishi. Einige dieser Fahrzeuge wurden umgebaut, doch manche sind mehr oder weniger original, abgesehen von Klima-anlagen auf dem Dach, Ausrüstung zur Fahrgelderhebung oder Tonband-Ansage-Geräten.

2) Hochflurwagen von den 1980er Jahren bis heute
   [40% aller Fahrzeuge]:
Der andauernde Verkauf von Gebrauchtwagen von stillge-legten Straßenbahnbetrieben sowie die düsteren Aussichten für die verbleibenden Systeme gab den inländischen Herstellern wenig Anreiz, moderne Fahrzeuge zu entwickeln, weshalb ab Mitte der 1960er bis Anfang der 1980er Jahre kaum neue Triebwagen in Dienst gestellt wurden. Erst nach der Ölkrise von 1973 begann die Zukunft der verbleibenden Straßenbahnen etwas sicherer zu werden, so dass 1980

be accommodated on longitudinal seating. Many of the cars still in service today were bought new in the 1950s and 60s but even then they were already technically dated with, for example, traditional Dick, Kerr/Mitsubishi drum controllers. Some of these cars have been re-bodied but others remain more-or-less as-built apart from the addition of roof-mounted air-conditioning units, fare col-lection equipment and tape-recorded stop announcement systems.

2) High-floor cars from the 1980s to the present
   [40% of all cars]:
The steady supply of second-hand cars from closed tramways and bleak prospects for the remaining systems gave domestic manufacturers little incentive to develop more modern designs and few new cars entered service between the mid-1960s and the early 1980s. However, the future of the remaining tramways began to appear somewhat more secure following the 1973 'oil shock' and in 1980 two prototypes of a proposed new standard Japanese tramcar design entered service in Hiroshima

Toyama - Omachi - #7022 (Nippon Sharyo, 1965) ► Minami Toyama-Ekimae

Hiroshima - Hatchobori – Hiroden #3908 (Alna Koki, 1996) ► R5

Toyama - Chitetsubiru-mae – #8001 (Nippon Sharyo, 1993) ▶ Minami-Toyama-Ekimae

zwei Prototypen eines geplanten japanischen Standard-
wagens nach Hiroshima (Gelenkwagen 3501) und Nagasaki
(Drehgestellwagen 2001) kamen. Man blieb bei der Hochflur-
konzeption, jedoch mit moderner Gestaltung und Ausrüstung
wie etwa Chopper-Steuerung oder elektrischen Bremsen.
Auch wenn sich der Standardwagen nicht überall durchset-
zen konnte, beschafften die meisten Betriebe während der
1980er und 1990er Jahre etwas modernere Fahrzeuge, einige mit neuer Antriebstechnik, andere jedoch mit traditioneller
Ausrüstung und Drehgestellen von älteren Wagen. Es han-
delte sich vor allem um Standard-Drehgestellwagen, doch
für die Miyajima Line in Hiroshima wurden auch Gelenkwagen hergestellt. Seit der Verabschiedung neuer Richtlinien
bezüglich Barrierefreiheit im Jahr 2000 (siehe unten) waren
die Auslieferungen neuer Hochflurwagen auf Strecken mit
Hochbahnsteigen wie die Arakawa Line in Tokyo beschränkt.

3) **Niederflurwagen von 1997 bis heute**
 [15% aller Wagen]:
Die ersten beiden modernen Niederflur-Gelenkwagen, die
von Niigata Engineering nach einem ADtranz-Design gebaut wurden, kamen 1997 in Kumamoto zum Einsatz (von
1955-69 verkehrten bereits Niederflur-Gelenkfahrzeuge auf
Tokyus Tamagawa Line in Tokyo). Japanische Hersteller
entwickelten aufgrund der begrenzten Inlandsnachfrage
und ausländischer Patente auf Niederflurtechnik nur lang-
sam eigene Niederflurwagen. Im November 2000 wurde
jedoch das Gesetz über Barrierefreiheit im Nahverkehr
verabschiedet, welches bei Neubeschaffungen Anwendung
findet, wobei zusätzliche Kosten für Niederflurfahrzeuge
durch Steuererleichterungen kompensiert werden. Dadurch
wurde die Entwicklung weiterer Modelle vorangetrieben,
auch wenn die meisten Betriebe aufgrund schwieriger
finanzieller Verhältnisse bislang nur geringe Stückzahlen an
Niederflurwagen bestellt haben. Der einzige völlig niederflurige Betrieb ist Toyamas Portram (7 Fahrzeuge); Hiroshima

*(articulated set 3501) and Nagasaki (bogie car 2001). The
new specification retained the standard high-floor con-
figuration but introduced modern styling and equipment
including chopper control and electric braking. Although
the standard design was not universally adopted, most
operators introduced some new vehicles with more
modern-styling during the 1980s and 90s, some with
modern traction equipment but others incorporating
traditional equipment and bogies from older cars. These
were mainly standard bogie cars but there were also
articulated cars for Hiroshima's Miyajima Line. Since
the introduction of new accessibility requirements in
2000 (see below) deliveries of new high-floor cars have
been limited to lines with high platforms such as Tokyo's
Arakawa Line.*

3) *Low-floor cars from 1997 to the present*
 [15% of all cars]:
*Japan's first two modern low-floor articulated trams, built
by Niigata Engineering to an ADtranz design, entered service in Kumamoto in 1997 (though low-floor articulated
cars previously operated on Tokyu's Tamagawa Line in Tokyo
from 1955-69). Japanese manufacturers were slow to
develop their own modern low-floor designs due to limited
domestic demand for new trams and patents on low-floor
technology being held by overseas companies. However,
in November 2000 the Barrier-Free Transportation Law
was enacted requiring operators to observe accessibility
standards when introducing new rolling stock, with tax
relief to compensate for the additional cost of low-floor
vehicles. This encouraged the development of further designs of low-floor cars and their gradual introduction into
most fleets, albeit in small numbers reflecting the difficult
financial circumstances of many operators. The only completely low-floor operation is Toyama's Portram (7 cars);
Hiroshima has the most low-floor cars (32 out of a total*

Toyama - Nishicho – Niederflur- | *low-floor* Santram #T103 (Alna Sharyo *'Little Dancer'*, 2015)
Loop Line ► Toyama-Eki

hat die meisten Niederflurwagen (32 von insg. 133), doch mehrere Betreiber haben nur 1-3 Niederflurwagen, z. B. Sapporo (3 von 33), Toyohashi (1 von 17), Kochi (1 von 65). In den Fahrplänen ist meist angegeben, welche Fahrten mit Niederflurwagen durchgeführt werden. Bei den ersten Niederflurwagen war man noch auf europäische Technologie angewiesen, einige Wagen wurden importiert (die ersten acht Siemens Combinos für Hiroshima), andere in Lizenz in Japan gebaut (z. B. Adtranz/Niigata-Wagen für Kumamoto). Niigata Transys produziert weiterhin Triebwagen basierend auf Bombardier-Modellen (z. B. für Takaoka, Toyama und Fukui), doch japanische Typen sind auch aufgetaucht – vor allem die „Little Dancer"-Serie von Alna Sharyo (Toyohashi, Toyama und Nagasaki) und Fahrzeuge von Kinki Sharyo/Mitsusbishi (Hiroshima). Während nach Hiroshima und Fukui längere Gelenkwagen (27-30 m) für ihre Überlandstrecken geliefert wurden, blieben die meisten Betreiber bei Fahrzeugen mit niedriger bzw. mittlerer Kapazität, von den 12 m langen teilniederflurigen Drehgestellwagen für Matsuyama für nur 47 Passagiere (20 Sitzplätze) bis zum neuesten 18,6 m langen dreiteiligen Gelenkwagen von Hiroshima mit einer Kapazität von 86 Passagieren (33 Sitzplätze).

fleet of 133) but several operators have only 1-3 low-floor cars e.g. Sapporo (3 out of 33), Toyohashi (1 out of 17), Kochi (1 out of 65). To assist passengers, most operators publish timetables which identify specific trips scheduled for operation by low-floor cars. The earliest low-floor cars relied on European technology, with some cars imported (the first eight Siemens Combino sets for Hiroshima) and others built under licence in Japan (e.g. Adtranz/Niigata cars for Kumamoto). Niigata Transys has continued to manufacture cars based on Bombardier designs (including deliveries to Takaoka, Toyama and Fukui) but Japanese designs have also appeared – notably Alna Sharyo's 'Little Dancer' series (Toyohashi, Toyama and Nagasaki) and Kinki Sharyo/Mitsusbishi cars (Hiroshima). Whilst Hiroshima and Fukui have taken delivery of longer (27-30 m) high-capacity articulated cars for their interurban routes, most operators have opted for low/medium capacity vehicles in various configurations. These range from Matsuyama's 12 m long partial low-floor bogie cars with a capacity of only 47 passengers (20 seated) to Hiroshima's latest 18.6 m long three-section articulated cars with a capacity of 86 (33 seated).

Matsuyama - Otemachi-Ekimae – Iyotetsu low-floor #2107 (Alna Sharyo *'Little Dancer S-type'*, 2005) ► Line 1

Sapporo - Shiseikan-Shogakko-mae > Suskino - *Polaris* #A1203 (Alna Sharyo, 2014) ► Inner Loop

Toyama - Minami-Toyama-Ekimae – #7018 (Nippon Sharyo, 1965) im alten Anstrich | *in former fleet livery*

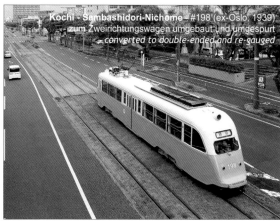

Kochi - Sambashidori-Nichome – #198 (ex-Oslo, 1939) zum Zweirichtungswagen umgebaut und umgespurt *converted to double-ended and re-gauged*

Eine gewisse Nostalgie für **alte Straßenbahnen** nutzen einige Betreiber, um neue Fahrgäste anzuziehen und so ihren veralteten Fuhrpark einsetzen zu können. So wird Hiroshima mit seiner Sammlung von Gebrauchtfahrzeugen aus ganz Japan als „lebendes Straßenbahnmuseum" vermarktet, während Kochi extra ältere ausländische Fahrzeuge übernommen hat. Neben dem regulären Einsatz älterer Wagen verfügen viele Betriebe über mindestens einen originalen Wagen oder historische Nachbauten für touristische Fahrten bzw. zur Anmietung für besondere Anlässe; einige haben „Blumenwagen", die für Festivals und Paraden geschmückt werden. Weitere Beispiele für Versuche, mehr Fahrgäste anzulocken, sind die Einführung von modernen Wagen im Retro-Look oder der Einsatz bei Sommerveranstaltungen von „Bier-Trams" mit entsprechender Ausschank.

Zusätzlich zu den oben beschriebenen „beweglichen Exponaten" sind in den Zustand von 1895 zurückversetzte Triebwagen aus Kyoto auf kurzen Straßenbahnstrecken im *Meiji-Mura Historic Village* in Inuyama in der Präfektur Aichi (zwei Wagen mit Oberleitungsbetrieb) sowie auf dem *City Tram Square* (*Shiden Hiroba*) im Umekoji Park in Kyoto (ein Wagen mit Lithiumbatterien) unterwegs. Historische Fahrzeuge kann man auch in den **Straßenbahnmuseen** in Sendai und Yokohama sehen. Verteilt im ganzen Land findet man außerdem Triebwagen, die in Parks, Museen oder außerhalb von Depots usw. aufgestellt sind.

Nostalgia for **old-style tramways** has been encouraged by some operators as a means of attracting business and making a virtue of their old rolling stock. Hiroshima, for example, with its collection of second-hand cars from around Japan is promoted as a 'moving streetcar museum' and Kochi has actively acquired older foreign cars as an attraction. In addition to scheduling older cars for regular service, many operators retain at least one genuine or rebuilt historic car for operation on special tourist services and for private hire and many have 'flower cars' which are decorated for festivals and parades. Other examples of attempts to attract patronage include the introduction of modern cars with retro-style bodywork and the operation of special events such as summer 'beer trams' which provide a tour with appropriate refreshments.

In addition to the 'on-street exhibits' described above, the Meiji-Mura Historic Village at Inuyama, Aichi Prefecture, and the City Tram Square, 'Shiden Hiroba', within Umekoji Park, Kyoto, each operates a short tramway with ex-Kyoto trams restored to 1895-appearance. Meiji-Mura has two trams with conventional overhead current collection whereas the single Umekoji tram is powered by lithium ion batteries. There are also static displays of old rolling stock at dedicated **tramway museums** in Sendai and Yokohama and at Sapporo Transportation Museum and Nagoya City Tram and Subway Museum, together with many examples of 'plinthed' tramcars around the country in parks, museums, outside depots etc.

Hakodate – #39 'Haikara-go' (1910; 1937-1993 Schneepflug | *snowplough*)

Tokyo - Toei Arakawa Line - #9002 (Alna Sharyo, 2009) - Retro style

RS

Nagoya - Kanayama – Meitetsu 3500-series *Semi-Express* ▶ Central Japan International Airport

Regionalbahnen

Wie in Band 1 haben wir die Definition des Titels „Metros
& Trams" auf alle städtischen Bahnen, inklusive Vorortbah-
nen von JR sowie private oder gemischte (staatlich/privat)
Unternehmen, ausgedehnt. JR ist zwar abgesehen von
Naha in allen Städten in diesem Buch präsent, doch variiert
der Umfang des Angebots erheblich: vom S-Bahn-Verkehr
in Sapporo von *JR Hokkaido* bis zu selten verkehrenden
Dieseltriebwagen auf ländlichen Strecken in Takaoka. In
den Städten entlang des *Hokuriku Shinkansen* (Nagano,
Toyama, Takaoka und Kanazawa) wurden die ehemaligen
JR-Strecken (1067 mm) auf neue Unternehmen übertragen,
an denen hauptsächlich die entsprechenden Präfekturen
und Kommunen beteiligt sind und die heute den Regionalverkehr durchführen. Weitere Mischunternehmen sind die
Echizen Railway in Fukui, gegründet zur Rettung einer
bankrotten Privatbahn, sowie die *Aichi Loop Railway* bei
Nagoya, die eine ehemalige
JR-Strecke übernahm.

Die wichtigste Privat-
bahn in diesem Band ist die
Nagoya Railway (*Meitetsu*),
ein Unternehmen, das
gleichbedeutend mit jenen
in den Ballungsgebieten von
Tokyo und Osaka ist. Es
betreibt ein umfangreiches
Netz von S-Bahn-Linien mit
metro-ähnlichen Fahrzeugen
und wechselseitigem Betrieb
mit der U-Bahn von Nagoya.
Bei den anderen privaten Be-
treibern, die in diesem Buch
behandelt werden, handelt

Local Railways

As in Volume 1, we have stretched the definition of
'Metros & Trams' to cover all urban/suburban railways
including JR, private and third-sector (public/private)
lines. JR companies have a presence in all the cities
covered in this book, apart from Naha, but the scale of
operation varies considerably; from JR Hokkaido's Sapporo area network of frequent EMU commuter services
to Takaoka's two infrequent DMU-operated semi-rural
lines. In those cities served by the Hokuriku Shinkansen
(Nagano, Toyama, Takaoka and Kanazawa), the former
JR main lines (1067 mm gauge) have been transferred
to new third-sector companies, mainly owned by the
relevant prefectures and local authorities, which now
operate many of the local trains serving these cities.
Other third-sector companies include Echizen Railway in
Fukui, set up to rescue a failing private railway, and the
Aichi Loop Railway near
Nagoya, set up to take over
a former JR line.

Foremost among the
private railways in this
volume is Nagoya Railway
(Meitetsu), a major operator on a par with those
serving the Tokyo and Os-
aka conurbations; it operates an extensive network
of frequent, heavily-used
services with metro-style
rolling stock and features
reciprocal through running
with the Nagoya metro.
The other private opera-

Fukui – Echizen Railway #6108 (ex-Aichi Loop Railway)
Local ▶ Katsuyama

Sapporo - Shin-Sapporo – JR Hokkaido 731-series *Local* ▶ Sapporo

es sich um kleinere Unternehmen, die in Provinzstädten mit viel geringerem Fahrgastaufkommen als in den Ballungsräumen unterwegs sind. Typischerweise entstanden deren Strecken als Überlandbahnen oder ländliche Bahnen, die sich mit Ausdehnung der Städte in Vorortlinien verwandelt haben. Auch wenn eine erhebliche Anzahl von Pendlern und Schülern befördert wird, sind die Fahrgastzahlen in den letzten Jahren gesunken, während die Anzahl der privaten Pkws gestiegen ist. Dadurch sind die Möglichkeiten für Investitionen in Infrastruktur und neue Fahrzeuge beschränkt. Bis auf die zweigleisige *Shizuoka Railway* sind die meisten dieser Bahnen überwiegend eingleisig und fast ausschließlich auf Gebrauchtfahrzeuge von größeren Betrieben angewiesen; meist verkehren 2- oder 3-Wagen-Einheiten. Einige Strecken haben metro-ähnliche Eigenschaften wie unterirdische Stationen oder automatische Zugangssperren, doch im Großen und Ganzen haben sie sich ihren traditionellen *Interurban*-Charakter zum Beispiel mit zahlreichen Bahnübergängen und alten Bahnhofsgebäuden erhalten.

tors covered in this book are smaller concerns, serving provincial cities with much lower passenger demand than the conurbations. Typically, these railways originated as interurban or rural lines which have transformed into commuter lines with the growth of suburban development. Although carrying significant numbers of commuters and school children, most have seen ridership decline as car ownership has risen, thus limiting opportunities for investment in infrastructure upgrades and new rolling stock. Except for the double-track Shizuoka Railway, these railways remain predominantly single-track and rely almost exclusively on second-hand rolling stock acquired from larger operators, usually formed as 2 or 3-car trains. Some have metro-like features such as underground stations or automatic ticket barriers but generally they retain their traditional interurban character with, for example, many level crossings and old-style station buildings.

Shizuoka - Naganuma - Shizutetsu 1000-series ▶ Shin-Shimizu

Takamatsu - Kotoden-Kotohira
- Kotoden 1100-series (Ex-Keio) ▶ Takamatsu-Chikko

Toyohira-Koen – Sapporo Subway Toho Line 9000-series ▶ Fukuzumi

SAPPORO

Sapporo ist die Hauptstadt von Hokkaido, Japans nördlichster Präfektur und zweitgrößter Insel. Diese Funktion übernahm Sapporo erst 1869 von Hakodate mit dem Ziel, die Entwicklung der Insel voranzutreiben; die *Hokkaido Development Commission* engagierte dazu amerikanische Berater, was sich am schachbrettartigen Straßenraster im Zentrum von Sapporo widerspiegelt. Die Stadt ist heute Japans fünftgrößte mit 1,9 Mio. Einwohnern auf einer Fläche von 1.121 km². Alljährlich fallen etwa 6 Meter Schnee, so dass im Februar immer das berühmte Snow Festival stattfinden kann. Die Stadt war auch Austragungsort der Olympischen Winterspiele (1972) sowie der Winter-Asienspiele (1986, 1990 und 2017).

Hokkaido ist mit der Hauptinsel Honshu durch den Seikan-Eisenbahntunnel verbunden, aber die meisten Fahrten zwischen Tokyo und Sapporo werden mit dem Flugzeug zurückgelegt. Die Eröffnung des *Hokkaido Shinkansen* bis Shin-Hakodate-Hokuto im März 2016 verkürzte die Bahnfahrt von Tokyo nach Sapporo (1.035 km) mit Umsteigen in Hakodate auf etwa acht Stunden. Der *Hokkaido Shinkansen* wird erst 2030 Sapporo erreichen.

Sapporo City Transportation Bureau [ST] (*Sapporo-shi Kotsu Kyoku*) betreibt nur Bahnen, nämlich drei U-Bahn-Linien und eine Straßenbahnlinie, nachdem zwischen 2001 und 2004 der defizitäre Busbetrieb an drei private Betreiber abgegeben worden war. Ein S-Bahn-Verkehr wird von *JR Hokkaido* durchgeführt, deren Tochtergesell-

Sapporo is the capital of Hokkaido, Japan's northernmost prefecture and second largest island. The city is relatively young having replaced Hakodate as the administrative centre of Hokkaido as part of a government drive to develop the island from 1869 onwards; the Hokkaido Development Commission engaged American advisors and this is reflected in the grid street pattern adopted in central Sapporo. The city is now Japan's fifth largest city by population with 1.9 million in an area of 1,121 km². The city experiences heavy snowfall of around 6 metres per year and is famous for its Snow Festival held in February each year. The city has also hosted the Winter Olympics (1972) and the Asian Winter Games (1986, 1990 and 2017).

Hokkaido is linked to the main island of Honshu by the Seikan rail tunnel but most travel between Tokyo and Sapporo is by air. The opening of the Hokkaido Shinkansen to Shin-Hakodate-Hokuto in March 2016 reduced the Tokyo — Sapporo train journey time but it still takes around eight hours with a change of trains for the 1,035 km journey. The Hokkaido Shinkansen is being extended but is not due to reach Sapporo until 2030.

Sapporo City Transportation Bureau [ST] (Sapporo-shi Kotsu Kyoku) operates rail modes only, three metro lines and one tram line, having disposed of its bus operations to three private operators between 2001 and 2004 due to mounting financial losses. Suburban rail services are

Susukino > Shiseikan-Shogakko-mae – Sapporo Streetcar 250-series (Outer Loop)

schaft *JR Hokkaido Bus* einige Stadtbus-Linien betreibt. Eine Luftseilbahn führt auf den Mount Moiwa. Die U-Bahn hält einen Anteil von 45,7% am öffentlichen Nahverkehr, der Bus 23,4%, JR Hokkaido 16,5%, Taxis 12,8% und die Straßenbahn 1,6%.

An *ST*-Stationen, Fahrzeugen und auf Infomaterialien findet man das mehrfarbige *ST*-Logo, mit dem ab 1993 das Image des Verkehrsbetriebs aufgebessert werden sollte. Gemeinsame Fahrscheine gibt es für die U-Bahn, Straßenbahn und die privaten Busse in Form von verschiedenen Tickets mit Umsteigeberechtigung sowie Tageskarten (nur U-Bahn - 830 Yen; U-Bahn/Tram/Bus - 1.000 Yen) bzw. ermäßigten Tageskarten an Wochenenden und Feiertagen (nur Tram - 310 Yen; nur U-Bahn - 520 Yen), Prepaid-Karten und der SAPICA IC Card.

run by JR Hokkaido which also operates some city bus services through its JR Hokkaido Bus subsidiary. An aerial cable car serves Mt Moiwa. The metro accounts for 45.7% of public transport mode share, bus 23.4%, JR Hokkaido 16.5%, taxi 12.8% and tram 1.6%.

ST stations, vehicles and publicity are branded with a multi-coloured ST symbol which was adopted in 1993 as part of an image improvement plan. A coordinated fares structure covers the metro, trams and private buses with a range of transfer tickets, 1-day cards (metro only - 830 Yen; metro/tram/bus - 1,000 Yen), discounted 1-day passes for weekends and holidays (tram only - 310 Yen; metro only 520 Yen), prepaid cards and the SAPICA IC Card.

Hassamu-Minami – Sapporo Subway Tozai Line

Odori

Nishi-Yon-Chome > Nishi-Hatchome – Sapporo Streetcar 3300-series ▶ Nishi-Yon-Chome

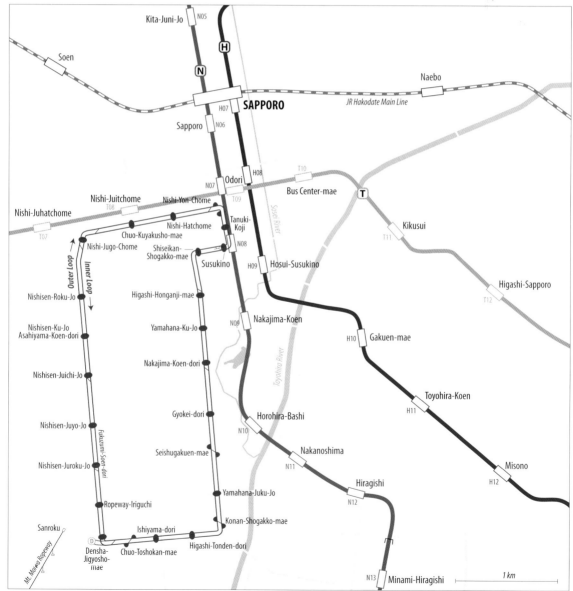

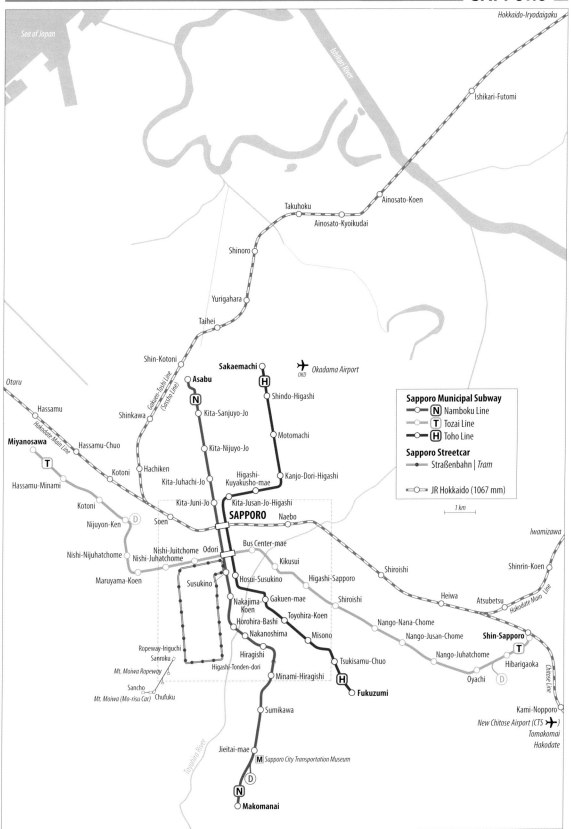

Sea of Japan

Hokkaido-Iryodaigaku

Ishikari-Futomi

Ishikari River

Ainosato-Koen

Takuhoku

Ainosato-Kyoikudai

Shinoro

Yurigahara

Taihei

Shin-Kotoni

Sakaemachi

Asabu

Shindo-Higashi

Okadama Airport
OKD

Shinkawa

Kita-Sanjuyo-Jo

Motomachi

Kita-Nijuyo-Jo

Hassamu

Otaru

Gakuen-Toshi Line
(Sassho Line)

Hokkaido Main Line

Hassamu-Chuo

Miyanosawa

Kotoni

Hachiken

Kita-Juhachi-Jo

Higashi-Kuyakusho-mae

Kanjo-Dori-Higashi

Hassamu-Minami

Kotoni

Kita-Juni-Jo

Kita-Jusan-Jo-Higashi

Nijuyon-Ken

Soen

SAPPORO

Naebo

Nishi-Nijuhatchome

Nishi-Juitchome

Odori

Bus Center-mae

Iwamizawa

Nishi-Juhatchome

Kikusui

Shiroishi

Shinrin-Koen

Maruyama-Koen

Hosui-Susukino

Higashi-Sapporo

Heiwa

Atsubetsu

Hokkaido Main Line

Susukino

Gakuen-mae

Shiroishi

Nakajima-Koen

Toyohira-Koen

Nango-Nana-Chome

Shin-Sapporo

Horohira-Bashi

Nakanoshima

Misono

Nango-Jusan-Chome

Nango-Juhatchome

Hibarigaoka

Ropeway-Iriguchi

Hiragishi

Tsukisamu-Chuo

Oyachi

Chitose Line

Sanroku

Higashi-Tonden-dori

Mt. Moiwa Ropeway

Minami-Hiragishi

Fukuzumi

Sancho

Kami-Nopporo

Mt. Moiwa (Mo-risu Car)

Chufuku

Sumikawa

New Chitose Airport (CTS)
Tomakomai
Hakodate

Toyohira River

Jieitai-mae

Sapporo City Transportation Museum

Makomanai

Sapporo Municipal Subway
— N — Namboku Line
— T — Tozai Line
— H — Toho Line

Sapporo Streetcar
— Straßenbahn | Tram

— JR Hokkaido (1067 mm)

1 km

Makomanai – Namboku Line 5000-series ► Asabu

RS

SAPPORO MUNICIPAL SUBWAY

Sapporo war nach Tokyo, Osaka und Nagoya die vierte Stadt in Japan mit einer U-Bahn. Aufgrund des starken Bevölkerungswachstums in den frühen 1960er Jahren verabschiedete die Stadt Sapporo ein langfristiges Metro-Projekt, und nachdem Sapporo den Zuschlag zur Austragung der Olympischen Winterspiele 1972 erhalten hatte, begann der Bau der ersten Phase im Jahre 1969. Der erste 12 km lange Abschnitt der Namboku Line [wörtlich Nord-Süd-Linie] wurde im Dezember 1971 eröffnet als Verbindung der nördlichen Stadtteile und des Stadtzentrums mit den

Sapporo was the fourth Japanese city to open a metro following Tokyo, Osaka and Nagoya. Rapid population growth in the early 1960s led Sapporo municipality to develop a long-term plan for a metro network and construction of the first phase was put into immediate effect in 1969 following the selection of Sapporo to host the 1972 Winter Olympics. The initial 12 km section of the Namboku (literally south-north) Line opened in December 1971 connecting north and central Sapporo with the main Olympic venue at Makomanai in the south. The system

SAPPORO SUBWAY: 3 U-Bahn-Linien | *metro lines*; 48 km; 46 U-Bahnhöfe (49, wenn man sie für jede Linie einzeln zählt) | *46 stations (49 if stations on each line counted separately)*; 368 Wagen | *cars*; 220 000 000 pax/a, 603 000 pax/d

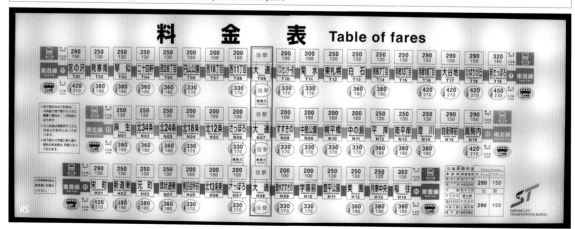

Sakaemachi – Toho Line   RS

Odori

wichtigsten olympischen Veranstaltungsorten in Makomanai im Süden. Das Netz wurde dann schrittweise bis 1999
erweitert und umfasst nun drei Linien. Allerdings lastet auf
der Metro ein hoher Schuldenberg infolge hoher Baukosten, so dass vorerst keine Erweiterungen geplant sind.

In Sapporo entstand weltweit die erste Metro mit
Gummireifen, bei der eine mittige Führungsschiene im
Gegensatz zum seitlichen Führungssystem in Paris und
anderswo verwendet wurde. Die Züge fahren mit Luftrei-
fen, werden jedoch durch zusätzliche horizontale Räder
entlang einer mittigen Schiene geführt. Diese Führungsschiene ist an Weichen beweglich. Die Gummireifen-
Technologie wurde aufgrund ihrer Vorteile bezüglich
Lärm, Fahrkomfort und Beschleunigung bzw. Bremsen
bei geringen Stationsabständen und Steigungen gewählt
– heute können moderne Stahlrad-Fahrzeuge in diesen
Bereichen jedoch weitgehend mithalten. Zwischen den
drei Linien gibt es einige technologische Unterschiede:
Die Namboku Line hat eine T-förmige Führungsschiene,
während die Tozai und Toho Line eine I-förmige aufweisen;
die Namboku Line verfügt über eine Betonfahrbahn, die
mit Harz bedeckt ist, während auf der Tozai Line Stahlplat-
ten auf den Beton gelegt wurden, um den Fahrkomfort zu
verbessern. Auf den äußeren Abschnitten der Tozai Line
(zwischen Shiroishi und Shin-Sapporo sowie zwischen
Kotoni und Miyanosawa) wie auch auf der gesamten
Toho Line liegt eine Stahlfahrbahn, die an Betonschwellen
befestigt ist, die wiederum im Unterbau eingebettet sind.
Auf der Namboku Line wurde eine seitliche Stromschiene
(750 V DC) eingebaut, wodurch die Baukosten aufgrund
eines kleineren Tunnelprofils verringert werden konnten.
Für die Elektrifizierung der Tozai und Toho Line wählte man
dennoch eine Oberleitung (1500 V DC).

has been gradually extended since then, with the most
recent section opening in 1999, and now comprises three
lines. However, the metro carries a heavy debt burden
owing to high construction costs and no further extensions are planned.

Sapporo adopted the world's first rubber-tyred metro
system with a central guideway as opposed to the side
guideway systems found in Paris and elsewhere. The
trains run on pneumatic tyres but are guided by additional horizontal wheels running along the central guideway.
The guideway is moved to direct trains at points. Rubber
tyre technology was chosen because of advantages of less
noise, better riding comfort and better control of accel-
eration and deceleration between closely spaced stations
and on gradients – characteristics which modern steel
wheel vehicles can now largely replicate. There are some
technological differences between the three lines: the
Namboku Line has a T-shaped guiderail whereas the Tozai
and Toho Lines have I-shaped guiderails; the Namboku
Line has a concrete roadbed covered with resin, whereas
on the Tozai Line steel plates are laid on the concrete to
improve riding comfort. The outer sections of the Tozai
Line (between Shiroishi and Shin-Sapporo and between
Kotoni and Miyanosawa) and the entire Toho Line have
a steel track fastened to concrete sleepers embedded in
the roadbed. The Namboku Line is equipped with third
rail 750Vdc current collection, which reduced construction costs by lowering the height of the tunnel. However,
overhead line electrification at 1500Vdc was adopted for
the Tozai and Toho Lines.

Each line is colour-coded and a line and station
numbering system is used; the three lines provide radial
links between central Sapporo and suburban areas up to
7-10 km from the city centre. The system was designed
from the outset to be coordinated with feeder bus
services and purpose-built bus terminals and boarding

Jieitai-mae – Namboku Line 5000-series ▶ Asabu

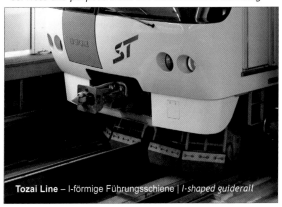

Tozai Line – I-förmige Führungsschiene | I-shaped guiderail

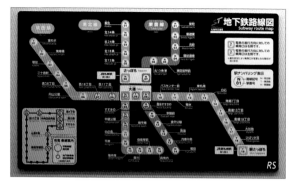

Jede Linie ist farblich gekennzeichnet, außerdem wird ein Linien- und Stationscodierungssystem verwendet. Alle drei Linien verbinden die Stadtmitte von Sapporo radial mit 7-10 km vom Zentrum entfernten Vororten. Das U-Bahn-Netz wurde von Anfang an so geplant, dass an wichtigen Stationen ein bequemes Umsteigen von Zubringerbussen zur U-Bahn möglich ist. Im zentralen Bereich verlaufen die Namboku und Toho Line auf etwa 2,5 km parallel (ca. 250 m bzw. zwei Häuserblocks voneinander entfernt), sie sind aber baulich nicht miteinander verbunden. An den Stationen Sapporo und Odori, den verkehrsreichsten im U-Bahn-Netz, kann jedoch zwischen den beiden Linien über ein weitreichendes Netz an Gängen durch unterirdische Einkaufszentren umgestiegen werden, die Wege werden auch auf dem Fußboden angezeigt. Die Ost-West-Linie (Tozai Line) kreuzt die beiden anderen Linien am Knoten Odori. Von der Namboku und Toho Line kann man außerdem am Bahnhof Sapporo zu den Zügen von *JR Hokkaido* umsteigen, während die Tozai Line an ihrer östlichen Endstelle Shin-Sapporo einen Übergang zur JR Chitose Line in die südöstlichen Vororte bietet. Wie man an der Wahl der inkompatiblen Schienentechnik erkennen kann, war die U-Bahn von Sapporo anders als viele japanische Metros nie für einen wechselseitigen Betrieb mit Vorortbahnen ausgelegt.

Die meisten U-Bahnhöfe haben eine ähnliche Struktur mit mehreren eher unauffälligen Eingängen (entweder überdacht oder in angrenzende Gebäude integriert), die in eine Verteilerhalle auf der Ebene -1 führen, wo die Zugangssperren angeordnet sind. Auf der Ebene -2 befinden sich entweder zwei Seitenbahnsteige oder ein Mittelbahnsteig. An ein paar Stationen sind die Zugangssperren wie die Bahnsteige auf Ebene -1, die jeweiligen Seitenbahnsteige sind dann mit einer oder mehreren Fußgängerunterführungen unter den Gleisen miteinander verbunden. Die Hochbahnhöfe auf der Namboku Line haben Seitenbahnsteige, die Zugangssperren befinden sich hier auf Straßenniveau unterhalb der Bahnsteigebene. Der U-Bahnhof Odori, wo sich alle drei Linien kreuzen, ist komplexer mit mehreren Sperrenanlagen, die Namboku Line liegt hier in Nord-Süd-Richtung auf Ebene -2, die Tozai Line kreuzt in Ost-West-Richtung auf Ebene -3 und die Toho Line wiederum in Nord-Süd-Richtung auf Ebene -4.

U-Bahn-Fahrzeuge

Die innovative Technologie der U-Bahn von Sapporo erforderte auch die Entwicklung von maßgeschneiderten Fahrzeugen. In den späten 1960er Jahren wurde eine Reihe von Prototypen produziert und in Higashi-Naebo getestet. Der dritte und der vierte Testwagen haben über-

areas are found adjacent to key stations. In the central area the Namboku and Toho Lines run parallel (about 250 m/two street blocks apart) for a distance of 2.5 km but do not physically connect with each other. However, at Sapporo and Odori stations, the busiest on the network, interchange between the two lines is available via an extensive network of underground shopping malls and walkways, with floor direction signs indicating the routes to follow. The east-west Tozai Line connects with the other two lines at Odori. The Namboku and Toho Lines provide interchange with JR Hokkaido services at Sapporo station and the Tozai Line connects with the JR Chitose Line at Shin-Sapporo in the south-east suburbs. Unlike many other Japanese metros, the system was not designed for reciprocal through running to suburban lines as evidenced by the choice of incompatible track technology.

Most stations have a similar layout comprising several relatively inconspicuous street-level entrances (either free-standing with canopies or incorporated into adjoining buildings) leading down to a basement-level (B1) concourse ticket hall with gatelines. Beyond the gatelines there are either two side platforms or a single island platform at B2-level. A few stations have a ticket hall and gatelines at the same B1 level as the platforms, with one or more pedestrian underpasses beneath the tracks connecting the two sides of the station. The elevated stations on the Namboku Line have side platforms with the ticket halls at ground level beneath the elevated structure. Odori station, which serves all three lines, is more complex with multiple ticket halls, the north-south Namboku tracks at B2-level, the east-west Tozai Line passing beneath at B3-level and the Toho Line at B4-level.

Rolling stock

The innovative design of the Sapporo metro required the development of bespoke vehicles and during the late 1960s a number of prototypes were produced and tested at the Higashi-Naebo car training centre. The third and fourth test cars have survived and are displayed at the Sapporo Transport Museum as are two articulated cars (#1001/1002) from the first batch of Namboku Line stock.

All Sapporo cars are Kawasaki-built and at 3080 mm are the widest metro cars in Japan. Most cars are equipped with electronic indicators to show the direction

Namboku Line 5000-series   RS

Odori – Toho Line 9000-series ▶ Fukuzumi

Toho Line 9000-series

lebt, sie sind neben zwei Gelenkwagen (1001/1002) der ersten Fahrzeuggeneration der Namboku Line im *Sapporo Transport Museum* zu sehen.

Alle Metro-Fahrzeuge stammen bisher von Kawasaki und sind mit 3080 mm die breitesten U-Bahn-Wagen in Japan. Die meisten Wagen sind mit elektronischen Anzeigen ausgestattet, Fahrtziel und die nächsten Stationen werden auf Japanisch und Englisch angezeigt. In einigen Fahrzeugen der Namboku Line sowie in den neuen des Typs 9000 auf der Toho Line findet man auch LCD-Bildschirme. Die Züge sind nicht klimatisiert.

Der aktuelle Wagenpark der Namboku Line besteht aus 20 Sechs-Wagen-Zügen der Serie 5000, die seit 1995 im Einsatz sind. Diese Züge haben eine VVVF-Wechselrichter-Steuerung und erstmals in Sapporo vier Türen pro Wagenseite. Die Fahrzeuge der Namboku Line haben Doppelreifen, die der Tozai und Toho Line hingegen aufgrund verbesserter Reifenleistung nur Einzelreifen. Der Tozai Line stehen 24 ab 1998 gelieferte Sieben-Wagen-Züge der Serie 8000 zur Verfügung, die auf der Serie 5000 basieren, jedoch mit nur drei Türen. Auf der Toho Line sind 20 Vier-Wagen-Züge im Einsatz. Die ursprüngliche Serie 7000 aus der Zeit der Eröffnung der Linie im Jahr 1988 sowie neuere Fahrzeuge dieser Serie, die zur Linienverlängerung im Jahr 1994 geliefert wurden, wurden alle 2015/16 durch neue Züge der Serie 9000 ersetzt. Seither verkehrt die gesamte Flotte im neuesten *ST*-Anstrich in Weiß, nur die Front- und Seitentüren tragen die entsprechende Linienfarbe.

of the train and the next stations in Japanese and English. In addition, in-car liquid crystal display indicators have been introduced in some of the Namboku Line cars and the new 9000-series Toho Line cars. Trains are not air-conditioned.

The current Namboku Line fleet consists of 20 six-car 5000-series trains introduced from 1995 onwards. These trains have VVVF inverter control and are the city's first with four-door cars. Namboku Line cars have double tyres on each wheel unlike Tozai and Toho Line cars which have single tyres due to improvements in tyre performance. The Tozai Line fleet comprises 24 seven-car 8000-series trains based on the 5000-series design but with three-door cars which were introduced from 1998 onwards. The Toho Line has a fleet of 20 four-car trains. The original 7000-series sets dating from the opening of the line in 1988 and new model 7000-series introduced when the line was extended in 1994 were all replaced during 2015 and 2016 by new 9000-series trains. Following the withdrawal of the older Toho Line cars, the whole fleet is now in the latest corporate livery of white with end and side doors in the appropriate line colour.

Sapporo Transport Museum – Namboku Line
Gelenkwagen | *articulated cars* #1001/1002

Sapporo Transport Museum
3. Testwagen | *3rd experimental car*
RS

Asabu

RS

Namboku Line

Sapporos erste Metro-Linie verläuft im Tunnel zwischen Asabu im Norden und Hiragishi südlich des Stadtzentrums, danach erklimmt sie einen Viadukt, der über der aufgelassenen Trasse der 1969 geschlossenen Jozankei-Privatbahn errichtet wurde. Dadurch konnten die Baukosten im Vergleich zum Tunnelbau um 50% gesenkt werden, doch zum Schutz vor starken Schneefällen und zur Lärmreduzierung wurde der gesamte Hochbahnabschnitt mit einem gewölbten Aluminiumdach mit seitlichen Fenstern eingehaust.

Die Fahrzeit auf der Gesamtstrecke beträgt 27½ Minuten, die Züge fahren alle 4-7 Minuten. Die wichtigsten Stationen sind Sapporo, Odori, Asabu sowie Susukino im Vergnügungsviertel der Stadt. Der Betriebshof Süd liegt zwischen Jieitai-mae und Makomanai. Das *Sapporo Transport Museum* mit diversen U-Bahn-Wagen, Straßenbahnen und Bussen befindet sich auch am Bahnhof Jieitai-mae unterhalb des Viadukts. Der Einbau von halbhohen Bahnsteigtüren wurde im März 2013 abgeschlossen, seit April 2013 wird im Ein-Mann-Betrieb mit ATO-Unterstützung gefahren.

Sapporo's first metro line runs in tunnel between Asabu in the north and Hiragishi, south of the city centre, after which it ascends onto an elevated structure built above the abandoned trackbed of the former Jozankei private railway which closed in 1969. This reduced costs by 50% compared to underground construction but in order to protect the metro from heavy snowfall and reduce noise, a curved aluminium shelter with side windows was installed over the entire elevated section.

The running time is 27.5 minutes from end to end and services operate every 4 to 7 minutes. The busiest stations are Sapporo, Odori, Asabu and Susukino, which serves the city's entertainment district. Rolling stock is housed at the South Depot situated between Jieitai-mae and Makomanai stations; the Sapporo Transport Museum is also at Jieitai-mae with various metro cars, trams and buses displayed in the open beneath the elevated structure. Platform edge gate installation was completed at all stations in March 2013 and ATO one-person operation commenced in April 2013.

Namboku Line (N)

Asabu (N01) – Makomanai (N16)
14.3 km, Ⓤ 9.9 km, 16 Bahnhöfe | stations
750Vdc ⚡: 228 000 pax/d

16-12-1971: Makomanai – Kita-Nijuyo-Jo
(12.1 km, 4.4 km Hochbahn | elevated)
16-03-1978: Kita-Nijuyo-Jo – Asabu (2.2 km)

RS

Minami-Hiragishi – 5000-series ► Asabu   RS

Sapporo – Ebene -1 | *B1 level*   RS

Odori

Kita-Juni-Jo   RS

Jieitai-mae – Transport Museum
- unter eingehauster Strecke
- *beneath covered route*

Oyachi – 8000-series ▶ Miyanosawa

Tozai Line

Diese Linie verläuft in Ost-West-Richtung unter dem Odori-Park durch das Zentrum von Sapporo und erschließt die Vororte im Nordwesten und Südosten. Sie befördert fast genauso viele Fahrgäste wie die Namboku Line, wobei Shin-Sapporo, wo man zur JR umsteigen kann, der wichtigste U-Bahnhof außerhalb des Stadtzentrums ist. Die Fahrzeit beträgt 35 Minuten, die Züge verkehren alle 4-7 Minuten. Seit 2009, als der Ein-Mann-Betrieb mit ATO eingeführt wurde, haben alle U-Bahnhöfe halbhohe Bahnsteigtüren.

Auf der Tozai Line wurde erstmals in Japan ein fahrerloser Betrieb für Züge ohne Fahrgäste eingeführt, nämlich auf der 1,3 km langen Strecke zwischen dem Betriebshof Ost und einem eigenen Bahnsteig im U-Bahnhof Hibarigaoka, der durch die Leitstelle überwacht wird. Die Fahrzeuge waren früher im Betriebshof West zwischen Nishi-Nijuhatchome und Nijuyonken untergebracht, doch dieser wird heute ausschließlich von den Zügen der Toho Line genutzt. Der Betriebshof West ist völlig unterirdisch, darüber wurde eine städtische Wohnanlage errichtet.

This line runs east-west through central Sapporo beneath Odori Park and serves the north-west and south-east suburbs. It carries almost as many passengers as the Namboku Line. Shin-Sapporo, an interchange with JR, is the busiest station outside central Sapporo. End-to-end running time is 35 minutes with all trains serving all stations every 4 to 7 minutes. All stations have had platform gates since 2009 when ATO one-person operation was introduced.

The Tozai Line features the first automatic driverless system for out-of-service trains in Japan. Trains run unmanned on a 1.3 km departure and return track between the East Depot and a dedicated platform at Hibarigaoka station monitored by the depot signal safety office. Rolling stock was previously housed at the West Depot situated between Nishi-Nijuhatchome and Nijuyonken stations but this is now used exclusively by Toho Line trains. The West Depot is entirely underground with a public housing development built above.

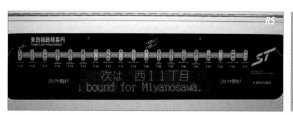

Tozai Line (T)

Miyanosawa (T01) – Shin-Sapporo (T19)
20.1 km ⓤ, 19 Bahnhöfe | *stations*
1500Vdc ⬆: 227 000 pax/d

10-06-1976: Kotoni – Shiroishi (9.9 km)
21-03-1982: Shiroishi – Shin-Sapporo (7.4 km)
25-02-1999: Kotoni – Miyanosawa (2.8 km)

Shin-Sapporo

RS

Oyachi

Bus Center-mae

RS

Nango-Jusan-Chome

RS

Bus Center-mae

RS

Odori – 7000-series ▶ Sakaemachi

Toho Line

Die Toho Line verbindet den Nordosten mit dem Südosten von Sapporo; sie ist nach den Bezirken Higashi und Toyohira benannt, die sie erschließt – „To" ist eine alternative Lesung für „higashi" (Ost) und „ho" für „Toyo". Diese Linie hat deutlich weniger Fahrgäste als die beiden anderen und wird derzeit mit 4-Wagen-Zügen betrieben. Aufgrund instabiler Bodenverhältnisse und einer Bauzeit während der japanischen *Bubble Economy* kostete der erste Abschnitt dieser Linie acht Mal so viel wie die Namboku Line. Bei der 1994 eröffneten Südverlängerung bemühte sich die Stadt, die Kosten zu senken, indem das Tunnelprofil verringert und alle Stationen mit Mittelbahnsteigen errichtet wurden. Während die Stationen des Ursprungsabschnitts für acht Wagen ausgelegt waren, sind die Bahnsteige der Südstrecke (Gakuen-mae bis Fukuzumi) nur für sechs Wagen ausgebaut, auch wenn baulich eine spätere Verlängerung berücksichtigt wurde.

Nördlich der Endstation Sakaemachi gibt es drei Abstellgleise mit begrenzten Wartungseinrichtungen, denn die Toho Line verfügt über keinen eigenen Betriebshof. Die

The Toho Line links north-east and south-east Sapporo; it is named after the Higashi and Toyohira Wards which it serves ('To' is an alternative reading for 'higashi' and 'ho' an alternative for 'Toyo'). This line has significantly lower ridership than the other lines and is currently operated with 4-car trains. The first section of the line cost eight times as much as the Namboku Line due to soft ground conditions and because it was built at the height of Japan's bubble economy. With the Toho Line southern extension, which opened in 1994, the city endeavoured to lower costs by reducing the tunnel profile and constructing all stations with island platforms. Furthermore, whilst the stations on the initial section were built at 8-car length from the outset the stations on the later extension (Gakuen-mae – Fukuzumi) have 6-car length platforms with additional foundation work to allow extension for 8-car trains in the future.

There are three sidings to the north of the Sakaemachi terminus with limited maintenance facilities but there is no depot on the Toho Line. Trains are stored and

さっぽろ・大通・福住 方面　1
For Sapporo,Odori,Fukuzumi
1st 10:49 for Fukuzumi
2nd 10:56 for Fukuzumi

RS

Toho Line (H)

Sakaemachi (H01) – Fukuzumi (H14)
13.6 km Ⓤ, 14 Bahnhöfe | *stations*
1500Vdc ⬆; 148 000 pax/d

02-12-1988: Sakaemachi – Hosui-Susukino (8.1 km)
14-10-1994: Hosui-Susukino – Fukuzumi (5.5 km)

Shindo-Higashi RS

Odori

Züge werden im Betriebshof West auf der Tozai Line abgestellt und gewartet; dieser wird über eine eingleisige Strecke in einem Röhrentunnel, der zwischen dem U-Bahnhof Nishi-Juitchome auf der Tozai Line und dem U-Bahnhof Sapporo auf der Toho Line verläuft, erreicht.

Die fahrplanmäßige Fahrzeit beträgt 24 Minuten, wobei die Züge alle 4 bis 7½ Minuten verkehren. Die wichtigste Station außerhalb des zentralen Bereichs ist Fukuzumi, in deren Einzugsbereich das Baseball- und Fußballstadion Sapporo Dome liegt. Bestimmte Stationen auf dieser Linie sind in Kennfarben gestaltet, Bahnsteigtüren sollen bis 2017/18 nachgerüstet werden.

maintained at the West Depot on the Tozai Line which out-of-service trains access via a single-track connector line in a shield-driven tunnel running between Nishi-Juitchome station on the Tozai line and Sapporo station on the Toho Line.

The scheduled end-to-end running time is 24 minutes with trains running every 4 to 7.5 minutes. The busiest station outside the central area is Fukuzumi which serves Sapporo Dome baseball and football stadium. Certain stations on the line have colour-coded decor and platform safety gates are due to be installed by 2017/18.

Mt. Moiwa Ropeway (Seilbahn | *Aerial Cable Car*)

Vom Mount Moiwa (531 m) kann man die wunderbare Aussicht über Sapporo genießen. Die Seilbahn stammt aus dem Jahr 1958, sie wurde aber 2012 modernisiert und verfügt nun über Kabinen für 66 Passagiere. Die Fahrt dauert 5 Minuten von der Talstation Sanroku bis zur Station Chufuku (1,2 km), von wo aus die Standseilbahn *Mo-risu Car* in 1 Minute 45 Sekunden die Bergstation Sancho erreicht. Der *Mo-risu Car* ist nach dem Mount-Moiwa-Maskottchen, einem Eichhörnchen, benannt und besteht aus zwei schwebenden Kabinen, die somit bei einer Steigungsänderung stets horizontal bleiben. Jede Kabine bietet Platz für 30 Passagiere. Ein kostenloser Shuttlebus verkehrt zwischen der Tram-Haltestelle Ropeway-Iriguchi und der Talstation Sanroku.

Mt Moiwa (531 m) provides panoramic views of Sapporo. The ropeway dates from 1958 but was refurbished and reopened with new 66-passenger capacity cars in 2012. It takes 5 minutes from Sanroku (the base station) to Chufuku station (1.2 km) from where 'Mo-risu Car', a mini-cable car (funicular), takes another 1 minute 45 seconds to travel 230 m to Sancho station for the summit. 'Mo-risu Car', named after the Mt Moiwa squirrel mascot, comprises two linked cabins which hang from supports, thus remaining horizontal as the track gradient changes; each cabin carries 30 passengers. A free shuttle bus operates between Ropeway-Iriguchi tram stop and Sanroku station.

Mt. Moiwa Ropeway

Mo-risu Car

RS   Nishi-Yon-Chome – Polaris A1200-series ▶ Inner Loop

SAPPORO STREETCAR

Die erste Pferdestraßenbahn fuhr in Sapporo im Jahr 1909, 1918 begann dann der elektrische Betrieb. Im Jahr 1927 übernahm die Stadt das Netz, das schließlich eine maximale Ausdehnung von 25 km erreichte. Eine Besonderheit war in den 1960er Jahren der Einsatz von Diesel-Trams auf der neuen Linie 7, um die Kosten für ein Unterwerk und Oberleitungen zu sparen. Einige dieser Fahrzeuge wurden später mit einem elektrischen Antrieb ausgerüstet.

Nach der Entscheidung für den U-Bahn-Bau schrumpfte das Tram-Netz zwischen 1971 und 1974. Einzelne Abschnitte von drei Straßenbahnlinien überlebten und wurden bis 2015 als eine einzige 8,46 km lange Linie betrieben, die fast eine Ringlinie darstellte, doch im Stadtzentrum blieb eine 0,45 km lange Lücke zwischen den beiden Endstellen Nishi-Yon-Chome und Susukino.

Bis 2002 sanken die Einnahmen aus dem Straßenbahnbetrieb und für Fahrzeuge und Infrastruktur waren teure Sanierungsarbeiten erforderlich. Eine Stilllegung des

Sapporo's first horse-drawn tram commenced operation in 1909 and electric traction was introduced in 1918. The municipality took over the system in 1927 and at its greatest extent it covered 25 km. A distinctive feature during the 1960s was the use of diesel trams on new route 7 to save on the cost of a sub-station and overhead line. Some of these cars were later converted to electric traction.

Following the decision to construct a metro, the tram network was gradually cut back with a series of line closures between 1971 and 1974. Sections of three tram lines survived and, until 2015, these were operated as a single 8.46 km route forming an almost complete loop apart from a 0.45 km gap between the two central termini at Nishi-Yon-Chome and Susukino.

By 2002, tramcar income had declined and the cars and infrastructure required expensive renovation works. Consideration was given to abandoning the trams alto-

Nishisen-Juyo-Jo – 8500-series ▶ Outer Loop   RS

Sapporo Streetcar (SC)

8.9 km, 24 Haltestellen | *stops*
1067 mm; 600Vdc ⊕

Elektrischer Betrieb* | *Electric operation*:
12-08-1918: Nishi-Yon-Chome – Nishi-Jugo-Chome (1.44 km)
25-08-1923: Susukino – Gyokei-dori (1.84 km)
16-07-1925: Gyokei-dori – Seishugakuen-mae (0.33 km)
20-11-1931: Seishugakuen-mae – Nishi-Jugo-Chome (4.85 km)
20-12-2015: Nishi-Yon-Chome – Susukino (0.45 km)

* ohne stillgelegte Strecken | *closed sections not listed*

Nishi-Yon-Chome (Inner Loop)   RS

Nishi-Hatchome – 216-series ▶ Outer Loop

gesamten Straßenbahnbetriebs wurde daher erwogen, doch schließlich wurde beschlossen, das Netz im Rahmen eines Stadtentwicklungsprogramms zu erhalten und zu modernisieren. Der *Sapporo City Streetcar Use Plan* wurde 2010 verabschiedet und anschließend wurden neue Niederflurwagen angeschafft. 2015 wurde die Neubaustrecke zwischen Nishi-Yon-Chome und Susukino mit einer Zwischenhaltestelle (Tanuki-Koji) in Betrieb genommen und der Ringbetrieb eingeführt. Mögliche Erweiterungen im Stadtzentrum, in Gebiete östlich des Sosei-Flusses oder nach Soen werden noch untersucht.

Die Straßenbahn ist durchgehend zweigleisig, meist in Straßenmitte mit engen Bahnsteigen, lediglich auf

gether but the decision was taken to retain and modernise the system as part of the city's urban development efforts. The *Sapporo City Streetcar Use Plan* was adopted in 2010 and since then new low-floor cars have been introduced and, in 2015, Nishi-Yon-Chome and Susukino were linked by a new section of line with one additional stop (Tanuki-Koji) and a full circular service was introduced. Possible extensions to the city centre, to east of the Sosei River and to Soen have been considered but these are not yet approved.

The tramway is double-track throughout, mostly in the centre of the road with narrow waiting islands at stops, apart from the new loop extension which has

RS   Nishisen-Juyo-Jo – 250-series ▶ Inner Loop

Shiseikan-Shogakko-mae – 8500-series ▶ Inner Loop

Nishisen-Juyo-Jo > Nishisen-Juichi-Jo – 240-series ▶ Inner Loop

der Neubaustrecke liegen die Gleise in Randlage und die Bahnsteige an der Haltestelle Tanuki-Koji sind in die Bürgersteige integriert. Um die Sicherheit der Fahrgäste im Winter zu gewährleisten, wurden an allen Haltestellen Geländer, Heizapparate und Dächer installiert. An einigen Haltestellen werden die nächsten Bahnen sowohl optisch als auch akustisch angekündigt. Die Haltestellen sind von Nishi-Yon-Chome (SC01) bis Tanuki-Koji (SC24) durchnummeriert.

Der Betriebshof liegt an der Haltestelle Densha-Jigyosho-mae, doch der Linieneinsatz beginnt und endet an der Haltestelle Chuo-Toshokan-mae. Die meisten Bahnen befahren die gesamte Ringstrecke, was 52 Minuten dauert, lediglich in der Morgenspitze gibt es Kurzläufer bis Susukino (im Uhrzeigersinn) und Nishisen-Juroku-Jo (gegen den Uhrzeigersinn). Die Straßenbahn verkehrt etwa alle 6-7 Minuten, während der Morgenspitze bisweilen alle 3 Minuten. Niederflurbahnen fahren etwa stündlich in jeder Richtung. Eine Einzelfahrt kostet 170 Yen, eine Tageskarte nur für die Tram gibt es an Wochenenden und Feiertagen für 310 Yen.

Die Straßenbahnflotte umfasst 33 Wagen. Die Typen 210/220/240/250 (18 Fahrzeuge) stammen aus den Jahren

kerbside tracks and pavement loading at Tanuki-Koji. To ensure passenger safety in winter, safety fences, road-heating elements and roofs have been installed at all stops. Some stops have visual and audio car approaching indicators. Stops are numbered from Nishi-Yon-Chome (SC01) to Tanuki-Koji (SC24).

The depot is adjacent to Densha-Jigyosho-mae tram stop but trams entering and leaving service do so at Chuo-Toshokan-mae. Most trams run the whole length of the line taking 52 minutes to complete the loop with some short workings during the AM peak to Susukino (clockwise) and Nishisen-Juroku-Jo (anti-clockwise). Trams operate approximately every 6-7 minutes, increasing up to every 3 minutes during the morning peak. Low-floor trams are scheduled to run approximately once an hour in each direction around the loop. A flat fare of 170 Yen applies and one-day tram tickets are available for 310 Yen on weekends and holidays.

The current fleet comprises 33 cars. The 210/220/240/250-series (18 cars) date from 1958-1961 and were built in Sapporo using some electrical components from earlier cars; 8500-series Kawasaki cars date from 1985-88

Nishisen-Juroku-Jo – 210-series ▶ Inner Loop

Nishi-Yon-Chome – M100-series ▶ Outer Loop

1958-1961, sie wurden in Sapporo mit einigen elektrischen Komponenten aus früheren Triebwagen gebaut; die Serie 8500 von Kawasaki (6 Wagen) stammt aus 1985-88 und verfügt über eine VVVF-Wechselrichter-Steuerung; die Serie 3300 (5 Wagen) wurde 1996-2001 mit Drehgestellen und Motoren älterer Fahrzeuge modernisiert. Die neuesten dreiteiligen Niederflurwagen vom Typ *Polaris* von Alna Sharyo (3 Wagen) wurden erstmals 2012 in Betrieb genommen. Unter den Arbeitsfahrzeugen sind vier Sasara-Schneefräsen mit Bambusbürsten vorn und hinten, um im Winter den Schnee von den Gleisen zu entfernen. Der eigentliche Anstrich ist grün mit einem weißen unteren Rand, aber rund die Hälfte aller Fahrzeuge ist mit Vollwerbung beklebt. Die *Polaris* tragen eine neue Schwarz-Weiß-Lackierung. Ein Einzelstück ist der 1961 von Nippon Sharyo gebaute Triebwagen M101, der erfolglos mit einem Beiwagen mit Fahrerkabine getestet wurde und der weiterhin eine ältere Version des grünen Anstrichs zeigt.

(6 cars) and have VVVF inverter control; 3300-series (5 cars) are refurbished cars dating from 1996-2001 with bogies and motors from earlier cars. The latest 'Polaris' 3-section articulated low-floor cars by Alna Sharyo (3 cars) first entered service in 2012. The works fleet includes four 'Sasara' rotary snow brooms with bamboo brushes at front and rear to remove snow from the tracks in winter. Fleet livery is green with a white skirt but around half the cars carry all-over advertising and a new black and white livery has been adopted for the 'Polaris' cars. The single 1961-built Nippon Sharyo motor car M101, unsuccessfully trialled with a control trailer, retains an older version of the green fleet livery.

Tanuki-Koji – 8500-series ▶ Inner Loop   RS

Susukino – 3300-series (ehem. Endstelle | *former terminus*)

Sapporo – JR Hokkaido - 731-series *Local* ▶ Otaru

JR Hokkaido (S-Bahn | *Suburban Rail*)

Das Streckennetz von *JR Hokkaido* in der Region Sapporo umfasst 55 Stationen und erstreckt sich bis Otaru (33,8 km) und Iwamizawa (40,6 km) auf der Hakodate Main Line, bis Shin-Chitose Airport (46,6 km) und Tomakomai (71,2 km) auf der Chitose Line und bis Hokkaido-Iryodaigaku (28,9 km) auf der Gakuen-Toshi (Sassho) Line. Auf diesen Strecken findet ein dichter S-Bahn-Verkehr statt, wobei die Gleise auch von Fernzügen genutzt werden; die IC Card „Kitaca" gilt innerhalb dieses Gebiets. Alle Linien und Stationen sind nach einem Hokkaido-weiten System ausgehend vom Bahnhof Sapporo (01) nummeriert.

Seit der Gründung von *JR Hokkaido* wurde mehr Augenmerk auf die Verbesserung der Infrastruktur, der Takte und der Fahrzeuge gelegt. Der Bahnhof Sapporo, der Knoten des Netzes, verfügt über zehn Gleise mit fünf Mittelbahnsteigen in Hochlage. Ein Großteil der Strecken im Stadtgebiet wurde aufgeständert und zusätzliche Gleise wurden verlegt, um Engpässe zu beseitigen. Erwähnenswert ist der südliche Abschnitt der Sassho-Linie, der nun als Gakuen-Toshi Line [etwa „Wissenschaftsstadt-Linie"]

JR Hokkaido's Sapporo area network covers 55 stations and extends to Otaru (33.8 km) and Iwamizawa (40.6 km) on the Hakodate Main Line, to Shin-Chitose Airport (46.6 km) and Tomakomai (71.2 km) on the Chitose Line and to Hokkaido-Iryodaigaku (28.9 km) on the Gakuen-Toshi (Sassho) Line. Frequent commuter services are operated within this area on tracks which are shared by longer distance services to other parts of Hokkaido. The Kitaca IC card is valid within this area and all lines and stations are numbered in accordance with a Hokkaido-wide numbering system radiating from Sapporo station (01).

Since the formation of JR Hokkaido, greater emphasis has been placed on meeting commuter demand by improving infrastructure, service frequencies and rolling stock. Sapporo station, the hub of the network, has ten elevated tracks with five island platforms. Much of the trackwork elsewhere in the city has been elevated and additional tracks have been provided to ease bottlenecks. Of note is the southern end of the Sassho Line,

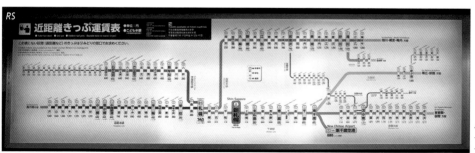

JR Hokkaido
- S-Bahn-Netz
- *Suburban Rail Network*

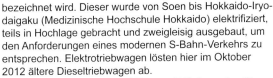

Shin-Sapporo

Otaru – JR Hokkaido - 733-series

bezeichnet wird. Dieser wurde von Soen bis Hokkaido-Iryo-daigaku (Medizinische Hochschule Hokkaido) elektrifiziert, teils in Hochlage gebracht und zweigleisig ausgebaut, um den Anforderungen eines modernen S-Bahn-Verkehrs zu entsprechen. Elektrotriebwagen lösten hier im Oktober 2012 ältere Dieseltriebwagen ab.

Eine Mischung aus *Local*-Zügen mit Halt an allen Stationen und *Rapid*-Zügen (Ishikari Liner) verkehrt durchgebunden von der Hakodate Main Line auf die Chitose Line und umgekehrt. Ab Sapporo fahren bis zu neun Züge pro Stunde Richtung Otaru, sechs Richtung Iwamizawa und acht Richtung Shin-Chitose/Tomakomai, wobei viele Fahrten bereits an Zwischenbahnhöfen enden. Vom Flughafen Shin-Chitose verkehren vier Züge pro Stunde als *Rapid Airport* mit Halt an bestimmten Zwischenstationen Richtung Sapporo, zwei davon fahren weiter nach Otaru und einer nach Asahikawa. Auf der Gakuen-Toshi Line verkehren bis zu vier Züge pro Stunde mit Halt an allen Stationen zwischen Sapporo und Ainosato-Kyoikudai, wo die zweigleisige Ausbaustrecke endet; zwei Züge pro Stunde fahren weiter bis Ishikari-Tobetsu oder Hokkaido-Iryodaigaku, bis wohin die Strecke elektrifiziert ist.

Im S-Bahn-Bereich von Sapporo wird eine Mischung aus Fahrzeugen der Baureihen 721, 731, 733 und 735 als Drei-Wagen-Einheiten eingesetzt, die ältesten stammen aus dem Jahr 1988. Alle Baureihen sind miteinander kompatibel und können in Doppeltraktion als Sechs-Wagen-Züge verkehren. Die *Rapid Airport*-Züge haben einen Wagen mit verstellbaren ‚u SEATS' für Fahrgäste mit Platzreservierung.

re-branded as the Gakuen-Toshi Line (meaning Academy-City Line), which has been electrified between Soen and Hokkaido-Iryodaigaku (Health Sciences University of Hokkaido), and partially elevated and double-tracked, to cater for increased commuting demand into Sapporo. EMUs replaced DMUs on this route in October 2012.

A mix of Local (all stations) and Rapid (Ishikari Liner) trains operate cross-city services on the Hakodate and Chitose Lines. Service frequencies from Sapporo are up to 9tph towards Otaru, 6tph towards Iwamizawa and 8tph towards Shin-Chitose/Tomakomai though many trains stop short of these final destinations. These frequencies include a 4tph Rapid Airport service linking Shin-Chitose Airport with Sapporo, calling at certain intermediate stations, of which 2tph continue to Otaru and 1tph continues to Asahikawa. The Gakuen-Toshi Line is served by an all-stations service of up to 4tph between Sapporo and Ainosato-Kyoikudai, the limit of double tracking, with 2tph continuing on to Ishikari-Tobetsu or Hokkaido-Iryodaigaku, the limit of electrification.

Sapporo area local services are operated by a mixture of 721/731/733 and 735-series three-car EMUs, the oldest dating from 1988, which are all compatible for multiple operation as six-car trains. Rapid Airport services include one car with reclining 'u SEATs' for reserved seat passengers.

Sapporo   RS

Sapporo – JR Hokkaido - 721-series

Shiyakusho-mae > Uoichiba-dori – 3000-series ► Yunokawa

HAKODATE

Die Hafenstadt Hakodate ist das Tor zu Hokkaido und mit 275.000 Einwohnern auf einer Fläche von 678 km² nach Sapporo und Asahikawa die drittgrößte Stadt der Insel. Sie liegt im Süden von Hokkaido und ist mit Aomori auf der Hauptinsel Honshu durch Fähren und den Shinkansen, der erst kürzlich herkömmliche Züge durch den Seikan-Tunnel ablöste, verbunden. Die erste Phase des *Hokkaido Shinkansen* von Shin-Aomori bis Shin-Hakodate-Hokuto (17,9 km nördlich von Hakodate) ist seit März 2016 in Betrieb, die schnellste Fahrt von Tokyo nach Hakodate konnte dadurch um etwa 50 Minuten auf 4 Stunden 30 Minuten verkürzt werden, wobei in Shin-Hakodate-Hokuto Richtung Innenstadt auf den „Hakodate Liner" von *JR Hokkaido* umgestiegen werden muss.

Die Stadt Hakodate betreibt ein Straßenbahnnetz mit zwei Linien, der Busverkehr wurde hingegen 2003 an den privaten Betreiber *Hakodate Bus* abgegeben. Neben dem oben erwähnten „Hakodate Liner" werden vom achtgleisigen JR-Bahnhof Hakodate aus Nahverkehrszüge von *JR Hokkaido* (Hakodate Main Line) sowie von der *South Hokkaido Railway* (Isaribi Line) betrieben. Eine Luftseilbahn führt auf den Mount Hakodate.

Hakodate is Hokkaido's gateway port and its third-largest city after Sapporo and Asahikawa, with a population of 275,000 in an area of 678 km². It is situated at the southern end of Hokkaido and is linked to Aomori on the main island of Honshu by ferries and by the Hokkaido Shinkansen which replaced the former conventional rail service through the Seikan tunnel. The first phase of the Hokkaido Shinkansen linking Shin-Aomori with Shin-Hakodate-Hokuto (17.9 km north of Hakodate) opened in March 2016, reducing fastest Tokyo — Hakodate journey times by around 50 minutes to 4h 30m, including transfer from Shin-Hakodate-Hokuto to the city centre via JR Hokkaido's connecting 'Hakodate Liner' EMU service.

Hakodate municipality operates a two-route tramway but disposed of its bus division to private operator Hakodate Bus in 2003 as part of a business revitalisation plan. Low-frequency local commuter services are operated by JR Hokkaido (Hakodate Main Line) and the third-sector South Hokkaido Railway (Isaribi Line) from JR's eight-track Hakodate terminus together with the aforementioned 'Hakodate Liner' service. An aerial cable car serves Mt Hakodate.

D Y 17 函館駅前
HAKODATE EKIMAE
函館站前 / 函館站前 / 하코다테에키마에

Hakodate City Tram (D/Y)

10.9 km, 26 Haltestellen | *stops*; 1372 mm; 600Vdc ⚡

Elektrischer Betrieb* | *Electric operation*:
17-06-1913/30-10-1913: Jujigai – Yachiyashita (1.4 km)
29-06-1913: Yunokawa – Matsukaze-cho (6.2 km)
30-10-1913: Matsukaze-cho – Hakodate Dock-mae (3.3 km)

* ohne stillgelegte Strecken | *closed sections not listed*

Yunokawa – 700-series

Goryokaku-Koen-mae – 9600-series – Hokkaido Shinkansen Werbeanstrich | promotional livery

HAKODATE CITY TRAM DEPARTMENT

1897 wurde in Hakodate eine privat betriebene Pferdebahn mit 1372 mm Spurweite in Betrieb genommen. Die Strecke wurde 1913 mit 600 V Gleichstrom elektrifiziert und 1943 von der Stadt übernommen. Das Netz erreichte eine maximale Größe von 17,9 km, nach einer ersten Stilllegung 1978 verblieben vier Linien mit einer Gesamtlänge von 16,3 km. Zu weiteren Rationalisierungen kam es in den Jahren 1992/93, als das Unternehmen seine finanzielle Lage durch die Schließung von zwei weiteren Abschnitten verbessern wollte, um sich auf ein Netz mit zwei Linien zu konzentrieren. Gleichzeitig wurde der frühere Einheitstarif zugunsten eines 4-Preisstufen-Tarifs abgeschafft.

Das übriggebliebene 10,9 km lange Netz umfasst eine Hauptstrecke von Yunokawa, einem Thermalbad in den östlichen Vororten, bis ins Zentrum von Hakodate sowie zwei kürzere westliche Äste. Die Linien 2 und 5 bieten

A privately-operated 1372 mm gauge horse tramway commenced operation in Hakodate in 1897. This was converted to 600Vdc electric traction in 1913 and was taken over by the municipality in 1943. Extending to 17.9 km at its maximum, the first closure occurred in 1978 leaving a 16.3 km system served by four routes. Further rationalisation occurred in 1992/93 when the undertaking sought to improve its financial position by closing two more sections of line to focus on a core two-route tram network; the former flat fare was also abolished in favour of a graduated four-stage system at this time.

The remaining 10.9 km network comprises a trunk line from Yunokawa, a hot spring resort in the eastern suburbs, into central Hakodate with two shorter branches at the western end. Routes 2 and 5 provide a combined 6-minute frequency service between Yunokawa and

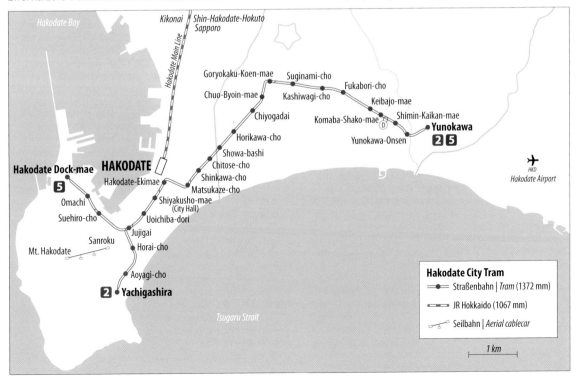

Hakodate City Tram
- ══●══ Straßenbahn | Tram (1372 mm)
- ▭▬▭ JR Hokkaido (1067 mm)
- Seilbahn | Aerial cablecar

1 km

Komaba-Shako-mae – 8000-series ► Yachigashira

einen kombinierten 6-Minuten-Takt zwischen Yunokawa und Jujigai über Hakodate-Ekimae (Bahnhof), auf den Ästen nach Yachigashira (Linie 2) und Hakodate Dock-mae (Linie 5) fährt somit alle 12 Minuten eine Bahn. Die meisten Bahnen fahren auf der Gesamtstrecke der jeweiligen Linie und benötigen dafür 46 Minuten; Kurzläufer sind vereinzelt zwischen Hakodate-Ekimae bzw. Yunokawa und dem Betriebshof bei Komaba unterwegs.

Abgesehen von den eingleisigen Stumpfendstellen ist das gesamte Netz zweigleisig in Straßenmitte. An den meisten Haltestellen sind schmale Bahnsteige und Unterstände vorhanden. Alle Haltestellen sind nummeriert – mit einem „D"-Präfix auf dem Ast nach Hakodate-Dock-mae und einem „Y"-Präfix auf dem Yachigashira-Ast; gemeinsam von den Linien 2 und 5 bediente Haltestellen werden mit „DY" gekennzeichnet. Die Nummern sind auf Netzplänen ersichtlich, an den Haltestellen jedoch bislang nur am Halt Hakodate-Ekimae, wo neue Unterstände errichtet wurden.

Der Fuhrpark besteht aus 32 neuen oder umgebauten Fahrzeugen. Die Haupttypen sind: die 700er Serie (8 Wagen) gebaut von Niigata Engineering 1960/61; die 8000er Serie (10 Wagen), die zwischen 1990 und 2012 durch Umbau aus der ehemaligen 800er Serie entstand; die 2000/3000er Serie (6 Wagen) von Alna Koki von 1993/96; die neueste 9600er Serie (3 Wagen) – 13,25 m lange „Rakkuru-go" Niederflur-Gelenkfahrzeuge von Alna Sharyo, ausgeliefert in den Jahren 2007, 2010 und 2014. Fast alle Fahrzeuge sind mit Vollwerbung beklebt. Die Wagen der Serien 3000 und 9600 sind klimatisiert.

Der Fuhrpark umfasst auch Museumswagen, einen Party-Wagen und Schneeräumfahrzeuge. Tw. 39 „Haikara-go", ein Nachbau von 1993 eines Zweiachsers von 1910 (1937-1993 als Schneepflug unterwegs), ist zwischen Mitte April und Ende Oktober im regelmäßigen Einsatz zu sehen.

Neben Wertkarten (Ikasu) werden Tageskarten nur für die Straßenbahn (600 Yen) oder kombiniert mit Stadtbussen (1 Tag - 1.000 Yen, 2 Tage - 1.700 Yen) angeboten.

Jujigai via Hakodate-Ekimae (station) with a 12-minute frequency on each of the branches to Yachigashira (route 2) and Hakodate Dock-mae (route 5). Most services operate over the full length of their respective routes taking 46 minutes for a single trip; there are, however, a few short workings to/from Hakodate-Ekimae and between Yunokawa and the depot at Komaba.

Apart from single-track stubs at the termini the whole system is double-track laid in the centre of the street. Narrow islands and shelters are provided at most stops. All stops are numbered – with a 'D' prefix on the Hakodate-Dock-mae branch, a 'Y' prefix on the Yachigashira branch and 'DY' for the stops shared by routes 2 and 5. These stop numbers appear on maps but not on the stops themselves, apart from Hakodate-Ekimae which has been refurbished with new shelters.

The tram fleet comprises 32 cars, both new and rebuilt. The main types are: the 700-series (8 cars) built by Niigata Engineering in 1960/61; the 8000-series (10 cars) which are former 800-series vehicles from 1962-65 re-built between 1990 and 2012; the 2000/3000-series (6 cars) built by Alna Koki between 1993/96; and, the latest 9600-series (3 cars), 13.25 m length 'Rakkuru-go' articulated ultra low-floor cars by Alna Sharyo, delivered in 2007, 2010 and 2014. Almost all cars are in all-over advertising liveries. The 3000 and 9600-series are air conditioned.

The fleet also includes museum cars, a party car and snow brooms. Car 39 'Haikara-go', a 1993-reconstruction of a 1910 four-wheeler (used as a snow plough, 1937-93), typically appears in regular service between mid-April and the end of October.

Tickets include one-day passes for the tram only (600 Yen) or combined with urban buses (1 day - 1,000 Yen; 2 days - 1,700 Yen) and pre-paid magnetic 'Ikasu' cards.

Komaba-Shako-mae – 700-series ▶ Yunokawa

Hakodate-Ekimae – 8000-series ▶ Yunokawa

Komaba Depot – 9600-series

Mt. Hakodate Ropeway (Seilbahn | *Aerial Cable Car*)

Die Aussicht bei Nacht vom Mount Hakodate (334 m) auf die Stadt gilt als eine der schönsten in Japan. Die Seilbahn wurde 1958 mit Kabinen für 31 Fahrgäste in Betrieb genommen. Die heutigen Kabinen von 1997 stammen von der österreichischen Firma Svoboda und können 125 Fahrgäste befördern. Die Seilbahn ist 787 m lang und überwindet einen Höhenunterschied von 278,5 m ohne Zwischenstützen. Sie verkehrt bis zu 12 Mal pro Stunde, eine Fahrt dauert drei Minuten. Die Talstation Sanroku ist etwa 10 Gehminuten von der Straßenbahnhaltestelle Jujigai entfernt. Eine Einzelfahrt kostet 660 Yen, die Hin- und Rückfahrt 1200 Yen.

The view of the city from Mt Hakodate (334 m) is reputed to be one of Japan's top three night-time views. The ropeway opened in 1958 with 31 passenger-capacity cars; the current cars came from Austrian company Svoboda in 1997 and can carry 125 passengers. The ropeway has a horizontal length of 787 m and covers a vertical distance of 278.5 m without any intermediate support poles. There are up to 12 departures per hour taking three minutes. The base station, Sanroku, is about 10 minutes by foot from Jujigai tram stop. The adult fare is 660 Yen single, 1200 Yen for a round trip.

Mt. Hakodate Ropeway

Mt. Hakodate Ropeway

SENDAI

Hirosegawa Bridge –
Kokusai (International) Center > Omachi-Nishi-Koen –
Sendai Subway Tozai Line 2000-series ► Yagiyama-Dobutsu-Koen

SENDAI

Sendai ist die Hauptstadt der Präfektur Miyagi und mit 1,07 Mio. Einwohnern auf einer Fläche von 786 km² mit Abstand die größte Stadt in der Region Tohoku. Sie liegt etwa 350 km nördlich von Tokyo, von wo aus sie in etwa 100 Minuten mit dem *Tohoku Shinkansen* erreicht werden kann. Sendai war die nächstgelegene Stadt zum Epizentrum des großen Erdbebens vom März 2011; der daraus entstandene Tsunami verwüstete Küstengebiete und brachte die Bahnen der Region zum Stillstand, auch wenn das Stadtzentrum selbst keine großen Schäden erlitt.

Sendai City Transportation Bureau (*Sendai-shi Kotsu Kyoku*) ist für zwei U-Bahn-Linien und ein umfangreiches Busnetz zuständig. *JR East* betreibt den *Tohoku Shinkansen* sowie auf dem konventionellen 1067-mm-Netz eine Mischung aus Nah- und Fernverkehrszügen; die *Senseki Line* verläuft im innerstädtischen Bereich unterirdisch und bietet einen metroartigen Betrieb. Eine Bahnverbindung zum Flughafen Sendai wurde 2007 eröffnet, der Betrieb wird gemeinsam durch *JR East* und *Sendai Airport Transit* durchgeführt.

Für die U-Bahn gibt es eine Tageskarte für 840 Yen (Sa/So und feiertags 620 Yen), außerdem den „Sendai Marugoto"-Pass für zwei Tage, gültig für U-Bahn, Busse, JR- und *Sendai Airport Transit*-Züge im Großraum Sendai (2.760 Yen). Die IC Card „icsca" der Stadt Sendai kann nur in der Region Sendai (Metro/Bus/JR East) genutzt werden. Die „Suica" von *JR East* und andere wechselseitig gültige Karten werden jedoch in der U-Bahn und den Bussen von Sendai akzeptiert.

Sendai is the capital of Miyagi prefecture and by far the largest city in Japan's Tohoku region, with a population of 1.07 million in an area of 786 km². It is situated about 350 km north of Tokyo from where it can be reached in around 100 minutes on the Tohoku Shinkansen. Sendai was the nearest city to the epicentre of the Great East Japan Earthquake of March 2011; the ensuing tsunami devastated coastal outskirts and disrupted rail and metro services though the city centre did not suffer from major damage.

Sendai City Transportation Bureau (Sendai-shi Kotsu Kyoku) operates two metro lines and an extensive bus network. JR East operates the Tohoku Shinkansen and a mix of suburban and longer distance services on its conventional 1067 mm gauge lines; its Senseki Line runs underground in central and inner Sendai, providing a metro-style service. A rail link to Sendai Airport opened in 2007, operated jointly by JR East and third-sector Sendai Airport Transit.

Ride-at-will tickets include a one-day metro pass (840 Yen; Sat/Sun/Hols - 620 Yen) and a two-day Sendai Marugoto pass which is valid on metro, bus, JR and Sendai Airport Transit services in the greater Sendai area (2,760 Yen). Sendai City's 'icsca' IC card can only be used in the Sendai area (metro/bus/JR East). However, JR East's 'Suica' and other cards in the national inter-operability scheme are accepted on Sendai's metro and buses.

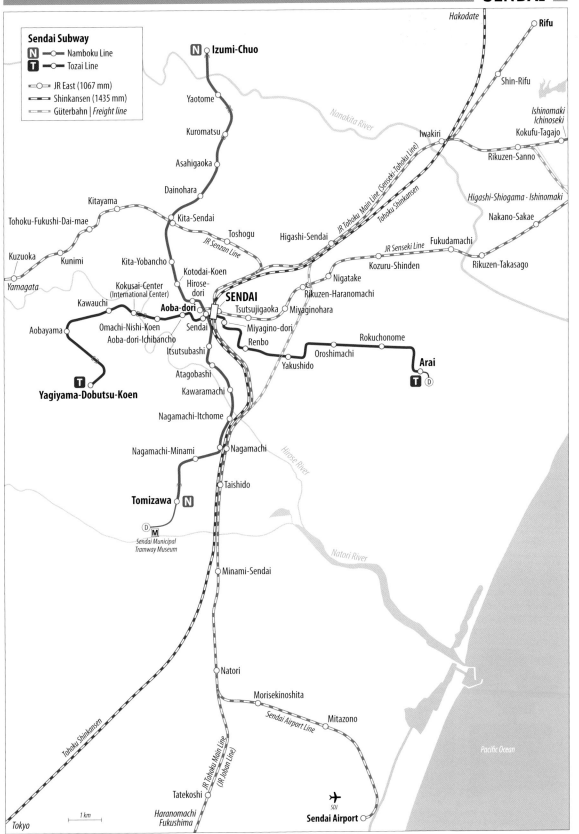

Sendai Subway
N ━━○━ Namboku Line
T ━━○━ Tozai Line

━○━ JR East (1067 mm)
━━━ Shinkansen (1435 mm)
━━━ Güterbahn | Freight line

Hakodate

N Izumi-Chuo
Rifu
Shin-Rifu

Yaotome
Nanakita River
Ishinomaki
Ichinoseki

Kuromatsu
Iwakiri
Kokufu-Tagajo

Asahigaoka
Rikuzen-Sanno

Dainohara
Higashi-Shiogama · Ishinomaki

Kitayama
Kita-Sendai
Toshogu
Nakano-Sakae

Tohoku-Fukushi-Dai-mae
Higashi-Sendai
Fukudamachi

JR Senzan Line
JR Senseki Line
Rikuzen-Takasago

Kuzuoka
Kunimi
Kita-Yobancho
Kozuru-Shinden

Yamagata
Kotodai-Koen
Nigatake

Kokusai-Center
(International Center)
Hirose-dori
Rikuzen-Haranomachi

Kawauchi
Aoba-dori
SENDAI
Tsutsujigaoka
Miyaginohara

Aobayama
Omachi-Nishi-Koen
Sendai
Miyagino-dori
Rokuchonome

Aoba-dori-Ichibancho
Renbo
Oroshimachi
Arai
T D

Itsutsubashi
Yakushido

T
Yagiyama-Dobutsu-Koen
Atagobashi

Kawaramachi

Nagamachi-Itchome

Hirose River

Nagamachi-Minami
Nagamachi

Tomizawa N
Taishido

D
M
Sendai Municipal
Tramway Museum

Natori River

Minami-Sendai

JR Tohoku Main Line (Senseki-Tohoku Line)
Tohoku Shinkansen

Tohoku Shinkansen

Natori

Morisekinoshita
Sendai Airport Line
Mitazono

JR Tohoku Main Line
(JR Joban Line)

Pacific Ocean

1 km

Tatekoshi

Haranomachi
Fukushima

✈
SDJ
Sendai Airport

Tokyo

41

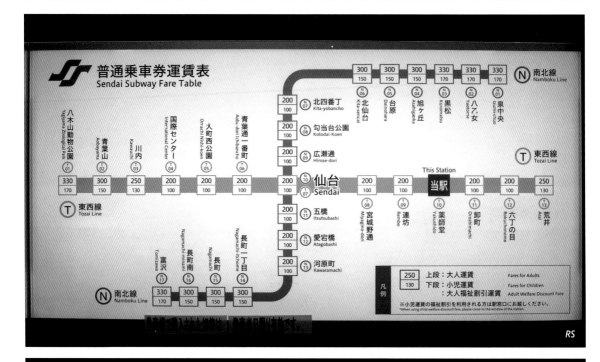

普通乗車券運賃表
Sendai Subway Fare Table

（N）南北線 Namboku Line

| 300 | 300 | 300 | 330 | 330 | 330 |
| 150 | 150 | 150 | 170 | 170 | 170 |

北四番丁 Kita-yobancho (N07) 200/100

北仙台 Kita-sendai (N06)
台原 Dainohara (N05)
旭ケ丘 Asahigaoka (N04)
黒松 Kuromatsu (N03)
八乙女 Yaotome (N02)
泉中央 Izumi-chuo (N01)

勾当台公園 Kotodai-Koen (N08) 200/100

（T）東西線 Tozai Line

広瀬通 Hirose-dori (N09) 200/100

This Station

八木山動物公園 Yagiyama Zoological Park (T01)
青葉山 Aobayama (T02)
川内 Kawauchi (T03)
国際センター International Center (T04)
大町西公園 Omachi Nishi-koen (T05)
青葉通一番町 Aoba-dori Ichibancho (T06)

| 330 | 300 | 250 | 200 | 200 | 200 |
| 170 | 150 | 130 | 100 | 100 | 100 |

仙台 Sendai (N10/T07) 200/100

| 200 | 200 | 当駅 | 200 | 200 | 250 |
| 100 | 100 | | 100 | 100 | 130 |

（T）東西線 Tozai Line

五橋 Itsutsubashi (N11) 200/100

宮城野通 Miyagino-dori (T08)
連坊 Rembo (T09)
薬師堂 Yakushido (T10)
卸町 Oroshimachi (T11)
六丁の目 Rokuchonome (T12)
荒井 Arai (T13)

愛宕橋 Atagobashi (N12) 200/100

河原町 Kawaramachi (N13) 200/100

富沢 Tomizawa (N17)
長町南 Nagamachi-minami (N16)
長町 Nagamachi (N15)
長町一丁目 Nagamachi-itchome (N14)

（N）南北線 Namboku Line

| 330 | 300 | 300 | 300 |
| 170 | 150 | 150 | 150 |

250	上段：大人運賃	Fares for Adults
130	下段：小児運賃	Fares for Children
凡例	：大人福祉割引運賃	Adult Welfare Discount Fare

※小児運賃の福祉割引を利用される方は駅窓口にお越しください。
*When using child welfare discount fare, please come to the window of the station.

RS

SENDAI SUBWAY

In den frühen 1970er Jahren wurde noch vor dem Ende des Straßenbahnbetriebs 1976 ein Metro-Netz mit sieben Linien entworfen. Später konzentrierte man die Planungen auf eine Nord-Süd-Strecke, eine Ost-West-Strecke mit durchgebundenem Betrieb auf die JNR (heute JR) Senseki Line sowie eine Monorail, die den Südwesten der Stadt erschließen sollte. Der Bau der Namboku Line (Nord-Süd-Linie) begann 1981 und wurde 1992 vollendet. 1991 wurden die ursprünglichen Pläne für eine Monorail aufgegeben und das Projekt für die Ost-West-Linie dahingehend verändert, dass daraus eine Kleinprofil-Metro entstand, deren Bau 2004 begann und die im Dezember 2015 als Tozai Line eröffnet wurde.

Mit Inbetriebnahme der Tozai Line wurde für 13 Stationen im zentralen Bereich ein Einheitstarif von 200 Yen eingeführt. Stationseingänge sind mit einem „SS"-Symbol gekennzeichnet, welches auch an Fahrzeugen und in Infomaterialien zu sehen ist.

Plans for a seven-route metro network were developed in the early 1970s prior to the end of tramway operations in 1976. These options were then narrowed down to a north-south route, an east-west route with through running to the JNR (now JR) Senseki Line and a monorail serving the south-west of the city. Construction of the north-south Namboku Line commenced in 1981 and the line was completed in 1992. In 1991 plans for the proposed monorail and east-west line were abandoned but plans for a revised east-west small-profile metro, the Tozai Line, were subsequently developed; construction commenced in 2004 and the line opened in December 2015.

A new fare structure was adopted to coincide with the opening of the Tozai Line with a flat 200 Yen fare covering 13 central area stations. Station entrances are denoted by an 'SS' symbol which also appears on rolling stock and publicity material.

Yagiyama-Dobutsu-Koen   RS

Aoba-dori-Ichibancho

SENDAI SUBWAY: 2 U-Bahn-Linien | *metro lines*; 28.7 km; 29 U-Bahnhöfe (30, wenn man sie für jede Linie einzeln zählt) | *29 stations (30 if stations on each line counted separately)*; 144 Wagen | *cars*; 67 900 000 pax/a, 186 000 pax/d

Yaotome > Izumi-Chuo – Namboku Line 1000N-series

Namboku Line

Diese Linie verbindet äußere Wohngebiete im Norden und Süden mit dem Stadtzentrum, der innerstädtische Abschnitt ersetzte ehemalige Nord-Süd-Straßenbahnlinien zwischen Kita-Sendai und Nagamachi.

Der nördliche Endpunkt Izumi-Chuo liegt unterirdisch auf Ebene -1 unter einem Vorstadt-Einkaufszentrum mit angeschlossenem Busbahnhof. Kurz nach Abfahrt erreichen die Züge ein Betonviadukt, fahren am Sendai-Stadion vorbei und halten am ursprünglichen Endpunkt Yaotome auf Ebene +2. Die Hochbahn verläuft weiter Richtung Süden durch den Mamizawa-Park bis Kuromatsu, wo die Züge im Tunnel verschwinden. Nach dem Durchqueren des Stadtzentrums taucht die Linie kurz vor der Endstation Tomizawa wieder auf und endet in Hochlage (+2). Die Hochbahntrasse führt 0,6 km weiter zum Depot, wo sich auch das *Sendai Municipal Tramway Museum* befindet, das drei Straßenbahnwagen sowie andere kleinere Exponate beherbergt.

Die Namboku und Tozai Line kreuzen sich im rechten Winkel am Bahnhof Sendai, wo die Bahnsteige auf den Ebenen -3 bzw. -4 liegen. Außerdem besteht hier eine Umsteigemöglichkeit zur JR Senseki Line im nahen unterirdischen Bahnhof Aoba-dori sowie über einen 200 m langen unterirdischen Korridor zum JR-Bahnhof Sendai. Von der Namboku Line kann man in Kita-Sendai zur JR

This line links outer suburban dormitory areas in the north and south via the city centre, the inner section replacing former north-south tram routes between Kita-Sendai and Nagamachi.

The northern terminus, Izumi-Chuo, is situated underground at B1-level beneath a district shopping centre with adjacent bus terminal. From here the line ascends onto a concrete viaduct, passing close to Sendai Stadium, to reach the original terminus at Yaotome which is situated above ground at second-floor level (3F). The viaduct continues southwards passing through the wooded Mamizawa Park to Kuromatsu where the line enters tunnel. After passing through Sendai city centre the line re-emerges onto viaduct shortly before Tomizawa terminus where the station is again at second-floor level. The viaduct continues for a further 0.6 km beyond Tomizawa to the depot, which is also home of the Sendai Municipal Tramway Museum which houses three tramcars and other smaller exhibits.

The Namboku and Tozai Lines cross at right angles at Sendai station where their platforms are at B3 and B4-levels respectively. There is also interchange with nearby Aoba-dori underground station on the JR Senseki Line and with JR Sendai Station via 200 m underground passageways. The Namboku Line also links with the JR Senzan

Namboku Line (N)

Izumi-Chuo (N01) – Tomizawa (N17)
14.8 km, Ⓤ 12 km, 17 Bahnhöfe | *stations*
1500Vdc ⭡; 1067 mm; 174 000 pax/d

15-07-1987: Tomizawa – Yaotome
15-07-1992: Yaotome – Izumi-Chuo

Nagamachi – 1000N-series ▶ Tomizawa

Senzan Line und in Nagamachi zur Tohoku bzw. Joban Line umsteigen, wobei in beiden Fällen ein kurzer Fußweg zurückzulegen ist.

Die Tunnel der Namboku Line sind rechteckig mit Mittelstützen und alle Stationen haben 130 m lange Mittelbahnsteige, auch wenn bislang nur 4-Wagen-Züge eingesetzt werden, denn Pläne für 6-Wagen-Züge wurden verworfen. Die U-Bahn-Stationen verfügen über mehrere Eingänge, von denen mindestens einer mit einem Aufzug ausgestattet ist. Direkt unterhalb der Straßenebene liegt das Verteilergeschoss. Am U-Bahnhof Asahigaoka ist die westliche Seite des Tunnels offen und erlaubt einen Blick in den Dainohara Forest Park. Auf der Bahnsteigebene sind Stationsschilder und die halbhohen Bahnsteigtüren je nach Fahrtrichtung farblich verschieden – blau Richtung Norden und dunkelrosa Richtung Süden. Die Bahnhofsgestaltung ist eher funktional mit vor allem gefliesten Oberflächen in Braun- und Beigetönen. Im U-Bahnhof Hirose-dori findet man allerdings ein bemerkenswertes gewölbtes Wandbild mit mythologischen Figuren und der U-Bahnhof Sendai

Line at Kita-Sendai and the Tohoku and Joban Lines at Nagamachi though in both cases there is a short walk between stations at street level.

Tunnels are rectangular in cross-section with pillars separating the tracks and all stations have 130 m long island platforms though only four-car trains are operated, plans for six-car operation having been frozen. The underground stations all have multiple street level entrances, with at least one having lift access, and subsurface ticket halls. At Asahigaoka the western side of the tunnel is open and looks over Dainohara Forest Park. At platform level, station signs and platform edge gates are colour-coded blue for northbound and dark pink for southbound. Station décor is functional with mainly tiled surfaces in brown and beige colours, though Hirose-dori has a noteworthy vaulted mural depicting mythological figures and Sendai (N10) has a green indirectly illuminated vaulted ceiling along the middle of the island platform.

The line is operated by 21 four-car sets of 1000N-series stock built by Kawasaki between 1987 and 2007. The cars were refurbished between 2004 and 2013 to include internal and external LED destination signs, space for wheelchairs, VVVF control and air conditioning. These trains have ATC/ATO control and were the first in the world to use fuzzy logic to control speed.

Seven of the outer suburban stations are designated transfer discount stations where bus/metro transfer tickets are available at a reduced rate. Running time is 27 minutes from end to end with a service frequency of approximately 5-7 minutes.

Sendai – 1000N-series ► Tomizawa

(N10) hat eine grüne, indirekt beleuchtete gewölbte Decke über dem Mittelbahnsteig.

Auf dieser Linie sind 21 Vier-Wagen-Einheiten vom Typ 1000N von Kawasaki, gebaut 1987-2007, im Einsatz. Diese Fahrzeuge wurden zwischen 2004 und 2013 modernisiert, sie verfügen nun über interne und externe LED-Anzeiger, Platz für Rollstühle, VVVF-Steuerung und eine Klimaanlage. Die Züge sind mit ATC/ATO ausgerüstet und nutzten als erste weltweit Fuzzy-Logik zur Geschwindigkeitskontrolle.

An sieben U-Bahnhöfen im äußeren Bereich kann vergünstigt zwischen Bus und Metro umgestiegen werden. Die Fahrzeit auf der Gesamtstrecke beträgt 27 Minuten, die Züge verkehren etwa alle 5-7 Minuten.

Hirose-dori – Zwischengeschoss | *mezzanine*   RS

Hirose-dori   RS

Namboku Line 1000N-series

RS   Arai

Tozai Line

Wie ihr Name vermuten lässt, verläuft die Tozai Line im Zentrum von Sendai in Ost-West-Richtung, von Arai in den flachen östlichen Vororten bis Yagiyama-Dobutsu-Koen (Zoo) in den hügeligen westlichen Vororten jenseits des Hirose-Flusses. Alle Bahnhöfe sind unterirdisch, lediglich zwei kurze Streckenabschnitte liegen im Freien – zur Überquerung des Hirose-Flusses (zwischen Kokusai Center und Omachi-Nishi-Koen) und des Tatsunokuchi-Tals (zwischen Aobayama und Yagiyama-Dobutsu-Koen). Die Züge verlassen auch den Tunnel, um das oberirdische Depot direkt hinter der Endstation Arai zu erreichen. Die Stationen Aobayama und Kawauchi erschließen den Campus der Universität Tohoku. Eine Umsteigemöglichkeit zur Namboku Line sowie zu den JR-Linien ist am Bahnhof Sendai gegeben, wo der Bahnsteig der Tozai Line auf Ebene -4 unterhalb der Namboku Line (-3) liegt.

As its name suggests, the Tozai Line runs east-west through central Sendai from Arai in the flat eastern suburbs to Yagiyama-Dobutsu-Koen (zoological park) in the hilly western suburbs beyond the Hirose River. The line and all stations are underground apart from two short open-air sections where the line crosses the Hirose River (between Kokusai [International] Center and Omachi-Nishi-Koen) and the Tatsunokuchi valley (between Aobayama and Yagiyama-Dobutsu-Koen). The line also emerges from tunnel to access the surface-level depot just beyond the Arai terminus. Aobayama and Kawauchi stations serve the Tohoku University campus and interchange with the Namboku and JR lines is available at Sendai station where the Tozai Line platform is at B4-level beneath the Namboku Line (B3-level).

For Ⓣ01 Yagiyama Zoological Park   Car No. 4

Aoba-dori Ichibancho · Sendai · Miyagino-dori · Rembo · Yakushido · Oroshimachi · Rokuchonome · Arai
T06 · T07 · T08 · T09 · T10 · T11 · T12 · T13
15 · 13 · 12 · 9 · 7 · 5 · 3

Estimated time

RS

Tozai Line (T)

Yagiyama-Dobutsu-Koen (T01) – Arai (T13)
13.9 km, Ⓤ 13.4 km, 13 Bahnhöfe | *stations*
1500Vdc ⬆; 1435 mm
54 000 pax/d

06-12-2015: Yagiyama-Dobutsu-Koen – Arai

Kawauchi   RS

Sendai – 2000-series ▶ Yagiyama-Dobutsu-Koen   RS

Die Tozai Line hat ein kleineres Tunnelprofil und wird mit 15 Vier-Wagen-Zügen vom Typ 2000 von Kinki Sharyo, mit Linearmotoren und ATO/ATC ausgerüstet, betrieben. Der Tunnel- und Stationsbau erfolgte durch eine Kombination aus offener Bauweise, Schildvortrieb und NÖT, wobei die Tiefenlage von knapp unterhalb der Oberfläche (Kokusai Center) bis Ebene -6 (Aobayama) variiert. Alle Stationen haben Mittelbahnsteige mit halbhohen Bahnsteigtüren, deren Farbe zusammen mit den Stationsschildern die Richtung anzeigt – grün nach Westen oder orange nach Osten. Die Bahnsteige sind in der Regel nur lang genug für 4-Wagen-Züge, auch wenn versteckte Vorleistungen für eine mögliche Verlängerung vorhanden sind; der U-Bahnhof Sendai (T07) hat einen längeren Bahnsteig, so dass die Züge versetzt zueinander halten können. Der Stationsgestaltung wurde mehr Aufmerksamkeit gewidmet als auf der Namboku Line, so dass alle Bahnhöfe irgendein ansprechendes Detail aufweisen, meist in Form einer speziellen Deckenstruktur mit indirekter Beleuchtung; es wurden aber auch unterschiedliche Farbkombinationen bzw. Wandverkleidungen angewandt sowie mancherorts in der Zwischenebene interessante Wandbilder angebracht. Für die Gestaltung der Hirosegawa-Brücke und des anschließenden Nishi-Koen-Viadukts durch eine reizvolle Parklandschaft wurde erstmals in Japan ein Wettbewerb durchgeführt.

Die Züge verkehren alle 6-8 Minuten, die Gesamtfahrzeit beträgt 26 Minuten. Beim Umsteigen an den Stationen Yagiyama-Dobutsu-Koen, Yakushido und Arai zahlt man für eine anschließende Busfahrt bis 1,5 km nur 100 Yen. Das Ziel ist, 80.000 Fahrgäste pro Tag zu befördern.

The line has small-profile tunnels and is operated by 15 four-car 2000-series linear-motor trains with ATO/ATC built by Kinki Sharyo. Tunnel and station construction was by a combination of cut-and-cover, shield and NATM, with station depth ranging from just below the surface (Kokusai Center) to as deep as B6-level (Aobayama). Stations have single island platforms with half-height gates which, together with station signs, are coloured green (westbound) or orange (eastbound). Platforms are generally just long enough to accommodate 4-car trains, with concealed provision for future platform lengthening; however, Sendai (T07) has a longer platform with staggered stopping positions for east and westbound trains. Station design and decor has received more attention than on the Namboku Line with all stations having some appealing elements, in most cases it is a special ceiling structure using indirect illumination, but also varying colour schemes, types of wall cladding and in some cases stylish murals at the intermediate level. The first design competition for railway bridges in Japan was held to select the design for the Hirosegawa Bridge and adjoining Nishi-Koen viaduct which are situated in a scenic parkland area.

Services operate every 6-8 minutes and take 26 minutes for the entire route. Yagiyama-Dobutsu-Koen, Yakushido and Arai are transit hub stations with flat 100 Yen bus fares within 1.5 km radius. Patronage is expected to reach 80,000 passengers/day.

Tozai Line 2000-series   RS

Yagiyama-Dobutsu-Koen   RS

SENDAI

Aobayama

Rokuchonome

Yagiyama-Dobutsu-Koen

Kokusai (International) Center

Miyagino-dori

Aoba-dori – JR East Senseki Line 205-series ▶ Higashi-Shiogama

VORORTBAHNEN

Die Senseki Line von *JR East* verbindet das Zentrum von Sendai mit Vororten und Küstengebieten im Nordosten, wobei auf dem inneren Abschnitt ein U-Bahn-artiger Betrieb mit 4-Minuten-Takt zu Spitzenzeiten angeboten wird. Die Strecke wurde von der *Miyagi Electric Railway* eingleisig mit einer Spurweite von 1067 mm von Sendai nach Ishinomaki (50 km) errichtet und mit 1500 V Gleichstrom elektrifiziert. Bei ihrer Eröffnung 1925 war sie quasi Japans erste U-Bahn, zwei Jahre vor der Ginza Line in Tokyo, denn die ursprüngliche Endstation in Sendai lag unterirdisch. Nach Verstaatlichung der Linie 1944 wurde diese jedoch 1952 durch eine oberirdische Anlage ersetzt. Doch im Jahr 2000 wurde die einst kurvenreiche eingleisige Strecke durch die inneren Vorstädte begradigt und zwischen Rikuzen-Haranomachi und Aoba-dori zweigleisig unter die Erde verlegt. Die 3,2 km lange Tunnelstrecke umfasst fünf U-Bahnhöfe einschließlich eines neuen unterirdischen Bahnsteigs am JR-Bahnhof Sendai. Es war beabsichtigt, die Züge der Senseki Line auf die geplante Ost-West-Metro durchlaufen zu lassen, doch dieses Vorhaben wurde später verworfen. Die Strecke ist heute zweigleisig bis Higashi-Shiogama (17,2 km), bis wohin ein dichter Verkehr angeboten wird. Die Küstenabschnitte dieser Strecke wurden durch den Tsunami von 2011 schwer beschädigt, so dass die Züge erst 2015 wieder bis Ishinomaki durchfahren konnten. Als *Local*- und (gelegentliche) *Rapid*-Züge verkehren Fahrzeuge der Baureihe 205-3100 aus dem Jahr 2004 als Vier-Wagen-Einheiten.

SUBURBAN RAIL

JR East's Senseki Line links central Sendai with suburban and coastal areas to the north-east of the city, providing a metro-style service with four minute headways during peak periods on its inner section. The line was built as a 1067 mm gauge single-track railway, electrified at 1500Vdc, between Sendai and Ishinomaki (50 km) by the Miyagi Electric Railway. It had the distinction of being Japan's first underground railway, opening in 1925 and pre-dating Tokyo's Ginza Line by two years, as its Sendai terminus was in tunnel. The line was nationalised in 1944 and the original underground terminus was replaced by a surface-level facility in 1952. However, in 2000 the line once again regained its underground status when the curvaceous single-track section through the inner suburbs was replaced by a new straighter double-track alignment in tunnel between Rikuzen-Haranomachi and Aoba-dori. The 3.2 km underground section has five stations including a new underground platform at JR Sendai station. It had been intended that Senseki Line trains would run through to the proposed east-west metro line but this plan was subsequently abandoned. The line is now double-tracked as far as Higashi-Shiogama (17.2 km) and frequent services operate to this point. The coastal sections of the line were severely damaged in the 2011 tsunami and through trains to Ishinomaki were not reintroduced until 2015. Local and (occasional) Rapid services are operated with a fleet of 205-3100 series 4-car EMUs dating from 2004.

Sendai – JR East E271-series (Senzan Line *Rapid* & *Local*)

JR East betreibt außerdem von Sendai aus Regionalbahnen auf der Joban, Senzan und Tohoku Line, die mit 20 kV AC 50 Hz elektrifiziert sind, während mit Batterien ausgerüstete Dieseltriebwagen auf der Senseki-Tohoku Line unterwegs sind, allerdings weniger häufig. Der Bahnverkehr zwischen Sendai und dem Flughafen wird gemeinsam mit *Sendai Airport Transit* (SAT) durchgeführt, einer Gesellschaft, die im März 2007 die 7,1 km lange Sendai Airport Access Line als Abzweig von der JR Tohoku Line eröffnete. An SAT sind die Präfektur Miyagi, die Städte Sendai und Natori sowie *JR East* beteiligt. Die Flughafen-Linie ist aufgeständert und einspurig mit einer einzigen Ausweiche und drei Stationen. Abgesehen von zwei *Rapid*-Zügen pro Tag fahren 2-3 *Local*-Züge pro Stunde, die für die 17,5 km ab Sendai bei sechs Zwischenhalten 25 Minuten benötigen. Die *JR East*-Baureihe E271-500 sowie die Baureihe SAT721 verkehren als 2-Wagen-Einheiten, sie haben einen verschiedenen Anstrich, sind sonst aber ähnlich.

JR East also operates local services from Sendai on the 20kVac 50Hz Joban, Senzan and Tohoku Lines and the hybrid DMU-operated Senseki-Tohoku Line albeit at lower frequencies. A service between Sendai and Sendai Airport is provided jointly with Sendai Airport Transit (SAT), a third-sector company which opened the 7.1 km Sendai Airport Access Line in March 2007 connecting with JR's Tohoku Line at Natori. SAT's main shareholders are Miyagi Prefecture, Sendai and Natori municipalities and JR East. The elevated airport line is single-track with a single passing loop and three stations. Apart from two Rapid service trains per day, a Local service is operated at a frequency of 2-3 tph and takes 25 minutes to complete the 17.5 km trip with six intermediate stops. The JR East E271-500 series and SAT721 series 2-car EMUs which operate the service have different liveries but are otherwise similar.

Kozuru-Shinden > Nigatake – JR East Senseki Line 205-series

Sendai – Sendai Airport Transit SAT721-series

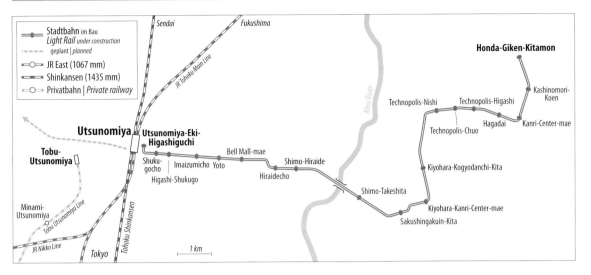

UTSUNOMIYA

Utsunomiya (518.000 Einwohner, 416.8 km²) ist die Hauptstadt der Präfektur Tochigi und ein wichtiger Industriestandort 100 km nördlich von Tokyo in der Kanto-Ebene. Die Stadt kann mit dem *Tohoku Shinkansen*, der Tohoku Main Line und Nikko Line von *JR East* sowie der Utsunomiya Line von *Tobu Railway* erreicht werden. Utsunomiya hatte zwar früher nie eine städtische Straßenbahn, doch demnächst entsteht hier die erste völlig neu entworfene Stadtbahn Japans (im Gegensatz zu Toyama, wo eine vorhandene Eisenbahn zur Stadtbahn umgebaut wurde).

Im Jahr 2015 wurde die Gesellschaft *Utsunomiya Light Rail Corporation* gegründet, an der die Städte Utsunomiya und Haga mit 41% bzw. 10% beteiligt sind. Der Bau soll 2017 beginnen, die Eröffnung ist für Dezember 2019 vorgesehen.

Der erste Abschnitt ist 14,6 km lang und verläuft in Ost-West-Richtung vom JR-Bahnhof Utsunomiya (Ostausgang) nach Haga (Honda Giken - Nordtor) mit insgesamt 19 Haltestellen, davon liegen vier in der Gemeinde Haga. Der Großteil der Strecke wird entlang bestehender Straßen errichtet, doch ca. 5,0 km werden eine eigene Trasse bekommen, dazu gehört eine neue, 643 m lange Brücke über den Fluss Kinu. Jenseits des Flusses erschließt die Linie das Utsunomiya Technopolis Center und mehrere Gewerbeparks, bevor sie am Haga-Takanezawa Industrial Park endet, wo Honda Motor und einige ihrer Tochterfirmen einen Standort haben. Die Strecke wird zweigleisig mit zusätzlichen Ausweichen, um Express-Fahrten zu ermöglichen.

Während der Hauptverkehrszeiten ist ein 6-Minuten-Takt, sonst ein 10-Minuten-Takt vorgesehen. Die Fahrzeit soll 38 Minuten (Express) bzw. 44 Minuten betragen. Es werden siebzehn 30 m lange Fahrzeuge (1067 mm Spurweite, 750 V DC) angeschafft. Man geht von 16.300 Passagieren pro Tag aus.

Später ist eine 3 km lange Westverlängerung durch die Innenstadt entlang der Haupt-Ost-West-Achse (Odori) geplant. Die Querung der JR-Strecke soll kreuzungsfrei erfolgen, indem die ebenerdigen 1067-mm-Gleise über- und die parallele Shinkansen-Hochstrecke unterquert wird.

Utsunomiya (518,000 population; 416.8 km²) is the capital of Tochigi Prefecture and an important industrial centre situated 100 km north of Tokyo in the Kanto plain. It is served by the Tohoku Shinkansen, JR East's Tohoku Main Line and Nikko Line and Tobu Railway's Utsunomiya Line. Although Utsunomiya never had a traditional urban tramway it looks set to become the first Japanese city to construct a completely new modern light rail system (as opposed to Toyama which has converted an existing railway to light rail operation).

In 2015 a third-sector company, Utsunomiya Light Rail Corporation, was formed with Utsunomiya and Haga municipalities holding 41% and 10% of shares respectively. Construction is due to commence in 2017 with opening scheduled for December 2019.

The authorised first stage is 14.6 km long, running in an east-west direction from JR Utsunomiya (East Exit) to Haga Town (Honda Giken - North Gate) with a total of 19 stops, 4 of which are in Haga Town. Most of the line is to be constructed along existing roads but approximately 5.0 km will be reserved-track including a new 643 m bridge over the Kinu River; beyond the river the line will serve the Utsunomiya Technopolis Center and several industrial parks, terminating at the Haga-Takanezawa Industrial Park where Honda Motor and affiliates are located. The line will be double-track with passing loops to permit the operation of express services.

The planned timetable envisages a 6-minute peak and 10-minute off-peak service taking 38 minutes (express) and 44 minutes (all-stops), operated by a fleet of seventeen 30 m long vehicles (1067 mm gauge, 750Vdc). Anticipated ridership is 16,300 passengers/day.

A planned but as yet unauthorised second stage would extend the line by 3 km westwards from JR Utsunomiya station through the city centre along the main east-west thoroughfare (Odori). At JR Utsunomiya station, it is envisaged that the LRT line would be vertically separated from the north-south JR lines, passing above the ground-level 1067 mm gauge tracks but below the elevated Shinkansen tracks.

Shiyakusho-mae – Nagaden 8500-series (ex-Tokyu) - *Local* ▶ Shinshu-Nakano

NAGANO

Nagano (387.146 Einwohner, 834.85 km²), Hauptstadt der Präfektur Nagano, liegt im flachen Tal des Chikuma-Flusses umgeben von Bergen der Northern Alps. Die Stadt entstand rund um Zenkoji, einen buddhistischen Tempel aus dem 7. Jahrhundert und heute eine bedeutende Touristenattraktion. Der *Nagano* (jetzt *Hokuriku*) *Shinkansen* wurde 1997 im Vorfeld der Olympischen und Paralympischen Winterspiele von 1998 eröffnet; der JR-Bahnhof Nagano wurde damals umgebaut und erweitert. Die aktuelle Shinkansen-Fahrt von Tokyo (222 km) dauert ca. 1 Stunde 20 Minuten. Die *Nagano Electric Railway* (Nagaden) betreibt eine einzige Linie mit einem metroartigen unterirdischen Abschnitt im Innenstadtbereich und einer Endstation neben dem JR-Bahnhof. Regionalverkehr wird außerdem von *JR East* sowie von der *Shinano Railway* durchgeführt.

Nagano (387,146 population; 834.85 km²), capital of inland Nagano Prefecture, is situated in the flat valley of the Chikuma River ringed by mountains of the Northern Alps. The city grew up around Zenkoji, a 7th century Buddist temple, which is today a significant tourist attraction. The Nagano (now Hokuriku) Shinkansen opened in 1997 in advance of the city hosting the Winter Olympics and Paralympics in 1998; JR Nagano station was rebuilt and expanded at the same time. The current Shinkansen journey time from Tokyo (222 km) is around 1hr 20mins. The Nagano Electric Railway (Nagaden) runs a single line with a metro-like underground section on the approach to its city terminus next to the JR station; other local rail services are operated by JR East and the third-sector Shinano Railway.

Gondo – Nagaden 1000-series (ex-Odakyu) - Limited-Express ▶ Nagano

Nagaden Nagano

Nagano – 3500-series (ex-Tokyo Hibiya Line) - Local ▶ Shinshu-Nakano

NAGANO ELECTRIC RAILWAY Nagano Dentetsu – 'Nagaden'

Die private Bahngesellschaft *Nagano Electric Railway* (Nagaden) eröffnete 1926 eine Strecke zwischen Gondo in Nagano und Suzaka. Im selben Jahr übernahm und elektrifizierte sie die *Kato Railway*, die 1922-25 als Dampfeisenbahn auf der östlichen Seite des Chikuma-Flusses zwischen Yashiro und Kijima über Suzaka und Shinshu-Nakano eröffnet worden war. Verlängerungen ins Zentrum von Nagano und zum Kurort Yudanaka folgten kurz danach.

Der Abschnitt Nagano – Shinano-Yoshida war von Anfang an zweigleisig, in den 1950er Jahren wurde auch zwischen Shinano-Yoshida und Asahi (6,3 km von Nagano)

The privately-owned *Nagano Electric Railway* (Nagaden) opened between Gondo in Nagano and Suzaka in 1926. In the same year it absorbed and electrified the Kato Railway which had opened (1922-25) as a steam railway running on the eastern side of the Chikuma River between Yashiro and Kijima via Suzaka and Shinshu-Nakano. Extensions to Nagano city centre and the hot spring resort of Yudanaka followed shortly thereafter.

The Nagano — Shinano-Yoshida section was built as double-track from the outset, and a second track was introduced between Shinano-Yoshida and Asahi (6.3 km from Nagano) in the 1950s; the remainder of the line is

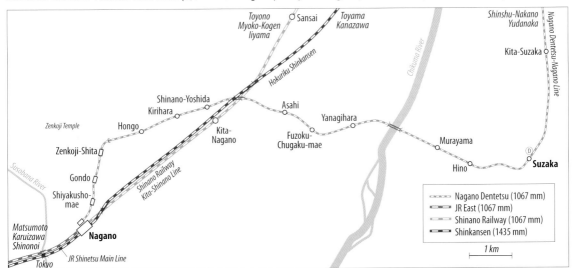

Legend:
- Nagano Dentetsu (1067 mm)
- JR East (1067 mm)
- Shinano Railway (1067 mm)
- Shinkansen (1435 mm)

1 km

ein zweites Gleis verlegt. Der Rest der Linie ist bis heute eingleisig. 1981 wurde der Abschnitt von Nagano bis kurz hinter Zenkoji-Shita (4 Stationen, 1,9 km) in einen Tunnel unter einer breiten Straße (Nagano-Odori) verlegt. Die unterirdischen Bahnsteige liegen auf der Ebene -2, darüber befindet sich eine Zwischenebene, die auch als Fußgängerunterführung dient. Die Endstation Nagano verfügt über drei Stumpfgleise und ist über Fahrtreppen und einen Aufzug zugänglich. Die übrigen drei U-Bahnhöfe haben Seitenbahnsteige nur mit festen Treppen. Die Unterführungen an der Station Zenkoji-Shita sind mit Nagaden-Wandbildern verziert, sonst scheinen die Bahnhöfe seit ihrer Inbetriebnahme nicht renoviert worden zu sein.

Die Kijima und Yashiro Line wurden aufgrund rückläufiger Fahrgastzahlen 2002 bzw. 2012 stillgelegt, so dass nur eine einzige Linie verbleibt, die Pendler nach Nagano und Ausflügler zu den heißen Quellen und Skigebieten in Yudanaka sowie in die benachbarten Alpen bringt. Der Großteil der Strecke verläuft durch das flache Tal durch vorstädtische und ländliche Siedlungen, erst hinter Shinshu-Nakano steigt die Strecke an und wird landschaftlich interessanter.

Pro Stunde verkehren zwischen Nagano und Suzaka 2-3 Züge mit Halt an allen Stationen in unregelmäßigen Abständen, von denen einer oder drei weiter bis Shinshu-Nakano fahren; zwischen Shinshu-Nakano und Yudanaka pendelt ein Zug 1-2 Mal pro Stunde. Das Angebot wird fast ganztags durch einen stündlichen *Limited Express* von Nagoya bis Shinshu-Nakano oder Yudanaka ergänzt, wobei abwechselnd an unterschiedlichen Stationen gehalten wird (*Limited Express A/B*).

Die Flotte besteht aus 45 Elektrotriebwagen, die alle gebraucht von größeren Betrieben beschafft wurden. Normale Fahrten werden im Ein-Mann-Betrieb mit herkömmlichen Vorortfahrzeugen mit Längssitzen durchgeführt, darunter fünf 2-Wagen-Einheiten und eine 3-Wagen-Einheit der Baureihe 3500/3600 (ex Tokyo Hibiya Line) und sechs 3-Wagen-Einheiten der Baureihe 8500 (ex Tokyu). Für *Limited Express*-Fahrten stehen vier Züge mit Quersitzen, darunter zwei 4-Wagen-Einheiten der Baureihe 1000 „Yukemuri" (ex Odakyu „Romancecar") und zwei 3-Wagen-Einheiten der Baureihe 2100 „Snow Monkey" (ex JR East Narita Express), zur Verfügung. Eine 3-Wagen-Einheit der Baureihe 2000 von 1964 ist an der Station Obuse ausgestellt.

Das „Nagaden Free Ticket" (1 Tag - 1.860 Yen, 2 Tage - 2.320 Yen) gilt in allen Zügen dieses Unternehmens; nicht eingeschlossen sind Zuschläge für Sitzplätze in Express-Zügen. Diese sind aber in der Bahn+Bus-Version dieses Tickets (2 Tage - 3.200 Yen, nur April bis November) enthalten. Die Fahrkartenkontrolle wird noch manuell durchgeführt, da die Stationen nicht mit automatischen Zugangssperren ausgestattet sind. IC Cards werden nicht akzeptiert.

single-track. In 1981, the section from Nagano to just beyond Zenkoji-Shita (4 stations, 1.9 km) was relocated underground in a cut-and-cover tunnel beneath a dual carriageway road (Nagano-Odori). The underground stations have B2-level platforms and B1-level ticket offices accessed via pedestrian underpasses. Nagano station has three tracks and bay platforms with escalator and lift access. The other three underground stations have side platforms with fixed stairs only; the underpasses at Zenkoji-Shita are decorated with Nagaden-themed murals but otherwise these stations do not appear to have been significantly refurbished since construction.

The Kijima and Yashiro Lines were closed due to declining ridership in 2002 and 2012 respectively, reducing the network to the current single line which carries commuters into Nagano and tourist traffic to hot springs and ski resorts at Yudanaka and in the Alps beyond. For the most part the line runs on the flat valley floor serving suburban and rural settlements but the line becomes more scenic as it ascends into upland terrain beyond Shinshu-Nakano.

A 2 or 3tph all-stations service operates between Nagano and Suzaka at irregular intervals of which 1 or 3tph continue to Shinshu-Nakano; a 1 or 2tph all-stations shuttle service runs between Shinshu-Nakano and Yudanaka. The all-stations service is supplemented by a 1tph limited-express service during most hours of the day; these trains run between Nagoya and Shinshu-Nakano or Yudanaka mostly following one of two stopping patterns (Limited Express A/B).

The operational fleet stands at 45 EMU cars, all acquired second-hand from larger operators. All-stations services are operated by driver-only commuter-style units with longitudinal seating comprising five 2-car and one 3-car 3500/3600-series (ex-Tokyo Hibiya Line) and six 3-car 8500-series (ex-Tokyu). Limited-express services are operated by four sets with transverse seating comprising two 4-car 1000-series 'Yukemuri' sets (ex-Odakyu 'Romancecar') and two 3-car 2100-series 'Snow Monkey' sets (ex-JR East - Narita Express). One 3-car 2000-series from 1964 is on static display at Obuse station.

The Nagaden Free Ticket (1 day - 1,860 Yen; 2 days - 2,320 Yen) covers the company's rail services excluding express seat supplements. A rail+bus version (2 days - 3,200 Yen; Apr-Nov only) includes express seat supplements. Manual ticket inspection/collection applies; stations are not equipped with automatic ticket barriers. IC cards are not accepted.

Nagano Dentetsu Line (N):

Nagano (N1) – Yudanaka (N24)

33.2 km (1.9 km Ⓤ), 24 Bahnhöfe | stations (4 Ⓤ); 1067 mm; 1500Vdc ⬆

26-03-1923: Suzaka – Shinshu-Nakano (13.1 km)
28-06-1926: Suzaka – Gondo (11.5 km)
28-04-1927: Shinshu-Nakano – Yudanaka (7.6 km)
24-06-1928: Gondo – Nagano (1.0 km)

Nagaden 3500-series (ex-Tokyo Hibiya Line)

Nagano – Shinano Railway 115-series (ex-JR East), *Local* ▶ Komoro

SONSTIGE REGIONALBAHNEN

Die Eröffnung des *Nagano Shinkansen* im Jahr 1997 und des *Hokuriku Shinkansen* im Jahr 2015 führte zur schritt-weisen Übertragung eines Großteils der Shinetsu Main Line (1067 mm Spurweite, 1500 V DC) in der Präfektur Nagano an die Bahngesellschaft *Shinano Railway*, nur der Abschnitt zwischen Nagano und Shinonoi (9,3 km) verblieb bei *JR East. JR East* betreibt *Local-* und *Rapid*-Züge nach Matsumoto und auf der Shinonoi Line darüber hinaus. Die elektrischen 3-Wagen-Züge der Baureihe 115 (ex JR) der *Shinano Railway* fahren im Ein-Mann-Betrieb mit Halt an allen Stationen von Nagano nach Süden Richtung Karui-zawa (1-4 Mal/Stunde) und nach Norden Richtung Myoko-Kogen (1-3 Mal/Stunde). Dieseltriebwagen verkehren als *Local* auf der JR Iiyama Line und erreichen Nagano ab Toyono auf den Gleisen der *Shinano Railway*.

OTHER LOCAL RAILWAYS

The opening of the Nagano Shinkansen in 1997 and the Hokuriku Shinkansen in 2015 led to the staged transfer of most of the Shinetsu Main Line (1067 mm gauge, 1500Vdc) in Nagano Prefecture to the third-sector Shinano Railway, though the section between Nagano and Shinonoi (9.3 km) remains in JR East ownership. JR East operates Local and Rapid services to Matsumoto and beyond via its connecting Shinonoi Line; Shinano Railway operates all-stations services south from Nagano towards Karuizawa (1-4tph) and north towards Myoko-Kogen (1-3tph) using driver-only 3-car 115-series EMU sets (ex-JR). DMU-operated Local services on JR East's Iiyama Line run through to Nagano over Shinano Railway tracks between Toyono and Nagano.

JR **Nagano** Station

Nagano – JR East Iiyama Line Kiha 110-series DMU - *Local* ▶ Echigo-Kawaguchi

Toyama-Eki — Santram #T103 (endet hier | *terminating*) & Chitetsu #7021 ▶ Daigaku-mae

TOYAMA

Die Hauptstadt der Präfektur Toyama hat 420.000 Einwohner auf einer Fläche von 1.241 km². Sie liegt in der Region Chubu im zentralen Honshu am Japanischen Meer und ist von Tokyo mit dem *Hokuriku Shinkansen* (395,5 km, schnellste Fahrt 2 Std. 8 Min.) zu erreichen. Der Jinzu fließt durch die Stadt und mündet im Norden in die Bucht von Toyama, während die Tateyama-Bergkette die Kulisse im Osten bildet. Auch wenn Toyama selbst für Touristen nicht so interessant ist, ist es ein guter Ausgangspunkt für zwei landschaftlich reizvolle Ziele – die Schmalspurbahn (762 mm) *Kurobe Gorge Railway* (*) und die „Tateyama-Kurobe-Alpen-Route" (**), ein Ausflug, der neben Bussen und Zügen auch zwei Obusstrecken durch Bergtunnel, zwei Standseilbahnen und eine Luftseilbahn umfasst.

In den letzten Jahren haben sich Stadtplaner bemüht, mit einer Reihe von Revitalisierungsprogrammen unter dem Motto „Compact City Toyama" Probleme wie Zersiedelung, starke Abhängigkeit vom Auto und sinkende Fahrgastzahlen im öffentlichen Nahverkehr anzugehen. Ziel ist es, Wohnungen sowie Gewerbe- und Kommunaleinrichtungen sowohl im Stadtzentrum als auch entlang von sechs aufgewerteten Bahn- bzw. Tramlinien sowie dreizehn Buskorridoren zu konzentrieren. Im Bereich öffentlicher Nahverkehr wurde bereits die erste richtige Stadtbahn Japans (Portram, 2006), eine neue Straßenbahnstrecke im Zentrum (2009) sowie der Umbau des JR-Bahnhofs Toyama zur Eröffnung des *Hokuriku Shinkansen* (2015) umgesetzt.

Neben dem städtischen Straßenbahnnetz und der Stadtbahn gibt es drei Gesellschaften, die Nahverkehrszüge betreiben: die private *Toyama Chiho Railway*, die *Ainokaze Toyama Railway* sowie *JR West*.

The capital of Toyama Prefecture has a population of 420,000 in an area of 1,241 km². It is situated within the Chubu region of central Honshu on the coast of the Sea of Japan, accessible from Tokyo via the Hokuriku Shinkansen (395.5 km, fastest journey time 2h 8 min). The Jinzu River flows through the city into Toyama Bay to the north and the Tateyama mountain range provides a backdrop to the east. Although not a tourist destination in itself, Toyama is a good starting point for visits to two scenic transport-related attractions - the 762 mm gauge Kurobe Gorge Railway (*) and the Tateyama Kurobe Alpine Route (**), an excursion involving the use of two tunnel trolleybus routes, two funiculars and an aerial ropeway as well as buses and trains.

In recent years, city planners have sought to address issues of low-density development, high car dependency, and declining public transport patronage through a series of revitalisation plans under the strap-line 'Compact City Toyama'. These plans seek to concentrate housing, commercial and community facilities in the city centre and along six improved rail/tram routes and thirteen bus corridors. Investment in public transport has included the opening of Japan's first full-scale LRT system (Portram, 2006), a new city centre tram line (2009) and the re-building of JR Toyama station for the opening of the Hokuriku Shinkansen (2015).

In addition to its urban tram network and light rail line, local/commuter rail services are provided by three operators - privately-owned Toyama Chiho Railway, third-sector Ainokaze Toyama Railway and JR West.

* www.kurotetu.co.jp/en   ** www.alpen-route.com/en

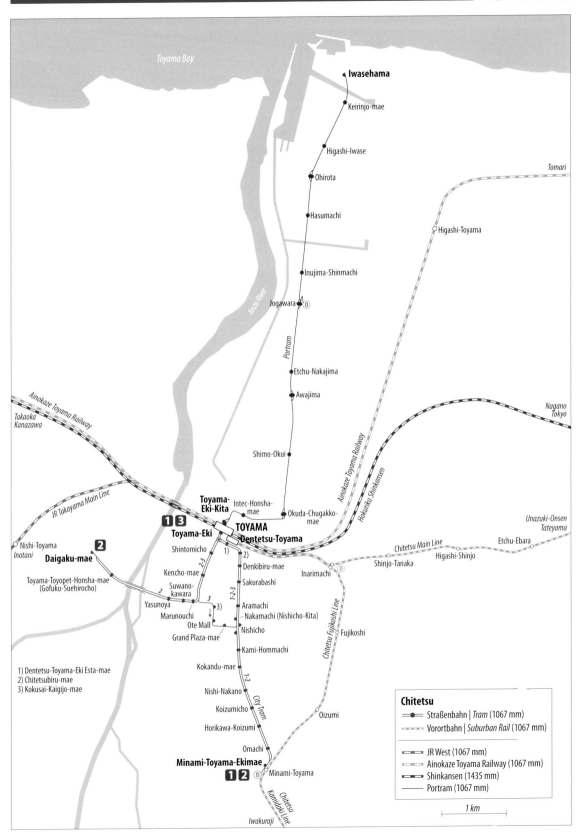

Toyama Bay

Iwasehama

Keirinjo-mae

Higashi-Iwase

Ohirota

Tomari

Hasumachi

Higashi-Toyama

Inujima-Shinmachi

Jinzu River

Jogawara Ⓓ

Portram

Etchu-Nakajima

Awajima

Nagano
Tokyo

Ainokaze Toyama Railway

Shimo-Okui

Hokuriku Shinkansen

Ainokaze Toyama Railway

Takaoka
Kanazawa

Unazuki-Onsen
Tateyama

JR Takayama Main Line

**Toyama-
Eki-Kita**

Intec-Honsha-
mae

Okuda-Chugakko-
mae

Etchu-Ebara

Chitetsu Main Line

Nishi-Toyama
Inotani

1 3

TOYAMA
Toyama-Eki

Dentetsu-Toyama

Higashi-Shinjo

2

Shintomicho

1)

2)

Shinjo-Tanaka

Inarimachi Ⓓ

Daigaku-mae

Kencho-mae

Denkibiru-mae

2-3

Toyama-Toyopet-Honsha-mae
(Gofuku-Suehirocho)

2

Suwano-
kawara

Sakurabashi

1-2-3

Chitetsu Fujikoshi Line

Yasunoya

3

3)

Marunouchi

Aramachi

Nakamachi (Nishicho-Kita)

Ote Mall

Nishicho

Fujikoshi

Grand Plaza-mae

Kami-Hommachi

Kokandu-mae

Nishi-Nakano

1-2

Koizumicho

City Tram

Oizumi

Horikawa-Koizumi

1) Dentetsu-Toyama-Eki Esta-mae
2) Chitetsubiru-mae
3) Kokusai-Kaigijo-mae

Omachi

Minami-Toyama-Ekimae

1 2 Ⓓ Minami-Toyama

Iwakuraji

Chitetsu
Kamidaki Line

Chitetsu

●━●	Straßenbahn | *Tram* (1067 mm)
◻◻◻	Vorortbahn | *Suburban Rail* (1067 mm)
◼━◼	JR West (1067 mm)
◻━◻	Ainokaze Toyama Railway (1067 mm)
◼◼◼	Shinkansen (1435 mm)
——	Portram (1067 mm)

1 km

Toyama-Eki – #7017 (endet hier | *terminating*) & Centram #9002 (Loop Line)

TOYAMA CHIHO RAILWAY   Toyama Chiho Tetsudo (Toyama Regional Railway) – 'Chitetsu'

Dieses private Unternehmen, bekannt als *Chitetsu*, betreibt die städtische Straßenbahn von Toyama sowie den Eisenbahn- und Bus-Verkehr im östlichen Teil der Präfektur Toyama. Das Unternehmen wurde 1943 gegründet, indem es fünf unabhängige Eisenbahngesellschaften und die kommunale Straßenbahn vereinigte; derartige Fusionen wurden während des Krieges von der Regierung gefördert. Das Unternehmen ist ein Großaktionär der *Tateyama Kurobe Kanko*, des Betreibers der Stand- und Luftseilbahn sowie der Obusse der „Alpen-Route"; zu *Chitetsus* Tochterfirmen gehören die *Kaetsuno Railway*, ehemaliger Betreiber der Straßenbahn von Takaoka, heute jedoch nur ein Busunternehmen.

Straßenbahn
Die private *Toyama Electric Tramway* nahm 1913 die erste Straßenbahnlinie von Toyama in Betrieb und erweiterte das Netz bis 1916 auf 8,4 km. 1920 übernahm die Stadt die Straßenbahn, bestimmte Abschnitte wurden daraufhin im Zuge des Baus neuer Straßen verlegt, so dass eine Ringlinie entstand. Ab 1943 wieder in privater Hand erreichte das Netz 1961 seine größte Ausdehnung (11,0 km). Der Ein-Mann-Betrieb wurde ab 1969 eingeführt, doch nach einer Reihe von Streckenkürzungen verblieb 1984 lediglich eine einzige 6,4 km lange Linie zwischen Daigaku-mae und Minami-Toyama-Ekimae.

Die nächsten 25 Jahre änderte sich nichts daran, bis im Jahr 2009 eine 0,9 km lange eingleisige Strecke, die Toyama Toshin Line, zwischen Marunouchi und Nishicho eröffnet wurde, womit eine neue eingleisige (gegen den

This private company, known as Chitetsu, operates Toyama's urban tramway and rail and bus services in the eastern part of Toyama Prefecture. The company was established in 1943, taking over five separate railways and the municipal tram system, as part of wartime mergers promoted by the government. It is a major shareholder in Tateyama Kurobe Kanko, operator of 'Alpine Route' funicular, ropeway and trolleybus services and its subsidiary companies include Kaetsuno Railway, former operator of the Takaoka tramway but now just a bus company.

Tram
The privately-owned Toyama Electric Tramway opened Toyama's first tram route in 1913, extending the system to 8.4 km by 1916. The municipality took over the tramway in 1920, re-aligning certain sections in connection with new road construction and creating a loop line. Under private ownership again from 1943 the network reached its greatest extent (11.0 km) in 1961. One-person operation was introduced from 1969 and a series of cut-backs reduced the system to a single 6.4 km line between Daigaku-mae and Minami-Toyama-Ekimae by 1984.

Things remained this way for 25 years until, in 2009, the City Council opened a 0.9 km single track connection, the Toyama Toshin Line, between Marunouchi and Nishicho creating a new one-way (anti-clockwise) central area loop line, albeit somewhat shorter than the original loop line. In 2015, the City Council opened a further 0.2 km spur, the Namboku Setsuzoku Line, to a new terminus be-

Nishicho – #8003 ▶ Toyama-Eki, #7020 ▶ Minami-Toyama-Ekimae

Uhrzeigersinn befahrene) Ringlinie durch die Innenstadt, etwas kürzer als die frühere, geschaffen wurde. Im Jahr 2015 entstand eine 200 m lange Stichstrecke, die Nam-boku Setsuzoku Line, zu einer neuen Endstelle unterhalb der erhöhten Eisenbahngleise am Bahnhof Toyama, die frühere Haltestelle Toyama-Ekimae wurde in Dentetsu-Toyama-Eki Esta-mae umbenannt. Diese neuen Strecken sind Eigentum der Stadt, werden aber von der Straßen-bahngesellschaft betrieben. Es gibt Pläne zur Einführung eines durchgehenden Betriebs auf die Portram sowie auf die eigene Kamidaki Line (siehe folgende Kapitel).

Der Großteil des Netzes verläuft straßenbündig in Mittellage, wobei die Trasse vom Autoverkehr durch weiße Linien abgetrennt ist; die einzigen Abschnitte mit eigenem Gleiskörper sind die Endstellen Toyama-Eki und Minami-Toyama-Ekimae. Die meisten Haltestellen haben schmale Bahnsteige, einige mit Unterständen. Die eingleisige Toyama Toshin (Loop) Line wurde für einen zukünftigen zweigleisigen Ausbau vorbereitet. Der Betriebshof liegt hinter der eingleisigen Endstelle Minami-Toyama-Ekimae.

Toyama City Tram Line (Toyama Shinai Kido-Sen)

7.5 km, 25 Haltestellen | stops; 1067 mm; 600Vdc ↑

01-09-1913: Horikawa-Koizumi – Marunouchi (4.0 km)**
13-03-1915: Horikawa-Koizumi – Minami-Toyama-Ekimae (0.6 km)
22-11-1916: Marunouchi – Daigaku-mae (1.8 km)***
23-12-2009: Marunouchi – Nakamachi (Nishicho-Kita) (0.9 km)
14-03-2015: Toyama-Ekimae (0.2 km)

* ohne stillgelegte Strecken | closed sections not listed
** 1934 im Stadtzentrum teils neu trassiert | partly re-routed in city centre in 1934
***05-08-1952: teils neu trassiert | partly re-routed

neath the elevated railway tracks at Toyama station, the previous Toyama-Ekimae stop being renamed Dentetsu-Toyama-Eki Esta-mae. These new lines are owned by the city authorities but operated by the tramway company. Further plans exist to introduce through-running services from the Portram Line and the company's Kamidaki Line (see subsequent entries).

Most of the network is on-street with centrally-placed tracks separated from general traffic by white lines; the only off-street sections are at Toyama-Eki and Minami-Toyama-Ekimae termini. Most stops have narrow platforms, some with shelters. The single-track Toyama Toshin (Loop) Line is designed for future conversion to double track. Depot access is via the single-track plat-form line at Minami-Toyama-Ekimae terminus.

Three routes are operated. For most of the day, routes 1 and 2 each run every 10 minutes providing a combined 5-minute frequency between Minami-Toyama-Ekimae and Toyama-Eki (taking 20 minutes), with route 2 continuing to Daigaku-mae every 10 minutes (total journey time 38 minutes). During peak periods a higher proportion of trams run through to Daigaku-mae on route 2. Route 3 (branded 'Centram') operates approximately every 13-16 minutes (weekdays) and up to every 10 minutes (weekends and holidays) taking 24-28 minutes to complete the anti-clockwise central area loop from/to Toyama-Eki.

The 22-strong tramway fleet comprises eleven 7000-series bogie cars (Nippon Sharyo 1960-65), five 8000-series bogie cars (Nippon Sharyo 1993), three 9000-series 'Centram' low-floor two-section 18.4 m articulated cars (Niigata Transys 2009, built to the same

Horikawa-Koizumi – Santram #T102 ▶ Minami-Toyama-Ekimae

Dentetsu-Toyama-Eki Esta-mae
Centram #9001 - Loop Line ▶ Toyama-Eki

Das Netz besteht aus drei Linien. Die Linien 1 und 2 verkehren fast den ganzen Tag alle 10 Minuten und bieten einen kombinierten 5-Minuten-Takt zwischen Minami-Toyama-Ekimae und Toyama-Eki (Fahrzeit 20 Minuten). Die Linie 2 fährt alle 10 Minuten weiter nach Daigaku-mae (insg. 38 Minuten), während der Hauptverkehrszeiten öfter. Die Linie 3 („Centram") verkehrt werktags etwa alle 13-16 Minuten und an Wochenenden und Feiertagen alle 10 Minuten. Für die Ringstrecke gegen die Uhrzeigersinn ab/bis Toyama-Eki benötigt sie 24-28 Minuten.

Die Tram-Flotte umfasst 22 Fahrzeuge: elf Drehgestellwagen der 7000er Serie (Nippon Sharyo 1960-65); fünf Drehgestellwagen der 8000er Serie (Nippon Sharyo 1993); drei niederflurige zweiteilige Gelenkwagen der 9000er Serie „Centram" (18,4 m, Niigata Transys 2009, basierend auf den Portram-Fahrzeugen); drei dreiteilige Gelenkwagen der Serie T100 „Santram" (16,3 m, Alna Sharyo 2010-15). Die drei „Centram"-Fahrzeuge gehören zwar der Stadt Toyama, sie werden aber von der Tramgesellschaft gewartet und betrieben. Die Drehgestellwagen haben einen Anstrich in Creme, Grün und Rot, nur Tw. 7018 trägt die ehemalige Lackierung in Beige/Grün und Tw. 7022 verkehrt im Retro-Design. Die drei „Centram"-Fahrzeuge sind jeweils weiß, silbern und schwarz; die „Santram"-Fahrzeuge sind überwiegend weiß, jedoch jeweils mit einer anderen Komplementärfarbe. Einige Wagen sind mit Vollwerbung beklebt.

Bei der Straßenbahn gilt ein Einheitstarif von 200 Yen (180 Yen mit IC Card). Für die Stadt Toyama gibt es Tageskarten für Tram/Bus (620 Yen) und Tram/Bus/Portram (820 Yen) – diese sind auch in Chitetsu-Zügen zwischen Dentetsu-Toyama und Minami-Toyama gültig. Der „Chitetsu 1-Day Free Pass" umfasst das gesamte Tram- und Eisenbahnnetz des Unternehmens (Dez.-März 2.000 Yen; Apr.-Nov. 2.500 Yen); die entsprechende 2-Tage-Karte (4.530 Yen) beinhaltet den Sitzplatzzuschlag für Express-Züge. Die IC Card „Ecomyca" des Unternehmens kann auch auf der Portram verwendet werden, gehört aber nicht zum landesweiten Kartensystem.

design as Portram cars) and three T100-series 'Santram' three-section 16.3 m articulated cars (Alna Sharyo 2010-15). The three 'Centram' cars are owned by Toyama municipality but maintained and operated by the company. The bogie cars have a fleet livery of cream, green and red but 7018 carries the former beige/green livery and 7022 is equipped with retro interior and livery. Each of the three Centram cars is in a different colour - white, silver, black; Santram cars are predominantly white, each with a different relief colour. Some cars carry advertising liveries.

A flat fare of 200 Yen applies (180 Yen with IC card). One-day ride-at-will passes are available for tram/bus (620 Yen) and tram/bus/Portram (820 Yen) within Toyama city; these are also valid on Chitetsu trains between Dentetsu-Toyama and Minami-Toyama only. The Chitetsu 1-Day Free Pass covers the company's entire tram and rail network (2,000 Yen, Dec-Mar; 2,500 Yen, Apr-Nov); a 2-Day version (4,530 Yen) includes the supplementary seat fee for express trains. The company's 'Ecomyca' IC card can also be used on Portram but is not part of the nationwide inter-operability scheme.

Horikawa-Koizumi – 7000-series ▶ Minami-Toyama-Ekimae

Dentetsu-Toyama – Chitetsu 10030-series (ex-Keihan)

Eisenbahn

Chitetsu betreibt ausgehend vom viergleisigen Kopf-
bahnhof Dentetsu-Toyama (neben dem JR-Bahnhof
Toyama) auch drei Vorortbahnlinien östlich von Toyama.
Teile des Netzes stammen aus dem Jahr 1913, der Rest
wurde vorwiegend in den 1920er und 1930er Jahren von
Vorgängern von *Chitetsu* gebaut. Der Bahnhof Dentetsu-
Toyama wurde 1931 eröffnet, auch wenn das heutige
Bahnhofsgebäude mit dem Kaufhaus Esta erst aus dem
Jahr 1987 stammt. Neben dem Pendlerverkehr hat die
Bahn große Bedeutung für den Tourismus, da sie sowohl
nach Unazuki-Onsen, einem Kurort und gleichzeitig Aus-
gangspunkt für Ausflüge auf der *Kurobe Gorge Railway*,
als auch nach Tateyama, Ausgangspunkt der „Tateyama-
Kurobe-Alpen-Route", führt.

Die Bahn ist eingleisig bis auf einen 1,7 km langen
Abschnitt zwischen Dentetsu-Toyama und Inarimachi, wo
sich der Betriebshof befindet. In der Regel wird an allen
Stationen gehalten, dazu kommen gelegentliche *Express-*
und *Limited Express*-Züge auf der Main Line und der
Tateyama Line.

Im Rahmen der Revitalisierungspläne der Stadt wird
die Umstellung der Fujikoshi-Kamidaki Line auf Stadtbahn-
betrieb mit Durchbindung auf das städtische Straßenbahnnetz über eine Verbindung bei Minami-Toyama in
Erwägung gezogen.

Der Wagenpark besteht aus 45 Elektrotriebwagen
vorwiegend in 2-Wagen-Einheiten, darunter welche,
die von Keihan und Tokyu übernommen wurden. Zwei
3-Wagen-Einheiten werden im Touristenverkehr eingesetzt
– der *Alps Express* (ex Seibu „Red Arrow"-Einheiten) und
der *Double-Decker Express* (ex Keihan Züge mit mittigem
Doppelstockwagen).

Rail

*Chitetsu's interurban division operates three routes
to the east of Toyama from its four-track ground-level
terminus, Dentetsu-Toyama, situated adjacent to JR
Toyama station. Part of the network dates back to 1913
but it was mostly constructed during the 1920s and 30s
by Chitetsu's predecessors; Dentetsu-Toyama terminus
opened in 1931, though the current station building,
which incorporates the company's Esta department store,
dates from 1987. In addition to commuter and other local
traffic, the railway attracts significant leisure and tourist
traffic heading for Unazuki-Onsen, a hot-spring town and
the departure point for sightseeing trips on the Kurobe
Gorge Railway, and Tateyama, starting point of the
Tateyama Kurobe Alpine Route.*

*The railway is single-track apart from 1.7 km of
double-track between Dentetsu-Toyama and Inarimachi
where the depot is situated. Most services call at all
stations supplemented by occasional Express and Limited-
Express services on the Main Line and Tateyama Line.*

*As part of the city's public transport revitalisation
plans, consideration is being given to the possible conversion of the Fujikoshi-Kamidaki Line for light rail operation with through-running to the urban tramway via a
connection at Minami-Toyama.*

*Rolling stock comprises 45 EMU cars mainly in 2-car
sets including ex-Keihan and ex-Tokyu vehicles. Two 3-car
sets operate tourist-oriented express services – the Alps
Express (ex-Seibu Red Arrow set) and the Double-Decker
Express (ex-Keihan set with centre double-deck car).*

93.2 km, 66 Bahnhöfe | *stations*, 1067 mm; 1500Vdc

Main Line: Dentetsu-Toyama – Unazuki-Onsen (53.3 km)
Tateyama Line: Terada – Tateyama (24.2 km)
Fujikoshi-Kamidaki Line: Inarimachi – Minami-Toyama – Iwakuraji (15.7 km)

Toyama-Eki-Kita – Portram TLR #0603

PORTRAM

Portram gilt als Japans erste moderne Stadtbahnlinie mit ertüchtigter Infrastruktur und komplett neuen Fahrzeugen. Die Bahn wird von *Toyama Light Rail* betrieben; diese Firma wurde gegründet, um die defizitäre Toyamako Line, die ursprünglich 1924 zum Anschluss des Hafens von Toyama eröffnet worden war, von *JR West* zu übernehmen und auszubauen. Durch die Wahl einer Stadtbahn konnte vermieden werden, dass die Strecke aufgeständert bzw. ganz geschlossen werden musste, als der JR-Bahnhof Toyama sowie die Hokuriku Main Line auf ein Viadukt verlegt wurden. Der JR-Betrieb endete im Februar 2006, doch die Strecke wurde bereits im April 2006 als Portram wiedereröffnet.

Die Stadtbahn beginnt an der Haltestelle Toyama-Eki-Kita an der Nordseite des JR-Bahnhofs Toyama und verläuft die ersten 1,1 km auf einer neuen straßenbündigen Trasse (teils mit Rasengleisbett) bis kurz vor Okuda-Chugakko-mae, ab wo die 6,5 km lange Trasse der ehemaligen JR Toyamako Line bis Iwasehama übernommen wurde; der 1,5 km lange Abschnitt der JR-Linie zwischen Okuda-Chugakko-mae und dem JR-Bahnhof Toyama wurde aufgegeben. Der Endpunkt Toyama-Eki-Kita ist zweigleisig, der Rest der Linie ist hingegen derzeit eingleisig und hat vier Ausweichen. Zwischen Intec-Honsha-mae und Okuda-Chugakko-mae soll jedoch ein zweites Gleis verlegt und

Portram is Japan's first modern light rail line with renovated infrastructure and entirely new rolling stock. It is operated by third-sector Toyama Light Rail which was established to take over and upgrade JR West's loss-making Toyamako Line, which originally opened in 1924 to serve Toyama port. Tramway conversion avoided the need to elevate or completely close the line when JR Toyama station and the Hokuriku Main Line were relocated to viaduct. JR services ceased in February 2006 and the line reopened as Portram in April 2006.

The light rail line commences at Toyama-Eki-Kita, to the north of JR Toyama station, and runs via 1.1 km of new street track (part on-carriageway, part on grassed roadside reservation) to just before Okuda-Chugakko-mae, from where it takes over 6.5 km of the former JR Toyamako Line to Iwasehama; the 1.5 km section of the JR line between Okuda-Chugakko-mae and JR Toyama station having been abandoned. Toyama-Eki-Kita terminus is double-track but the rest of the line is currently single-track with four passing loops; however, an additional track and intermediate stop are to be constructed between Intec-Honsha-mae and Okuda-Chugakko-mae and a double-track extension is due to open in 2020 connecting Toyama-Eki-Kita with the city tram terminus at Toyama-Ekimae, permitting through running between the two systems.

Portram

Toyama-Eki-Kita – Iwasehama
7.6 km; 13 Haltestellen | *stops*; 1067 mm; 600Vdc ↑

29-04-2006: Toyama-Eki-Kita – Iwasehama (7.6 km)

Intec-Honsha-mae ✕ Toyama-Eki-Kita – Portram TLR #0604 ▶ Iwasehama

eine Zwischenhaltestelle eingerichtet werden; außerdem soll bis 2020 eine zweigleisige Verbindung zur Tram-Endstation Toyama-Ekimae hergestellt werden, so dass ein durchgehender Betrieb möglich wird.

Die Portram führt durch eine Mischung aus Wohn- und Gewerbegebieten und erschließt auch einige neue Büroviertel wie den Hauptsitz von Intec (Intec-Honsha-mae). Die ursprünglichen acht JR-Stationen wurden mit niedrigen Bahnsteigen und Unterständen ausgestattet und fünf neue Haltestellen hinzugefügt – zwei auf der neuen Straßenbahnstrecke und drei (Okuda-Chugakko-mae, Awajima und Inujima-Shinmachi) auf der ehemaligen Eisenbahnstrecke. Zubringerbusse von *Chitetsu* fahren im Auftrag von *Toyama Light Rail* Hasumachi und Iwasehama an. Das Depot und die Verwaltung befinden sich in Jogawara. Die Wartung der Strecke und der Fahrzeuge übernimmt *Chitetsu*.

Die Flotte besteht aus 7 zweiteiligen Niederflurwagen (18,4 m lang) der TLR-Serie 0600, die von Niigata Transys unter Lizenz von Bombardier produziert wurden. Die Grundlackierung ist weiß, wobei jedes Fahrzeug ein andersfarbiges Band um die Türen aufweist.

The line passes through mixed residential and industrial areas and serves some new commercial developments such as the Intec head office (Intec-Honsha-mae). The original eight JR stations were re-equipped with low platforms and shelters and five new stations added - two on the new street-running section and three (Okuda-Chugakko-mae, Awajima and Inujima-Shinmachi) on the former rail line. Feeder buses serve Hasumachi and Iwasehama, operated by Chitetsu on behalf of Toyama Light Rail. The depot and head office are at Jogawara. Day-to-day line and rolling stock maintenance is contracted out to Chitetsu.

The fleet comprises seven TLR 0600-series low-floor two-section articulated cars (18.4 m long) built by Niigata Transys under licence from Bombardier. The basic livery is white with each car having a different coloured band around the doors.

Portram TLR 0600-series

Okuda-Chugakko-mae – Portram TLR #0605 ▶ Toyama-Eki-Kita

Etchu-Nakajima - Portram TLR #0602 ▶ Toyama-Eki-Kita

Wie bei der Straßenbahn gilt ein Einheitstarif von 200 Yen (180 Yen mit IC Card). Das Unternehmen gibt eine eigene „Passca" IC Card aus, die auch bei *Chitetsu* genutzt werden kann, aber nicht Teil des landesweiten Systems ist. Mit „Passca" erhält man Ermäßigungen für Stadtbahn+ Zubringerbus, außerdem werden pro Tag maximal 540 Yen (3 x 180 Yen) abgebucht. Der „Toyama Machinaka Iwase 1 Day Free Pass" (820 Yen) gilt bei Portram und *Chitetsu* (Tram/Bus/Bahn - nur Dentetsu-Toyama – Minami-Toyama).

Vor der Schließung fuhren die Züge auf der JR Toyamako Line etwa stündlich mit zusätzlichen HVZ-Fahrten. Portram verkehrt hingegen tagsüber alle 15 Minuten, in Spitzenzeiten alle 10 Minuten, und der Betrieb endet abends erst später.

As with the city trams, a flat fare of 200 Yen applies (180 Yen with IC card). The company issues its own Passca IC card which can also be used on Chitetsu services but is not part of the nationwide inter-availability scheme. Discounted tram/feeder bus fares are available with Passca and there is an auto 1-day facility which caps fares at 540 Yen (3x180 Yen). The Toyama Machinaka Iwase 1 Day Free Pass (820 Yen) is valid on Portram and Chitetsu tram/bus/rail (Dentetsu-Toyama – Minami-Toyama only).

Prior to closure, JR Toyamako Line services operated approximately hourly with additional peak trips. Portram by comparison runs every 15 minutes in the daytime, every 10 minutes during peak periods, and service continues until later in the evening.

Okuda-Chugakko-mae

Okuda-Chugakko-mae > Intec-Honsha-mae
- Portram TLR #0606 ▶ Iwasehama

Toyama – Ainokaze Toyama Railway 521-series (ex-JR West) - *Local* ▶ Tomari

SONSTIGE BAHNEN

Mit Eröffnung des *Hokuriku Shinkansen* im Jahr 2015 wurde der 100,1 km lange Abschnitt der Hokuriku Main Line von *JR West* (1067 mm, 20 kV AC) zwischen Ichiburi (Präfektur Niigata) und Kurihara (Präfektur Ishikawa) an das Unternehmen *Ainokaze Toyama Railway* übertragen, an dem die Präfektur Toyama (63%), verschiedene Kommunen (27%) und private Unternehmen (10%) beteiligt sind.

Auf dieser Strecke werden 21 Züge der ex-JR-Baureihen 413 (3-Wagen-Einheiten) bzw. 521 (2-Wagen-Einheiten) eingesetzt. Der Takt ist unregelmäßig mit 1-4 Zügen pro Stunde, meist mit Halt an allen Stationen, doch mit einzelnen *Rapid*-Fahrten. Die meisten Fahrten beginnen in Tomari (42,5 km nordöstlich von Toyama) und führen über die *Ishikawa Railway* durch bis Kanazawa (59,4 km südwestlich von Toyama). Die „ICOCA" IC Card von *JR West* kann auf der Linie verwendet werden.

Abgesehen vom *Hokuriku Shinkansen* betreibt *JR West* im Bereich Toyama nur noch die nicht elektrifizierte eingleisige 1067-mm-Strecke der Takayama Main Line, allerdings mit nur 11 Regionalbahnen pro Tag bis Inotani (36,6 km) sowie vier *Limited Express*-Zügen, die weiter bis Takayama und Nagoya fahren.

OTHER RAIL SERVICES

Coinciding with the opening of the Hokuriku Shinkansen in 2015, the 100.1 km section of JR West's parallel 1067 mm gauge 20kVac Hokuriku Main Line between Ichiburi (Niigata Prefecture) and Kurihara (Ishikawa Prefecture) was transferred to a new third-sector company, Ainokaze Toyama Railway, owned by Toyama Prefecture (63%), local authorities (27%) and private businesses (10%).

Services are operated by 21 ex-JR West 413-series (3-car) and 521-series (2-car) sets. An irregular-interval service of 1-4tph operates, mainly all-stations but with a few limited-stop Rapid services. Most services commence at Tomari (42.5 km north-east of Toyama) and continue to Kanazawa (59.4 km south-west of Toyama) over the Ishikawa Railway. JR West's ICOCA IC card can be used on the line.

Apart from the Hokuriku Shinkansen, the only other remaining JR West line serving Toyama is the 1067 mm gauge un-electrified single-track Takayama Main Line which has an infrequent all-stations service of 11 trains per day as far as Inotani (36.6 km) and four limited-expresses which continue to Takayama and Nagoya.

Suchirocho – Manyosen MLRV #1003 ▶ Takaoka-Eki

TAKAOKA

Takaoka (172.000 Einw., 209.5 km²) ist eine Industrie- und Hafenstadt im Westen der Präfektur Toyama. Sie liegt 19 km nordwestlich von Toyama nahe der Mündung der Flüsse Sho und Oyabe in die Bucht von Toyama. Die Stadt hat eine einzige Straßenbahnlinie, die bis in die angrenzende Stadt Imizu führt, sowie Nahverkehrszüge auf drei JR- bzw. ehemaligen JR-Strecken. Am neuen Bahnhof Shin-Takaoka, 1,8 km südlich des Stadtzentrums, hält seit März 2015 der *Hokuriku Shinkansen*, allerdings nur langsamere Züge von Tokyo nach Kanazawa bzw. regionale von Toyama nach Kanazawa mit Halt an allen Stationen.

Takaoka (population 172,000, 209.5 km²) is an industrial and port city in western Toyama Prefecture, situated 19 km north-west of Toyama on the lower reaches of the Sho and Oyabe Rivers where they enter Toyama Bay. The city has a single tram route which extends into the adjoining city of Imizu and local rail services operate on three JR / former-JR lines. The Hokuriku Shinkansen, which opened in March 2015, serves a new station, Shin-Takaoka, situated 1.8 km south of the city centre; semi-fast Tokyo — Kanazawa and all-stations Toyama — Kanazawa Shinkansen services call at Shin-Takaoka.

MANYOSEN

Auch wenn die Manyosen von Takaoka durchgehend betrieben wird, handelt es sich offiziell um zwei Linien: die **Shinminato-ko Line** auf eigenem Gleiskörper (Rokudoji – Koshinokata, 4,9 km) und die vorwiegend straßenbündige **Takaoka Kido Line** (Takaoka-Eki – Rokudoji, 8,0 km). Die Shinminato-ko Line wurde in den frühen 1930er Jahren gebaut und war ursprünglich Teil der Imizu Line der *Etchu Railway*, einer Überland-Küstenstraßenbahn von Toyama nach Imizu, die 1943 mit der *Toyama Chiho Railway* („*Chitetsu*") vereinigt wurde. *Chitetsus* Takaoka Kido Line wurde zwischen Takaoka-Ekimae, Yonejimaguchi und Fushiki-ko im Jahr 1948 eröffnet, womit Takaoka die letzte japanische Stadt war, die eine städtische Straßenbahn erhielt. 1951 wurde eine 3,6 km lange Verbindungsstrecke zwischen Yonejimaguchi und der Endstelle der Imizu Line

*Although operated as a single tram route, Takaoka's Manyosen is officially two lines: the reserved-track **Shinminato-ko Line** (Rokudoji — Koshinokata, 4.9 km) and the mainly street-running **Takaoka Kido Line** (Takaoka-Eki — Rokudoji, 8.0 km). The Shinminato-ko Line, built in the early 1930s, was originally part of the Etchu Railway's Imizu Line, an interurban coastal tramway linking Toyama and Imizu, which was merged into the Toyama Chiho Railway ('Chitetsu') in 1943. Chitetsu's Takaoka Kido Line opened between Takaoka-Ekimae, Yonejimaguchi and Fushiki-ko in 1948, Takaoka becoming the last Japanese city to gain an urban tramway. In 1951, a 3.6 km connecting line was opened between Yonejimaguchi and the Imizu Line terminus (today's Rokudoji) permitting the introduction of a through inter-*

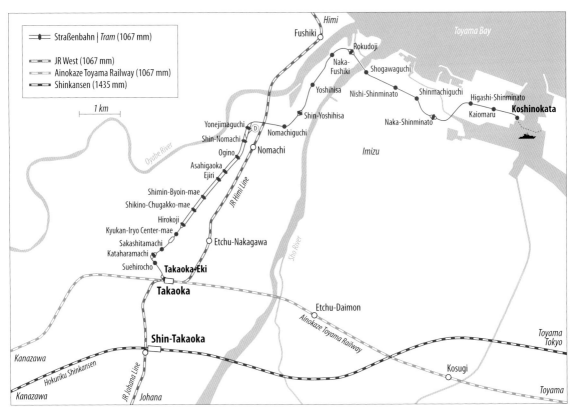

(heute Rokudoji) in Betrieb genommen, so dass ein durchgehender Verkehr zwischen Takaoka und Toyama möglich wurde. Im Jahr 1959 wurde die Takaoka Kido Line an die *Kaetsuno Railway* übertragen, einer Tochtergesellschaft von *Chitetsu*, die für den Bahn- und Busverkehr im Westen der Präfektur Toyama gegründet worden war.

Der durchgehende Betrieb nach Toyama endete jedoch 1965, als die Imizu Line östlich von Koshinokata als Folge des Baus eines neuen Hafens geteilt wurde, wobei der Abschnitt Rokudoji – Koshinokata von *Chitetsu* 1966 in den Besitz der *Kaetsuno Railway* überging. Heute verbindet noch eine Fähre die Manyosen-Endstelle Koshinokata mit der anderen Seite, doch *Chitetsus* Anschlussbahn nach Toyama ist seit 1980 außer Betrieb. Der 2,9 km lange Abschnitt Yonejimaguchi – Fushiki-ko der Takaoka Kido Line wurde 1971 stillgelegt.

Nach einem lang anhaltenden Fahrgastrückgang und finanziellen Schwierigkeiten überließ die *Kaetsuno Railway* im Jahr 2002 die Straßenbahn einem neuen Unternehmen, an dem hauptsächlich die Städte Takaoka

urban service between Takaoka and Toyama. In 1959 the Takaoka Kido Line was transferred to Kaetsuno Railway, a Chitetsu subsidiary established to run rail and bus services in western Toyama Prefecture.

The through service to Toyama ceased in 1965 when the Imizu Line was severed to the east of Koshinokata as the result of the construction of a new harbour, the Rokudoji – Koshinokata section being transferred from Chitetsu to Kaetsuno Railway ownership in 1966. Today, a ferry still operates across the harbour entrance from Manyosen's Koshinokata terminus but Chitetsu's connecting rail service to Toyama ceased in 1980. The 2.9 km Yonejimaguchi – Fushiki-ko section of the Takaoka Kido Line closed in 1971.

In 2002, after a long period of declining ridership and financial difficulties, Kaetsuno Railway divested the tramway to a new third-sector company owned mainly by Takaoka and Imizu municipalities and Toyama Prefecture (30.6% each). The new company adopted the line's nickname, Manyosen (Manyo Line), as its official name; it comes from 'Manyoshu', a major compilation of historic poems assembled by a former provincial governor. The new management has halted the decline in ridership by gradually upgrading infrastructure and modernising the fleet with low-floor light rail vehicles. However, the service frequency remains every 15 minutes for most of the day, limited by the preponderance of single track. Apart from depot workings, most trams run the full length of the line taking 47 minutes for a single trip.

In 2014, Takaoka-Ekimae terminus (renamed Takaoka-Eki) was relocated a short distance from the JR station forecourt to a double-track ground-floor facility within

Manyosen

12.9 km, 25 Haltestellen | *stops*; 1067 mm; 600 Vdc ⬆

12-10-1930: Nishi-Koshinokata (x) – Shinminato-Higashiguchi (x) (1.3 km)
23-12-1930: Nishi-Koshinokata (x) – Koshinokata (0.2 km)
09-11-1932: Shinminato-Higashiguchi (x) – Shogawaguchi (2.7 km)
25-12-1933: Shogawaguchi – Rokudoji (0.6 km)
10-04-1948: Takaoka-Ekimae (x) – Yonejimaguchi (4.3 km)
01-04-1951: Yonejimaguchi – Rokudoji (3.6 km)
05-04-1966: Koshinokata verlegt | *relocated* (0.1 km)
29-03-2014: Takaoka-Ekimae (x) – Takaoka-Eki (0.1 km)

(x) Haltestelle nicht mehr vorhanden | *Stop closed*

Rokudoji – MLRV #1004 'Doraemon Tram' ▶ Takaoka-Eki, #7074 ▶ Koshinokata

und Imizu sowie die Präfektur Toyama (jeweils 30,6%) beteiligt sind. Die neue Firma übernahm den Spitznamen der Linie, Manyosen (Manyo-Linie), als offizielle Bezeichnung; diese leitet sich von „Manyoshu", einer historischen Gedichtesammlung eines ehemaligen Provinzgouverneurs, ab. Das neue Management konnte den Fahrgastschwund stoppen, indem die Infrastruktur schrittweise erneuert und die Flotte modernisiert wurde. Allerdings herrscht meist nur ein 15-Minuten-Takt, da die Strecke größtenteils eingleisig ist. Abgesehen von Depotfahrten verkehren die Straßenbahnen auf der ganzen Länge der Linie und benötigen dafür 47 Minuten.

2014 wurde die Endstation Takaoka-Ekimae vom Bahnhofsvorplatz zu einer zweigleisigen Anlage im Erdgeschoss des neuen Bahnhofsgebäudes verlegt und in Takaoka-Eki umbenannt. Von hier aus verläuft die Linie entlang der Haupteinkaufsstraße von Takaoka und dann zur Küste durch ein flaches Gebiet mit einer Mischung aus Wohnhäusern, Industriebauten und Hafeneinrichtungen. Die Strecke ist vorwiegend eingleisig mit Ausweichen, lediglich ein 2,8 km langer Abschnitt zwischen Hirokoji und dem Depot an der Haltestelle Yonejimaguchi ist zweigleisig, seit dieser in den 1950er Jahren in Randlage neu gebaut und dann in den 1960er Jahren im Zuge einer Straßenverbreiterung in die Straßenmitte verlegt wurde. Zwischen Yonejimaguchi und Nomachiguchi, wo die JR Himi Line kreuzt, sowie ab Naka-Fushiki bis zur Endstation Koshinokata (5,4 km) steht ein eigener Gleiskörper zur Verfügung. Die meisten Haltestellen haben niedrige Bahnsteige mit Unterständen, doch an drei Stationen muss direkt von der Straßenebene eingestiegen werden. Der Fluss Sho wird auf einer 416 m langen Tram-Brücke überquert.

Die Flotte besteht aus 11 Fahrzeugen: fünf Drehgestellwagen der Serie 7070, die 1967 von Nippon Sharyo

a newly-built station building. From here the line runs along Takaoka's main shopping street and then towards the coast via a generally flat landscape of mixed residential, industrial and port-related development. The line is mainly single-track with passing loops apart from the 2.8 km section between Hirokoji and the depot at Yonejimaguchi where roadside double track was introduced in the 1950s and later moved to the centre of the road when it was widened in the 1960s. There is a section of private right-of-way where the line crosses the JR Himi Line between Yonejimaguchi and Nomachiguchi and a further 5.4 km section from Naka-Fushiki to the terminus at Koshinokata. Reserved-track stations have low platforms and shelters. Most on-street stops have safety islands, mainly with shelters, but at three stops passengers board/alight directly from the street. A 416 m long tram-only bridge carries the line over the Sho River.

The fleet comprises 11 cars: five 7070-series bogie cars built in 1967 by Nippon Sharyo, of similar design to Toyama's cars, and six MLRV1000-series two-section low-

Takaoka-Eki – #7071 ▶ Koshinokata

gebaut wurden und den Fahrzeugen von Toyama ähneln, sowie sechs zweiteiligen Niederflurwagen vom Typ MLRV1000, die 2003-09 von Niigata Transys produziert wurden. Vier der älteren Triebwagen tragen Vollwerbung, nur einer den eigentlichen Anstrich in Orange; die Niederflurwagen sind alle rot, nur einer ist blau und mit Motiven von „Doraemon", einer bekannten Cartoon-Katze, verziert. Einzelfahrten kosten 150-350 Yen, eine Tageskarte 800 Yen. IC Cards werden nicht akzeptiert.

floor articulated cars built in 2003-09 by Niigata Transys. Four of the older cars are in advertising liveries with only one in orange fleet livery; the low-floor cars are in all-over red livery, apart from one in blue livery featuring graphics of 'Doraemon', a popular cartoon cat. Stage fares range from 150-350 Yen and 1-day tickets (800 Yen) are available. IC cards are not accepted.

Shogawaguchi > Rokudoji – MLRV #1003 ▶ Koshinokata

■ TAKAOKA

Kataharamachi – #7074 ▶ Takaoka-Eki

Nomachiguchi > Yonejimaguchi – #7071 ▶ Koshinokata

#7076 ▶ Takaoka-Eki

Rokudoji – #7076 ▶ Koshinokata

Yonejimaguchi – #7075 ▶ Takaoka-Eki

Shin-Takaoka – JR West Kiha 47-series DMU ▶ Johana

REGIONALBAHNEN

Mit Eröffnung des *Hokuriku Shinkansen* wurde die Hokuriku Main Line (1067 mm) in der Präfektur Toyama von *JR West* an das neue Unternehmen *Ainokaze Toyama Railway* (siehe Kapitel Toyama) übertragen. Zu *JR West* gehören jedoch weiterhin zwei Nebenstrecken, die mit der Hokuriku Main Line am Bahnhof Takaoka verbunden sind. Diese sind eingleisig, nicht elektrifiziert und werden mit Dieseltriebwagen der Baureihe Kiha 40/47 von 1977-82 betrieben; die Züge verkehren annähernd stündlich. Die 16,5 km lange Himi Line (8 Stationen) führt von Takaoka nach Norden über das Hafenviertel Fushiki und erschließt kleine Küstenorte entlang der Bucht von Toyama. Die Johana Line (29,5 km, 14 Stationen) im Landesinnern führt durch vorstädtische und ländliche Siedlungen südlich von Takaoka; am Bahnhof Shin-Takaoka, der im März 2015 eröffnet wurde, kann zwischen der Johana Line und dem *Hokuriku Shinkansen* umgestiegen werden.

LOCAL RAILWAYS

To coincide with the opening of the Hokuriku Shinkansen, JR West's 1067 mm gauge Hokuriku Main Line in Toyama Prefecture was transferred to a new third-sector company, Ainokaze Toyama Railway (see Toyama entry). JR West, however, retains control of two branch lines which connect with the Hokuriku Main Line at Takaoka station. Both lines are 1067 mm gauge single-track, un-electrified, and served by a common pool of Kiha 40/47-series DMU cars dating from 1977-82; separate services operate on each line at irregular, approximately hourly, intervals. The 16.5 km Himi Line (8 stations) heads north from Takaoka via the port district of Fushiki and serves small coastal settlements along Toyama Bay. The inland Johana Line (29.5 km, 14 stations) serves suburban and rural settlements to the south of Takaoka; Shin-Takaoka, which opened in March 2015, is an interchange between the Johana Line and the Hokuriku Shinkansen.

Takaoka

Takaoka – Ainokaze Toyama Railway 521-series (ex-JR West) - *Local* ▶ Tomari

Hokutetsu-Kanazawa – Hokutetsu Asanogawa Line (ex-Keio EMUs)

KANAZAWA

Kanazawa (462.478 Einw., 467,8 km²), die Hauptstadt der Präfektur Ishikawa, ist eine historische Burgstadt, die 1945 von Brandbomben verschont blieb und deshalb einige Viertel mit traditionellen Holzhäusern bewahrt, auch wenn die Stadt sonst durchaus modern ist. Sie liegt in der Region Hokuriku am Japanischen Meer und ist mit Tokyo durch den *Hokuriku Shinkansen* verbunden, nach Nagoya und Kyoto/Osaka fahren Express-Züge auf der konventionellen Hokuriku Main Line.

Der Bahnhof Kanazawa, etwa 2 km nordwestlich des historischen Stadtzentrums gelegen, verfügt über vier Shinkansen- und sieben konventionelle Gleise in Hochlage. Zur besonderen Gestaltung gehören eine große Glaskuppel sowie ein hölzernes Eingangstor in Form einer Handtrommel, beides aus dem Jahr 2005.

Der öffentliche Nahverkehr wird vor allem mit Bussen abgewickelt, in der Stadt fahren jedoch auch zwei privat betriebene S-Bahn-Linien sowie Nahverkehrszüge auf der Hokuriku Main Line.

Kanazawa (population 462,478; 467.8 km²), capital of Ishikawa Prefecture, is a historic castle-town which escaped fire-bombing in 1945 and, though mainly modern, has retained some districts with traditional wooden buildings. It lies in the Hokuriku region on the Sea of Japan coast, connected to Tokyo by the Hokuriku Shinkansen and to Nagoya and Kyoto/Osaka by limited-express trains on the conventional Hokuriku Main Line.

Kanazawa station, located about 2 km north-west of the historic city centre, is an elevated station with four Shinkansen and seven conventional tracks. It has a distinctive design with a large glass 'welcome' dome and a hand-drum-shaped wooden entrance gate, both completed in 2005.

Buses are the mainstay of the public transport network, but the city is also served by two privately-owned suburban rail lines and JR/third-sector local rail services on the Hokuriku Main Line.

HOKURIKU RAILWAY — Hokuriku Tetsudo – 'Hokutetsu'

Die private *Hokuriku Railway* (*Hokutetsu*) wurde 1943 durch eine während des Krieges staatlich geförderte Fusion fast aller privaten Bus- und Bahngesellschaften in der Präfektur Ishikawa gegründet, darunter die von der *Kanazawa Electric Tramway* im Jahr 1919 eröffnete Straßenbahn (13 km, 6 Linien), die im Jahr 1966 stillgelegt wurde. Das Unternehmen betreibt heute neben den zwei verbleibenden S-Bahn-Linien hauptsächlich Busse. Seit den 1960er Jahren gehört das Unternehmen zur *Meitetsu*-Gruppe, die rund 14% der Anteile von *Hokutetsu* hält.

Die **Ishikawa Line** entstand 1915 als Dampfeisenbahn mit 762-mm-Spurweite zwischen Shin-Nishi-Kanazawa

The privately-owned Hokuriku Railway ('Hokutetsu') was founded in 1943 through a government-promoted wartime merger of almost all private bus and rail operators in Ishikawa Prefecture, including the city tram network originally opened by the Kanazawa Electric Tramway in 1919. The city tramway (13 km, 6 routes) closed in 1966 and the company is today primarily a bus operator with only two remaining suburban railway lines. Since the 1960s the company has been part of the Meitetsu Group which owns around 14% of Hokutetsu's shares.

*The **Ishikawa Line** originated as a 762 mm gauge steam railway which opened in 1915 between Shin-Nishi-*

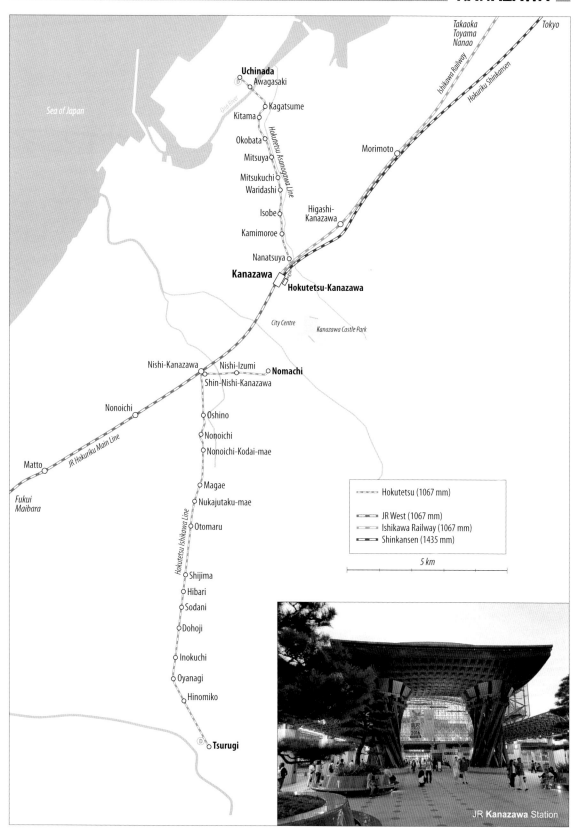

Takaoka
Toyama
Nanao

Tokyo

Ishikawa Railway

Hokuriku Shinkansen

Sea of Japan

Ono River

Uchinada
Awagasaki

Kagatsume

Kitama

Hokutetsu Asanogawa Line

Okobata

Mitsuya

Morimoto

Mitsukuchi
Waridashi

Isobe

Higashi-
Kanazawa

Kamimoroe

Nanatsuya

Kanazawa

Hokutetsu-Kanazawa

City Centre

Kanazawa Castle Park

Nishi-Kanazawa   Nishi-Izumi   **Nomachi**

Shin-Nishi-Kanazawa

Nonoichi

Oshino

Nonoichi

Nonoichi-Kodai-mae

Matto

JR Hokuriku Main Line

Fukui
Maibara

Magae

Nukajutaku-mae

Hokutetsu Ishikawa Line

Otomaru

Shijima

Hibari

Sodani

Dohoji

Inokuchi

Oyanagi

Hinomiko

Tsurugi

Legend:
- Hokutetsu (1067 mm)
- JR West (1067 mm)
- Ishikawa Railway (1067 mm)
- Shinkansen (1435 mm)

5 km

JR **Kanazawa** Station

KANAZAWA

Shin-Nishi-Kanazawa – Hokutetsu Ishikawa Line (ex-Tokyu EMUs, #7202 ► Nomachi; 7201 ► Tsurugi)

(Übergang zur Hokuriku Main Line) und Tsurugi südlich von Kanazawa. Die Strecke wurde 1921 umgespurt und elektrifiziert und 1922 nach Norden bis Shiragiku-cho verlängert, was zwar außerhalb des Stadtzentrums lag; an der Station Nomachi konnte jedoch zur Straßenbahn umgestiegen werden; die Linie wurde 1923 von der *Kanazawa Electric Tramway* erworben. 1926/27 baute die *Kinmei Railway* eine Verlängerung von Tsurugi bis Hakusan-Shita (16,8 km) als Teil eines ehrgeizigen, aber nie verwirklichten Plans für eine durchgehende Strecke von Kanazawa bis Nagoya. Diese Verlängerungsstrecke wurde jedoch schrittweise (1983-84 und 2009) stillgelegt, so dass die Linie heute wie zuvor in Tsurugi endet, wo sich auch der Betriebshof befindet. Der Fahrgastbetrieb auf dem nördlichsten 0,9 km langen Abschnitt bis Shiragiku-cho wurde 1970 eingestellt; Nomachi wurde somit Endstation, auch wenn bereits damals keine Straßenbahnverbindung ins Stadtzentrum mehr bestand.

Heute erschließt die eingleisige Strecke locker bebaute Wohngebiete, die hinter Shijima sehr ländlich werden. Im März 2015 wurde die Station Hibari in einem Entwicklungsgebiet am Stadtrand eingefügt. Die Lage der Endstation und der damit verbundene Umsteigezwang verringern das Potenzial dieser Linie. Die Züge verkehren unregelmäßig etwa 1-3 Mal pro Stunde mit Halt an allen Stationen und benötigen 29 Minuten für die Gesamtstrecke; Nomachi ist eingleisig, Ausweichen gibt es an den Stationen Shin-Nishi-Kanazawa, Nukajutaku-mae und Dohoji. Im Einsatz sind sechs elektrische 2-Wagen-Einheiten der Serie 7000 (ex Tokyu) und eine 2-Wagen-Einheit der Serie 7700 (ex Keio); seit 1990 herrscht Ein-Mann-Betrieb.

Kanazawa (interchange with Hokuriku Main Line) and Tsurugi to the south of Kanazawa. The line was re-gauged and electrified in 1921 and extended northwards in 1922 to Shiragiku-cho, outside the city centre but providing a connection with the city tramway at Nomachi; the line was acquired by Kanazawa Electric Tramway in 1923. In 1926/27 the Kinmei Railway built an extension from Tsurugi to Hakusan-Shita (16.8 km) as part of an ambitious but unrealised plan for a through line between Kanazawa and Nagoya; however, the extension was closed in stages (1983-84 and 2009), cutting the line back to its original terminus at Tsurugi, also the location of the line's depot. Passenger service on the northernmost 0.9 km section to Shiragiku-cho ceased in 1970 with Nomachi becoming the terminus, though by this time it had lost its tram connection into the city.

Today the single-track line serves mainly low-density residential suburbs which give way to semi-rural settlements beyond Shijima; a new station opened at Hibari in March 2015 to serve an industrial estate and expanding suburban development at the edge of the built-up area. However, the line's potential is hampered by its out-of-centre terminus and the need to change to JR or buses for onward travel to central Kanazawa. An irregular-interval all-stations service of 1-3tph takes 29 minutes for a single trip; Nomachi is a single-track terminus but passing loops are present at Shin-Nishi-Kanazawa, Nukajutaku-mae and Dohoji. Services are provided by a fleet of six 2-car 7000-series (ex-Tokyu) and one 2-car 7700-series (ex-Keio) EMU sets. Trains have been driver-only operated since 1990.

Hokutetsu

Ishikawa Line: Nomachi – Tsurugi
  13.8 km, 17 Haltestellen | *stations*; 1067 mm; 600Vdc ⬆

22-06-1915: Shin-Nishi-Kanazawa – Tsurugi (11.7 km)
01-10-1922: Shin-Nishi-Kanazawa – Nomachi (2.1 km)

Asanogawa Line: Hokutetsu-Kanazawa – Uchinada
  6.8 km (Ⓤ 0.2 km), 12 Haltestellen | *stations* (1 Ⓤ); 1067 mm; 1500Vdc ⬆

10-05-1925: Nanatsuya – Shin-Susaki (5.3 km)
18-05-1928: Nanatsuya – Hokutetsu-Kanazawa (0.7 km)
14-07-1929: Shin-Susaki – Uchinada (0.8 km)

Awagasaki > Kagatsume – Hoketetsu Asanogawa Line - 8800-series ► Uchinada

Nishi-Kanazawa - JR West 521-series - Local ► Komatsu

Die eingleisige **Asanogawa Line** wurde zwischen 1925 und 1929 von der *Asanogawa Electric Railway* eröffnet und verbindet Kanazawa mit Awagasaki-Kaigan an der Küste (8,6 km). Die Linie wurde 1946 von *Hokutetsu* übernommen und 1974 um 1,8 km bis Uchinada verkürzt. 1996 wurde die Stromversorgung von 600 V auf 1500 V erhöht und der Ein-Mann-Betrieb eingeführt. Im Zuge eines Umbaus des JR-Bahnhofs Kanazawa und dessen Umgebung wurde die Endstation Hokutetsu-Kanazawa im März 2001 unter die Erde verlegt; die neue Station hat einen Mittelbahnsteig und ist unterirdisch mit dem JR-Bahnhof verbunden. Die Linie erschließt Wohngebiete und verläuft teilweise in Straßenrandlage. Sie quert den Fluss Ono bei Awagasaki auf einer eigenen Brücke. Diese S-Bahn-Linie verkehrt alle 22 bis 30 Minuten, die Fahrzeit beträgt 17 Minuten; Zugbegegnungen finden an der Station Mitsuya statt. Im Einsatz sind fünf elektrische 2-Wagen-Einheiten (ex Keio Inokashira Line), das Depot befindet sich in Uchinada.

Hokutetsus „1-Day Free Ticket" (1.000 Yen) gilt an allen Tagen auf beiden Bahnstrecken; das „1-Day Free Eco Ticket" nur Sa/So und an Feiertagen (Ishikawa Line - 500 Yen, Asanogawa Line - 400 Yen). Die „Ica" IC Card des Unternehmens ist nur zusammen mit einem entsprechenden Abo gültig.

OTHER LOCAL RAILWAYS

Als der *Hokuriku Shinkansen* im März 2015 von Nagano nach Kanazawa verlängert wurde, übergab *JR West* den parallelen Abschnitt der Hokuriku Main Line (1067 mm, 20 kV AC 60Hz) in der Präfektur Ishikawa (Kanazawa – Kurihara, 17,8 km, 5 Stationen) an die Bahngesellschaft **Ishikawa Railway**. Gemeinsam mit der *Ainokaze Toyama Railway* wird ein durchgehender Regionalverkehr zwischen Kanazawa und Tomari (90,7 km) über Takaoka und Toyama angeboten. Die *Ishikawa Railway* verfügt über fünf 2-Wagen-Einheiten der Baureihe 521 für Gleich- und Wechselstrom von 2009-15 (3 ex JR, 2 neu). *JR West*-Züge der Nanao Line nutzen heute die Gleise der *Ishikawa Railway*, um den Bahnhof Kanazawa zu erreichen.

Die Hokuriku Main Line südwestlich von Kanazawa verblieb im Besitz von *JR West* – einige Vorortzüge mit Halt an allen Stationen erreichen Tsuruga in der Präfektur Fukui (130 km), doch der typische Fahrplan enthält 2-3 Züge pro Stunde bis Komatsu (28,4 km) oder Fukui (76,7 km).

The single-track **Asanogawa Line** was opened by the Asanogawa Electric Railway between 1925 and 1929, linking Kanazawa with Awagasaki-Kaigan on the coast (8.6 km). The line was taken over by Hokutetsu in 1946 and cut back by 1.8 km to Uchinada in 1974. In 1996 the power supply was upgraded from 600 to 1500Vdc and driver-only operation started. In March 2001, its Hokutetsu-Kanazawa terminus was relocated underground in connection with the redevelopment of JR Kanazawa station and the surrounding area; the new station has an island platform serving two tracks and is linked to the nearby JR station via an underground square. The line serves residential suburbs and features some roadside running and a bridge over the Ono River at Awagasaki. It supports a 22 to 30-minutes frequency all-stations service taking 17 minutes from end to end; trains pass each other at Mitsuya. Rolling stock comprises five 2-car EMUs (ex-Keio Inokashira Line); the depot is at Uchinada.

Hokutetsu's 1-Day Free Ticket (1,000 Yen) is valid at any time on both rail lines; the 1-Day Free Eco Ticket is valid Sat/Sun/Hols only (Ishikawa Line, 500 Yen; Asanogawa Line, 400 Yen). The company's 'Ica' IC card is only valid on its rail services if loaded with an appropriate season ticket.

OTHER LOCAL RAILWAYS

When the Hokuriku Shinkansen was extended from Nagano to Kanazawa in March 2015, the parallel section of JR West's 1067 mm gauge Hokuriku Main Line (20kVac 60Hz) in Ishikawa Prefecture (Kanazawa – Kurihara; 17.8 km, 5 stations) was transferred to the third-sector **Ishikawa Railway**. A reciprocal through-running service is provided with the Ainokaze Toyama Railway between Kanazawa and Tomari (90.7 km) via Takaoka and Toyama. Ishikawa Railway rolling stock comprises five 2-car 521-series dual voltage AC/DC EMU cars dating from 2009-15 (3 from JR, 2 newly built). JR West Nanao Line services also run into Kanazawa over Ishikawa Railway tracks.

The Hokuriku Main Line to the south-west of Kanazawa remains in JR West ownership; some all-stations Local services extend as far as Tsuruga in Fukui Prefecture (130 km) but the usual daytime all-stations service pattern is 2-3 tph to either Komatsu (28.4 km) or Fukui (76.7 km).

Echizen-Takefu (Fukutetsu Fukubu Line) – Echitetsu 'ki-bo' L-01 Niederflurbahn / *low-floor tram* & Fukutetsu 770-series

FUKUI

Auch wenn sich das Stadtgebiet bis ans Japanische Meer erstreckt, befindet sich die eigentliche Stadt Fukui (266.000 Einw., 536,17 km²) im Zentrum der Fukui-Ebene am Zusammenfluss der Flüsse Asuwa, Hino und Kuzuryu. Die Hauptstadt der gleichnamigen Präfektur ist ein wichtiger Industriestandort und wurde durch Luftangriffe im Jahr 1945 und ein starkes Erdbeben im Jahr 1948 weitgehend zerstört, weshalb die Stadt als modernes Symbol den Phönix für den Wiederaufbau „aus der Asche" wählte.

Fukui liegt an der Hokuriku Main Line von *JR West*, hier halten *Limited Express*-Züge von Kanazawa nach Nagoya bzw. Kyoto/Osaka. Der *Hokuriku Shinkansen* soll die Stadt 2022/23 erreichen. Der Schienennahverkehr wird von der *Fukui Railway* (Straßenbahn) und der *Echizen Railway* betrieben. Diese Unternehmen haben keine eigenen IC Cards und akzeptieren auch keine, es gibt jedoch eine Tageskarte für die *Fukui Railway* (nur Sa/So/Feiertage - 500 Yen) bzw. für *Fukui Railway* + *Echizen Railway*, das „Common One-Day Free Ticket" (Sa/So/Feiertage - 1.400 Yen). *JR West* bietet auch Regionalzüge auf der Hokuriku Main Line (stündlich nach Kanazawa oder Tsuruga) und seltener auf der nicht elektrifizierten Etsumi-Hoku Line (Fukui – Kuzuryuko, 55,1 km) an.

Although its administrative boundary extends to the Sea of Japan coast, the actual city of Fukui (266,000 population; 536.17 km²) is located approximately 15 km inland in the centre of the Fukui plain at the confluence of the Asuwa, Hino, Kuzuryu rivers. An industrial centre and capital of Fukui Prefecture, the city was largely destroyed by air raids in 1945 and a massive earthquake in 1948; the modern city's symbol is the Phoenix, signifying its reconstruction 'from the ashes' of the destroyed city.

Fukui lies on JR West's Hokuriku Main Line, served by Limited-Expresses running between Kanazawa and Nagoya or Kyoto/Osaka; the Hokuriku Shinkansen is due to reach the city by 2022/23. Local rail services are operated by Fukui Railway (urban tramway/interurban line) and Echizen Railway. These companies do not issue or accept IC cards but the following ride-at-will tickets are available: Fukui Railway - One-day Free Ticket (Sat/Sun/Hols - 500 Yen); Fukui Railway and Echizen Railway - Common One-day Free Ticket (Sat/Sun/Hols - 1,400 Yen). JR West also operates all-stations services on the Hokuriku Main Line (generally hourly to Kanazawa or Tsuruga) and infrequently on the un-electrified Etsumi-Hoku Line (Fukui – Kuzuryuko, 55.1 km).

FUKUI RAILWAY   Fukui Tetsudo – 'Fukutetsu'

Die **Fukubu Line** ist eine Mischung aus Überlandstraßenbahn auf eigenem Gleiskörper und konventioneller straßenbündiger Tram. Der Überlandabschnitt wurde 1924/25 eröffnet und verband die Stadt Takefu mit Fukui-Shin (heute Sekijuji-mae), einer Endstation außerhalb des Zentrums an der Südseite des Flusses Asuwa. Die Linie wurde 1933 straßenbündig über den Fluss und entlang einer neuen Nord-Süd-Straße (später Phoenix-dori genannt) zum Bahnhof Fukui verlängert; die Straße wurde im Rahmen

*The **Fukubu Line** is partly reserved-track interurban and partly street-running urban tramway. The interurban section opened in 1924/25 linking the town of Takefu with Fukui-Shin (since renamed Sekijuji-mae), an out-of-centre terminus on the south side of the Asuwa River. Street-running commenced in 1933 when the line was extended across the river to Fukui station along a new north-south highway (later named Phoenix-dori); the highway and tramway were extended further northwards*

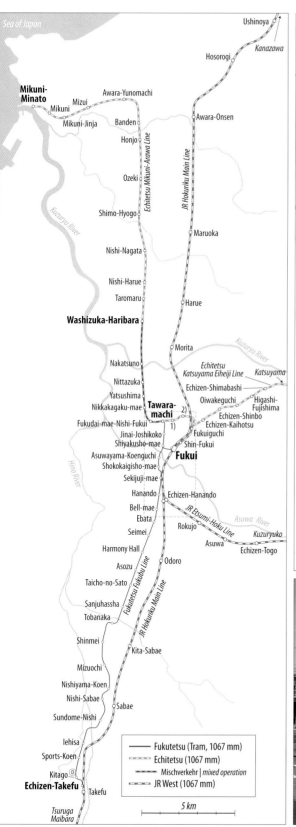

Sea of Japan

Ushinoya

Kanazawa

Hosorogi

Mikuni-Minato

Mizui

Awara-Yunomachi

Mikuni

Mikuni-Jinja

Banden

Awara-Onsen

Honjo

Ozeki

Shimo-Hyogo

Maruoka

Nishi-Nagata

Nishi-Harue

Taromaru

Harue

Washizuka-Haribara

Morita

Nakatsuno

Echitetsu Katsuyama Eiheiji Line

Katsuyama

Nittazuka

Echizen-Shimabashi

Yatsushima

Oiwakeguchi

Higashi-Fujishima

Nikkakagaku-mae

Tawara-machi

2)

Echizen-Shinbo

Fukudai-mae-Nishi-Fukui

1)

Echizen-Kaihotsu

Jinai-Joshikoko

Fukuiguchi

Shiyakusho-mae

Shin-Fukui

Fukui

Asuwayama-Koenguchi

Shokokaigisho-mae

Sekijuji-mae

Echizen-Hanando

Hanando

Bell-mae

JR Etsumi-Hoku Line

Ebata

Rokujo

Seimei

Asuwa

Kuzuryuko

Harmony Hall

Odoro

Echizen-Togo

Asozu

Taicho-no-Sato

Sanjuhassha

Tobanaka

Shinmei

Kita-Sabae

Mizuochi

Nishiyama-Koen

Nishi-Sabae

Sabae

Sundome-Nishi

Iehisa

Sports-Koen

Kitago

Echizen-Takefu

Takefu

Tsuruga Maibara

Echitetsu Mikuni-Arawa Line

JR Hokuriku Main Line

Kuzuryu River

Hino River

Fukutetsu Fukubu Line

JR Hokuriku Main Line

Asuwa River

	Fukutetsu (Tram, 1067 mm)
	Echitetsu (1067 mm)
	Mischverkehr | *mixed operation*
	JR West (1067 mm)

5 km

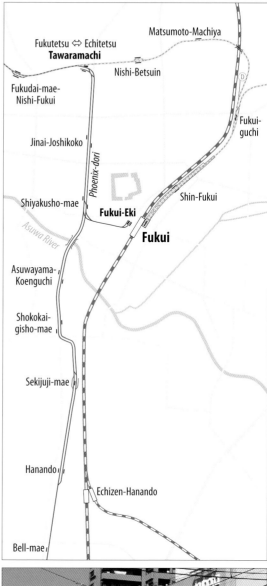

Fukutetsu ⇔ Echitetsu
Tawaramachi

Matsumoto-Machiya

Nishi-Betsuin

Fukudai-mae-Nishi-Fukui

Fukui-guchi

Jinai-Joshikoko

Phoenix-dori

Shin-Fukui

Shiyakusho-mae

Fukui-Eki

Asuwa River

Fukui

Asuwayama-Koenguchi

Shokokai-gisho-mae

Sekijuji-mae

Hanando

Echizen-Hanando

Bell-mae

Jinai-Joshikoko > Tawaramachi – Fukutetsu 'Fukuram'
#F1002 ► Echizen-Takefu

Fukui-Eki
– Fukutetsu 735-series (ex-Stuttgart)

Asozu - Fukutetsu 770-series - *Local* ▶ Tawaramachi via
Fukui-Eki (überdachte Weiche | *snow shelter over points*)

des Wiederaufbaus der Stadt nach Norden ausgeweitet und die Tram bis 1950 von Shiyakusho-mae (Rathaus) bis Tawaramachi verlängert. Daraufhin verkehrte bis 1972 auf den Gleisen zwischen Fukui-Ekimae und Tawaramachi auch eine eigene städtische Straßenbahn.

Die Strecke ist von Echizen-Takefu bis Hanando eingleisig mit Ausweichen, nördlich davon zweigleisig. Südlich von Shokokaigisho-mae, am Übergang von Eigentrasse zu Straßenmittellage entlang der Phoenix-dori, wechselt auch die Klassifizierung von Eisenbahn zu Straßenbahn. Von der Südstrecke gibt es keine direkte Gleisverbindung zum kurzen eingleisigen Abzweig zum Bahnhof Fukui, weshalb an der Haltestelle Shiyakusho-mae ein Richtungswechsel erforderlich ist. Auf der Uberlandstrecke schützen kurze gewölbte Dächer die Weichen vor starkem Schneefall.

Die Gleislage an beiden Endstellen in Fukui wurde 2016 geändert. Die eingleisige Stumpfendstelle Fukui-Ekimae wurde durch eine zweigleisige Anlage ersetzt, diese liegt etwa 100 m näher am Eingang des Bahnhofs Fukui und wurde im Rahmen der Neugestaltung des Bahnhofswestausgangs in Fukui-Eki umbenannt. Die eingleisige Stumpfendstelle Tawaramachi wurde ebenfalls zweigleisig ausgebaut, um einen durchgehenden Betrieb auf die Mikuni-Awara Line der *Echizen Railway* zu ermöglichen.

Im Jahre 1963 wurde *Nagoya Railway* (*Meitetsu*) Hauptaktionär, doch starke Verluste veranlassten *Meitetsu*, ihren Anteil von 33% im Jahr 2008 an ein Konsortium aus Kommunen und anderen Unternehmen abzugeben. 2009 genehmigte die Zentralregierung Finanzhilfen zur Modernisierung der Bahn, was zu Verbesserungen im Fahrplan und bei den Tarifen führte, außerdem wurden drei

as part of post-war and post-earthquake reconstruction works, the street-running section between Shiyakusho-mae (City Hall) and Tawaramachi opening in 1950. A dedicated urban tram service operated between Fukui-Ekimae and Tawaramachi but was withdrawn in 1972.

The line is single-track with passing loops from Echizen-Takefu to Hanando and double-track north of Hanando. Its official designation changes from railway to tramway just south of Shokokaigisho-mae where it switches from private right-of-way to street-running along the centre of Phoenix-dori. An interesting feature of the tramway layout is the absence of a direct track connection from the south to the short single-track branch serving Fukui station, a change of direction being necessary at Shiyakusho-mae for services undertaking this manoeuvre. Short tunnel-like shelters protect the points on the interurban section from heavy snowfall.

Track arrangements at both Fukui termini were altered in 2016; the single-track stub terminus at Fukui-Ekimae was replaced by a double-track facility located approximately 100 m closer to the entrance of Fukui station and renamed Fukui-Eki as part of the redesign of the west exit station square; and, the single-track off-street stub terminus at Tawaramachi was also converted to double-track to facilitate through running to Echizen Railway's Mikuni-Awara Line.

In 1963 Nagoya Railway (Meitetsu) became the major shareholder but heavy losses led Meitetsu to transfer its 33% share of the company to a consortium of local municipalities and support organisations in 2008. In 2009 central government authorised a package of financial assistance to upgrade the railway; subsequent improve-

Fukui-Eki > Shiyakusho-mae – Fukutetsu 800-series
▶ Tawaramachi via Fukui-Eki

Fukubu Line
Echizen-Takefu – Fukui-Eki/Tawaramachi

21.5 km, 25 Haltestellen | *stops/stations*; 1067 mm; 600Vdc ⊕
Fukubu Line (N) ⇔ Echitetsu Mikuni-Arawa Line

23-02-1924: Echizen-Takefu – Shinmei (8.5 km)
26-07-1925: Shinmei – Sekijuji-mae (9.3 km)
15-10-1933: Sekijuji-mae – Fukui-Ekimae (2.3 km)
27-11-1950: Shiyakusho-mae – Tawaramachi (1.3 km)
01-10-1989: Bell-mae
20-09-1997: Harmony Hall
03-2010: Sports-Koen
03:2011: Taicho-no-Sato
03:2011: Seimei
27-03-2016: Fukui-Ekimae (geschlossen | *closed*) – Fukui-Eki (0.1 km)

Tawaramachi - Fukutetsu Fukuram #F1001 ▶ Echizen-Takefu

neue Haltestellen eingerichtet (Sport-Koen, Taicho-no-Sato und Seimei), Zubringerbuslinien und Park-&-Ride-Anlagen geschaffen, neue Niederflurstraßenbahnen geliefert und die Haltestellen entlang der Phoenix-dori modernisiert. Die Möglichkeit, den Fukui-Eki-Ast zu einer Schleife durch die Innenstadt zu verlängern, wird ebenfalls untersucht. Zwischen 2008 und 2014 erhöhten sich die Fahrgastzahlen um 20%.

Ein „Tram-Train" nach europäischem Vorbild wurde im März 2016 geschaffen, als die Verbindung zwischen *Fukutetsus* Straßenbahn und der *Echizen Railway* an der Station Tawaramachi in Betrieb ging. Ein wechselseitiger, durchgehender Verkehr, die sog. „Phoenix-Tawaramachi Line", wird seither bis Washizuka-Haribara (6 km von Tawaramachi) mit Fahrzeugen beider Gesellschaften durchgeführt, wobei das Personal an der Station Tawaramachi wechselt.

Tagsüber (10.00-18.00 Uhr) fährt *Fukutetsu* 4 Mal pro Stunde zwischen Echizen-Takefu und Tawaramachi, darunter sind zwei *Express*-Fahrten ohne Halt an zehn Stationen der Überlandstrecke und ohne den Abstecher zum Bahnhof Fukui, welcher somit nur zweimal pro Stunde bedient wird. Die *Express*-Fahrten benötigen 42 Minuten, die *Local*-Fahrten sogar 68 Minuten, da 17 Minuten für den Umweg von Shiyakusho-mae bis Fukui-Eki und zurück in Anspruch genommen werden. Eine der beiden *Express*-Fahrten pro Stunde führt weiter auf der *Echizen Railway* bis Washizuka-Haribara. Abends verkehrt halbstündig eine *Local*-Tram, wobei der Bahnhof nur in Fahrtrichtung Süden angefahren wird.

Ein Großteil der Flotte stammt von *Meitetsu* und wurde von Nippon Sharyo produziert. Diese Fahrzeuge übernahm *Fukutetsu* nach der Schließung der Straßenbahn von Gifu im Jahr 2005. Darunter sind neun zweiteilige Hochflurwagen der Serie 770/880 (1980/87/88) sowie zwei teilniederflurige Drehgestellwagen der Serie 800, alle mit ausfahrbaren Trittbrettern. Zu den sonstigen älteren Fahrzeugen

ments have included timetable and ticketing changes, opening of three new stations (Sports-Koen, Taicho-no-Sato and Seimei), a bus feeder service, new park and ride facilities, new low-floor trams and upgraded tram stops along Phoenix-dori. The possibility of extending the Fukui-Eki branch into a city centre loop is also under consideration. Ridership increased by 20% between 2008 and 2014.

European-style tram-train operation commenced in March 2016 with the opening of a connection between Fukutetsu's tramway and the Echizen Railway at Tawaramachi. A reciprocal through-running tram service, branded 'Phoenix-Tawaramachi Line', runs to Washizuka-Haribara (6 km from Tawaramachi) using rolling stock from both operators, with crew changeover at Tawaramachi.

During the daytime (10.00-18.00) Fukutetsu operates a 4tph service between Echizen-Takefu and Tawaramachi comprising a 2tph Express service, which skips ten interurban stations but serves all tramway stops except Fukui-Eki, plus a 2tph Local service which calls at all-stations including a detour via Fukui-Eki. The Expresses take 42 minutes and the Locals take 68 minutes of which 17 minutes is taken up with the detour from Shiyakusho-mae to Fukui-Eki and back again. One of the two Expresses each hour is the reciprocal through-running tram-train service to/from Washizuka-Haribara on the Echizen Railway. A half-hourly Local service operates in the evenings with Fukui-Eki only served in the southbound direction; northbound passengers need to change at Shiyakusho-mae for Fukui-Eki.

Most of the fleet are ex-Meitetsu cars built by Nippon Sharyo which were transferred to Fukutetsu following the closure of the Gifu tram network in 2005. They comprise nine 2-section 770/880-series high-floor articulated cars (1980/87/88) plus two 800-series part-low-floor bogie cars (2000), all with retractable steps. Other

FUKUI

gehören eine 2-Wagen-Einheit sowie ein Einzelwagen (ex *Nagoya Municipal Subway*), außerdem ein GT4-Gelenkwagen der Serie 735 aus Stuttgart von 1965, der aus Kochi übernommen wurde und bei besonderen Anlässen im Einsatz ist. Neuere Zugänge umfassen vier dreiteilige Niederflurwagen vom Typ F1000 (27 m), die 2013-16 von Niigata Transys nach einem Entwurf von Bombardier produziert wurden. Jeder dieser Wagen hat eine andere Farbe und trägt die Bezeichnung „FUKURAM" mit dem Zusatz „Fukui Light Rail Transit". Alle Wagen sind für den Ein-Mann-Betrieb ausgerüstet. Ein kleines Eisenbahnmuseum ist im Bahnhofsgebäude von Kitago untergebracht.

older cars include a 2-car set and single car (ex-Nagoya Municipal Subway) and one 735-series ex-Stuttgart 2-section GT4 articulated car dating from 1965, acquired from Kochi, which is used for special services. Recent additions to the fleet are four F1000-series 27 m long 3-section articulated low-floor cars built by Niigata Transys to a Bombardier design (2013-16). Each of these cars is in a different colour and carries 'FUKURAM' branding with the strap-line 'Fukui Light Rail Transit'. All cars are equipped for driver-only operation. A small railway museum is housed in Kitago station building.

ECHIZEN RAILWAY   Echizen Tetsudo – 'Echitetsu'

Das Unternehmen *Echizen Railway* wurde von der Präfektur Fukui und anderen Kommunen und Geschäftspartnern gegründet, um das defizitäre Fukui-Netz der *Keifuku Electric Railway* (die weiterhin die Randen-Straßenbahn in Kyoto betreibt) zu übernehmen. Nach zwei Unfällen in den Jahren 2000 und 2001 kam es zu einer Betriebseinstellung, woraufhin sich *Keifuku* aus dem Eisenbahngeschäft zurückzog; die *Echizen Railway* nahm 2003 den Betrieb auf zwei Strecken wieder auf, lediglich der 6,2 km lange Ast der Katsuyama-Eiheiji Line blieb geschlossen.

Echizen Railway is a third-sector company which was established by Fukui Prefecture and local authority/business partners to take over the loss-making Fukui division of the Keifuku Electric Railway (which continues to operate Randen trams in Kyoto). Two accidents, in 2000 and 2001, forced the suspension of all services and led Keifuku to withdraw from the railway business; Echizen Railway recommenced operations on both lines during 2003, apart from a 6.2 km branch of the Katsuyama-Eiheiji Line which remained closed.

Tawaramachi – Echitetsu Mikuni-Arawa Line #6109 (ex-Aichi Loop Railway) ▶ Mikuni-Minato

Mikuni-Awara Line: Fukuiguchi – Mikuni-Minato
25.2 km, 22 Haltestellen | *stations*; 1067 mm; 600Vdc ⊕
Mikuni-Arawa Line (S) ⇔ Fukutetsu Fukubu Line

30-12-1928: Fukuiguchi – Awara-Yunomachi (20.0 km)
31-01-1931: Awara-Yunomachi – Mikuni (4.2 km)
11-10-1944: Mikuni – Mikuni-Minato (1.0 km)

Katsuyama-Eiheiji Line: Fukui – Katsuyama
27.8 km, 23 Haltestellen | *stations*; 1067 mm; 600Vdc ⊕

11-02-1914: Shin-Fukui – Echizen-Takehara (19.0 km)
11-03-1914: Echizen-Takehara – Katsuyama (8.8 km)

Washizuka-Haribara
- Hoch- und Niedrigbahnsteig
- *high and low-level platforms*

Since 2015 the former surface-level Echitetsu terminus adjacent to JR Fukui station has been temporarily
relocated onto the future Hokuriku Shinkansen viaduct
pending construction of a parallel viaduct for the company's own use, which is due for completion in 2018. The
new viaduct will extend for 3.0 km with three elevated
stations (Fukui, Shin-Fukui and Fukuiguchi). The current
temporary station has two tracks serving a single island
platform; Shin-Fukui, also relocated to the viaduct, has
side platforms. Trains return to ground-level before
reaching Fukuiguchi where the depot is located and
where the Mikuni-Awara Line branches off the main **Katsuyama-Eiheiji Line**. The main line becomes single-track
with passing loops beyond Echizen-Kaihotsu (2.4 km from
Fukui), heading inland and serving a mix of suburban and
rural settlements along the scenic Kuzuryu River valley.
The **Mikuni-Arawa Line** is also single-track and serves
small towns on the coastal plain towards Mikuni-Minato
(port) at the mouth of the Kuzuryu River.

Both lines have a half-hourly all-stations train service
to/from Fukui throughout the day supplemented by a
few short workings and limited-stop services during the
morning peak. Since March 2016, Echitetsu and Fukutetsu
have operated a 1tph reciprocal through-running service
between Washizuka-Haribara on the Mikuni-Awara Line
and Echizen-Takefu on the Fukubu Line by making use
of a new track connection at Tawaramachi. The through
service runs from approximately 10.00 until 18.00 with
two additional AM peak trips to/from Fukudaimae-Nishifukui only.

Only one car of Keifuku-era rolling stock remains in
service. The remainder have been replaced by second-
hand cars from JR Central (six 2-car EMU sets, built
1982/83) and the Aichi Loop Railway (14 single railcars,
built 1987); these vehicles carry 'E-Line' branding. Two
18.7 m long low-floor two-section articulated trams
from Niigata Transys (L-series, named 'ki-bo') operate
the reciprocal services over the Fukutetsu Line. Stations
from Tawaramachi to Washizuka-Haribara have high and
low-level platforms to handle both trains and low-floor
trams. Trains and trams are driver-only operated but
some carry passenger attendants.

Im Jahr 2015 wurde die ehemalige ebenerdige *Echitetsu*-Endstelle in der Nähe des JR-Bahnhofs Fukui
vorübergehend auf die Hochtrasse für den zukünftigen
Hokuriku Shinkansen verlegt. Bis 2018 soll *Echitetsu*
parallel dazu einen eigenen Viadukt bekommen, der mit
3,0 km Länge drei Hochbahnstationen umfassen wird (Fukui, Shin-Fukui und Fukuiguchi). Die heutige provisorische
Endstation ist zweigleisig mit Mittelbahnsteig, während
Shin-Fukui auch auf dem Viadukt liegt, jedoch Seitenbahnsteige aufweist. Die Züge erreichen kurz vor Fukuiguchi
die Straßenebene; hier, wo die Mikuni-Awara Line von der
Hauptstrecke, der Katsuyama-Eiheiji Line, abzweigt, befindet sich das Depot. Die Hauptlinie wird hinter Echizen-Kaihotsu (2,4 km von Fukui) eingleisig und führt entlang des
malerischen Flusses Kuzuryu ins Landesinnere durch eine
Mischung aus vorstädtischen und ländlichen Siedlungen.
Die Mikuni-Arawa Line ist auch eingleisig, sie erschließt
kleine Orte in der Küstenebene Richtung Mikuni-Minato
(Hafen) an der Mündung des Flusses Kuzuryu.

Auf beiden Linien herrscht ganztags ein Halbstunden-
takt mit Halt an allen Stationen, dazu kommen während
der Morgenspitze einzelne Kurzläufer bzw. Express-Züge.
Seit März 2016 fährt tagsüber (ca. 10.00-18.00) zusätzlich
eine gemeinsam von *Echitetsu* und *Fukutetsu* betriebene
Bahn pro Stunde unter Nutzung der neuen
Gleisverbindung an der Station Tawaramachi
von Washizuka-Haribara bis Echizen-Takefu
(plus zwei Morgen-HVZ-Fahrten von/nach
Fukudaimae-Nishifukui) .

Aus der *Keifuku*-Ära ist nur noch ein
Wagen im Einsatz. Der Rest wurde durch
Gebrauchtfahrzeuge von *JR Central* (sechs
elektrische 2-Wagen-Einheiten von 1982/83)
und der *Aichi Loop Railway* (14 Einzeltrieb-
wagen, Baujahr 1987) ersetzt; diese Fahrzeuge tragen die Marke „E-Line". Für den
wechselseitigen Betrieb mit *Fukutetsu* stehen
zwei 18,7 m lange zweiteilige Niederflurwagen von *Niigata Transys* (L-Serie, genannt
„ki-bo") zur Verfügung. Die Stationen von
Tawaramachi bis Washizuka-Haribara haben
hohe und niedrige Bahnsteige, so dass sowohl Züge als auch Niederflurstraßenbahnen
halten können. In der Regel ist nur ein Fahrer
an Bord, doch in manchen Bahnen fährt ein
Fahrgastbetreuer mit.

Shiyakusho-mae (Fukutetsu Fukubu Line) – Echitetsu 'ki-bo' L-01
- als durchgehender Express | *on through-running Express service*
▶ Washizuka-Haribara

Nagoya Municipal Subway – Hisaya-odori – Meijo Line (im Uhrzeigersinn | *clockwise*)

NAGOYA

Nagoya liegt in der Tokai-Region am nördlichen Zipfel der Ise-Bucht an der Pazifikküste etwa 340 km westlich von Tokyo. Es ist die Hauptstadt der Präfektur Aichi und Japans viertgrößte Stadt mit 2,27 Mio. Einwohnern auf einer Fläche von 326,4 km². Nagoya ist auch das Zentrum von Japans drittgrößter Metropolregion, der *Chukyo Metropolitan Area*, in der 8,74 Menschen leben. Die schnellsten *Tokaido Shinkansen*-Züge benötigen für die Fahrt von Tokyo bis Nagoya 1 Stunde 40 Minuten, der jetzt im Bau befindliche *Chuo Shinkansen* (Magnetschwebebahn) soll das ab 2027 in nur 40 Minuten schaffen.

Nagoya ist eine wichtige Hafen-, Handels- und Industriestadt und besonders als Standort zahlreicher im Automobilsektor tätiger Firmen bekannt. Die Stadt wurde während der Bombenangriffe im Jahr 1945 stark zerstört und anschließend schachbrettartig mit breiten, mehrspurigen Straßen für das autogerechte Zeitalter wiederaufgebaut. Die Bevölkerungsdichte und die Nutzung öffentlicher Verkehrsmittel sind niedriger als in Tokyo und Osaka, der Anteil von Privatautos hingegen höher. Innerhalb der Stadt Nagoya entfallen lediglich 23% aller Fahrten auf den Schienenverkehr (verglichen mit 78% in Tokyo und 59% in Osaka), was 938 Mio. Bahnfahrten pro Jahr entspricht.

Nagoyas traditionelles Geschäfts- und Einkaufszentrum liegt im Bereich Sakae, wo sich die beiden ursprünglichen Metro-Linien der Stadt kreuzen. Allerdings hat sich in den letzten Jahren um den 2,4 km weiter westlich gelegenen Bahnhof Nagoya (Meieki) durch den Bau von Bürohochhäusern, darunter die 55- bzw. 59-stöckigen Twin Towers von *JR Central*, mehreren Hotels und umfangrei-

Nagoya is situated in the Tokai region at the head of Ise Bay on the Pacific coast around 340 km to the west of Tokyo. It is the capital of Aichi Prefecture and Japan's fourth largest city with a population of 2.27 million in an area of 326.4km²; it is also the centre of Japan's third largest metropolitan region, the Chukyo Metropolitan Area, which has a population of 8.74 million. Nagoya is 1hr 40 min from Tokyo by the fastest Tokaido Shinkansen trains but the Chuo Shinkansen (maglev line) now under construction is due to cut this to 40 minutes by 2027.

Nagoya is a major port, commercial and industrial centre with a wide range of manufacturing activities including a concentration of companies in the automotive sector. Much of the city was destroyed during bombing raids in 1945 and an extensive reconstruction plan was implemented with a grid of wide multi-lane roads designed for the motor age. Population density and public transport mode share are lower than in Tokyo and Osaka and car ownership is higher. Rail accounts for only 23% of motorised passenger journeys in Nagoya City (compared to 78% in Tokyo and 59% in Osaka) constituting 938 million rail passenger journeys per year.

Nagoya's traditional central business and retail district is centred on Sakae where the city's original two metro lines intersect. However, in recent years the Nagoya station area (Meieki), 2.4 km to the west, has seen the construction of major high-rise office buildings including the twin 55 and 59 storey JR Central Towers, hotels and extensive underground shopping malls so that it now rivals the importance of Sakae. JR Nagoya

chen unterirdischen Einkaufspassagen neben Sakae ein zweites Zentrum etabliert. Der JR-Bahnhof Nagoya mit den angrenzenden unterirdischen Stationen von *Meitetsu* und *Kintetsu* bilden das Zentrum des Schienennetzes der Stadt, hier halten neben dem Shinkansen auch konventionelle Nah- und Fernverkehrszüge, zwei U-Bahn-Linien sowie die metroähnliche Aonami Line.

Auch wenn Nagoya einen Ruf als Autostadt hat (neben Toyota sind viele Zulieferfirmen in der Region ansässig), eröffnete die Stadt bereits 1957 ihre erste städtische U-Bahn-Linie; heute gibt es sechs Linien, von denen zwei direkt mit der gemeinhin als *Meitetsu* bekannten Privatbahn *Nagoya Railway* verknüpft sind. Die U-Bahn hält einen Anteil von 45% am städtischen Schienenverkehr, die Privatbahnen 35% und *JR Central* (*JR Tokai* auf Japanisch) 20%; der JR-Anteil ist niedriger als in Tokyo (38%) oder Osaka (31%), da das JR-Netz von Nagoya vergleichsweise klein ist. Bis auf den Bahnhof Akaike liegt das U-Bahn-Netz innerhalb des Stadtgebiets von Nagoya, während die äußeren Gebiete des Ballungsraums von *JR Central*, *Meitetsu* und *Kintetsu* erschlossen werden. Daneben verkehren noch die Aonami Line, die Magnetschwebebahn Linimo sowie die tangentiale Johoku und Aichi Loop Line.

Auf Korridoren ohne Schienenverkehr wurden Busspuren eingerichtet, darunter ein Busway auf einer Hochtrasse. Für Bahnfreunde interessant ist der „SCMAGLEV and Railway Park" von *JR Central* in der Nähe der Station Kinjo-Futo auf der Aonami Line, denn hier kann man nicht nur die Maglev-Technologie näher kennen lernen, sondern auch konventionelle Fahrzeuge sehen.

Das *Transportation Bureau* und einige andere Betreiber bieten Tageskarten für ihre eigenen Bahnen an, es gibt jedoch keine übergreifende für die ganze Region. Allerdings akzeptieren die meisten Betreiber verschiedene landesweite IC Cards, dazu gehören die von *Transportation Bureau* zusammen mit *Meitetsu* und anderen ausgegebene „manaca"-Karte sowie die „TOICA"-Karte von *JR Central*.

station and the adjoining underground Meitetsu and Kintetsu stations form the hub of the city's rail network, being served by Shinkansen, conventional inter-city and suburban services as well as by two metro lines and the third-sector Aonami Line.

Although having a reputation as a motor city (Toyota and other vehicle/component manufacturers are based in the region), Nagoya opened its first municipal metro line in 1957 and the city is now served by six lines, two of which feature reciprocal through running with the private Nagoya Railway commonly known as 'Meitetsu'. The metro accounts for 45% of rail passenger journeys in the city itself, with 35% carried by private railways and 20% by JR Central (JR Tokai in Japanese); the JR share is lower than in Tokyo (38%) or Osaka (31%) reflecting Nagoya's more limited JR network. The metro is confined to Nagoya city (apart from Akaike station) with outer suburban and interurban services operated by JR Central, Meitetsu and Kintetsu. The city and surrounds are also served by the third-sector Aonami Line, the Linimo maglev and the orbital Johoku and Aichi Loop lines.

A network of key bus priority routes and an elevated bus rapid transit line have been introduced on corridors without metro or rail services. Of note for rail enthusiasts is the 'SCMAGLEV and Railway Park' run by JR Central which has displays of 'super-conducting' maglev and conventional rolling stock situated close to Kinjo-Futo station on the Aonami Line.

The Transportation Bureau and some other operators sell unlimited-ride tickets for their own services but there is no comprehensive multi-operator ticket for the Nagoya area. However, most operators accept prepaid IC cards within the national inter-operability scheme, including the 'manaca' card issued by the Transportation Bureau, Meitetsu and others and the 'TOICA' card issued by JR Central.

Linimo – Irigaike-Koen ▶ Fujigaoka

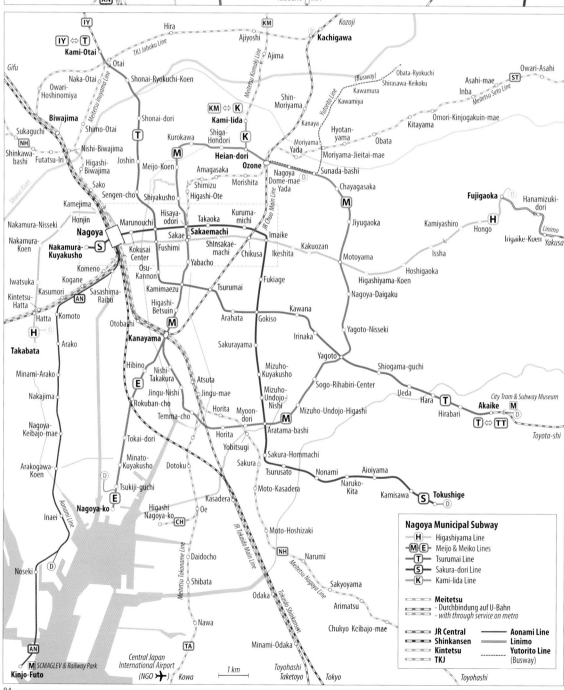

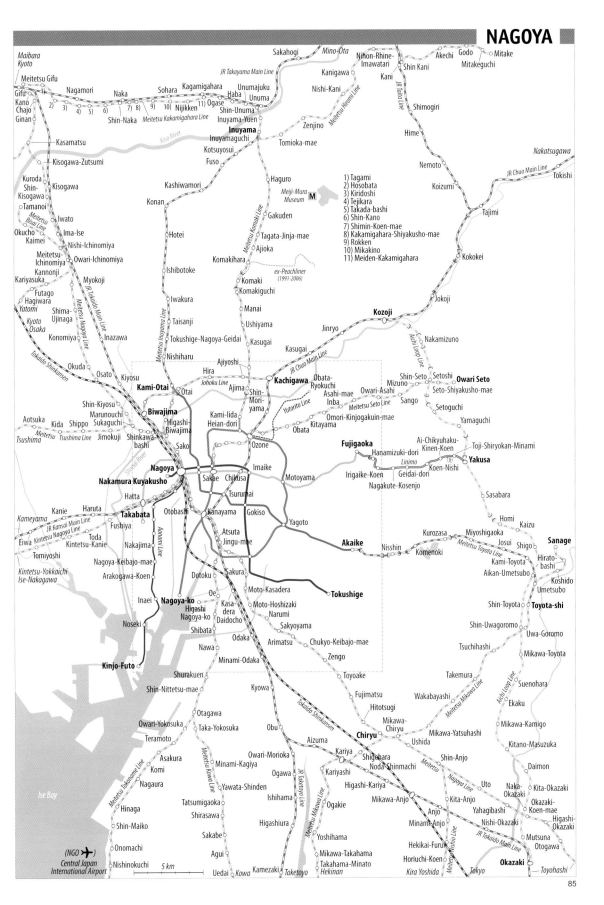

Maibara
Kyoto
Meitetsu Gifu
Gifu
Kano
Chajo
Ginan
Sakahogi
Mino-Ota
Nihon-Rhine-Imawatari
Shin Kani
Akechi
Godo
Mitake
Mitakeguchi

JR Takayama Main Line
Nagamori
Naka
Sohara
Kagamigahara
Haba
Kanigawa
Kani

Nishi-Kani
Shimogiri

Nagoya-ko

2) 3) 4) 5) 6) 7) 8) 9) 10) Nijikken 11) Ogase
Shin-Unuma
Unuma
Unumajuku

Hime

Shin-Naka
Meitetsu Kakamigahara Line
Inuyama-Yuen
Zenjino
Nemoto
Koizumi

Kasamatsu
Kiso River
Inuyama
Inuyamaguchi
Tomioka-mae
JR Chuo Main Line
Tokishi

Kisogawa-Zutsumi
Kotsuyosui
Tajimi

Kuroda
Shin-Kisogawa
Tamanoi
Kisogawa
Iwato
Kashiwamori
Konan
Fuso
Haguro
Meiji-Mura Museum M
Kokokei

Okucho
Kaimei
Ima-Ise
Hotei
Gakuden
Jokoji

Nishi-Ichinomiya
Meitetsu
Bisai Line
Owari-Ichinomiya
Myokoji
Ishibotoke
Tagata-Jinja-mae
Ajioka
Komakihara
ex-Peachliner
(1991-2006)
Komaki
Komakiguchi

1) Tagami
2) Hosobata
3) Kiridoshi
4) Tejikara
5) Takada-bashi
6) Shin-Kano
7) Shimin-Koen-mae
8) Kakamigahara-Shiyakusho-mae
9) Rokken
10) Mikakino
11) Meiden-Kakamigahara

Meitetsu
Ichinomiya
Kannonji
Kariyasuka
Futago
Hagiwara
Yatomi
Kyoto
Osaka
Shima-Ujinaga
Konomiya
Inazawa
Iwakura
Taisanji
Manai
Ushiyama
Jinryo
Nakamizuno
Kozoji

Okuda
Osato
Kiyosu
Nishiharu
Tokushige-Nagoya-Geidai
Kasugai
Kasugai

Kami-Otai
Otai
Hira
Ajiyoshi
Johoku Line
Ajima
Kachigawa
Obata-Ryokuchi
Asahi-mae
Shin-Seto
Mizuno
Owari-Asahi
Setoshi
Owari Seto
Seto-Shiyakusho-mae

Aotsuka
Kida
Shippo
Marunouchi
Sukaguchi
Shin-Kiyosu
Biwajima
Higashi-Biwajima
Shinkawa-bashi
Sako
Kami-Iida
Heian-dori
Shin-Moriyama
Inba
Meitetsu Seto Line
Sango
Setoguchi

Meitetsu
Tsushima
Tsushima Line
Jimokuji
Ozone
Obata
Kitayama
Omori-Kinjogakuin-mae
Yamaguchi

Nagoya
Sakae
Imaike
Fujigaoka
Ai-Chikyuhaku-Kinen-Koen
Toji-Shiryokan-Minami
Yakusa

Nakamura Kuyakusho
Chikusa
Motoyama
Hanamizuki-dori
Linimo
Geidai-dori
Koen-Nishi

Hatta
Tsurumai
Irigaike-Koen
Nagakute-Kosenjo
Sasabara

Kanie
Haruta
Takabata
Otobashi
Kanayama
Gokiso
Yagoto
Akaike
Kurozasa
Miyoshigaoka
Homi
Kaizu
Sanage

Kameyama
JR Kansai Main Line
Meitetsu
Nagoya Line
Fushiya
Atsuta
Jingu-mae
Nisshin
Komenoki
Josui
Shigo
Hiratobashi

Eiwa
Toda
Kintetsu-Kanie
Nakajima
Kami-Toyota
Aikan-Umetsubo
Koshido
Umetsubo

Tomiyoshi
Nagoya-Keibajo-mae
Sakura
Shin-Toyota
Toyota-shi

Kintetsu-Yokkaichi
Ise-Nakagawa
Arakogawa-Koen
Dotoku
Moto-Kasadera
Tokushige
Shin-Uwagoromo
Uwa-Goromo

Inaei
Nagoya-ko
Higashi
Nagoya-ko
Oe
Kasa-dera
Daidocho
Moto-Hoshizaki
Narumi
Tsuchihashi
Mikawa-Toyota

Noseki
Shibata
Odaka
Sakyoyama
Takemura
Suenohara

Nawa
Minami-Odaka
Arimatsu
Chukyo-Keibajo-mae
Zengo
Ekaku

Kinjo-Futo
Shurakuen
Kyowa
Toyoake
Wakabayashi
Meitetsu Mikawa Line
Mikawa-Kamigo

Shin-Nittetsu-mae
Fujimatsu
Hitotsugi
Mikawa-Chiryu
Kitano-Masuzuka

Otagawa
Obu
Aizuma
Chiryu
Ushida
Mikawa-Yatsuhashi
Daimon

Owari-Yokosuka
Taka-Yokosuka
Owari-Morioka
Kariya
Shigehara
Noda-Shinmachi
Shin-Anjo
Naka-Okazaki
Kita-Okazaki

Teramoto
Asakura
Minami-Kagiya
Ogawa
Kariyashi
Higashi-Kariya
Meitetsu
Nagoya Line
Uto
Kita-Anjo
Okazaki-Koen-mae

Komi
Nagaura
Yawata-Shinden
Ishihama
Mikawa-Anjo
Anjo
Yahagibashi
Nishi-Okazaki
Higashi-Okazaki

Hinaga
Tatsumigaoka
Shirasawa
Ogaki
Minami-Anjo
Mutsuna
Otogawa

Shin-Maiko
Higashiura
Yoshihama
Hekikai-Furui
Horiuchi-Koen
JR Tokaido Main Line

Sakabe
Mikawa-Takahama
Okazaki

Onomachi
Agui
Takahama-Minato
Hekinan
Kira Yoshida
Tokyo
Toyohashi

Ise Bay

(NGO ✈)
Central Japan
International Airport
Nishinokuchi
5 km
Uedai
Kowa
Kamezaki
Taketoyo

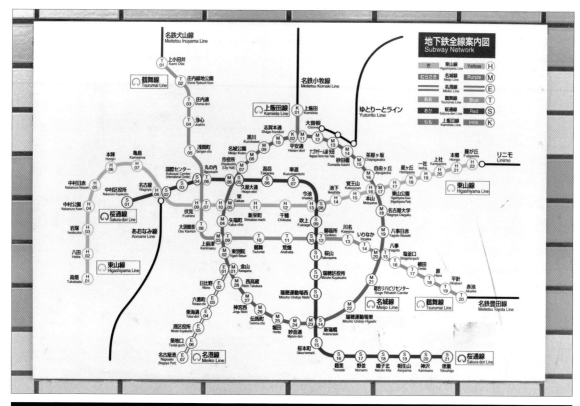

NAGOYA MUNICIPAL SUBWAY

Das *City of Nagoya Transportation Bureau (Nagoya-shi Kotsu Kyoku)* betreibt nicht nur die *Nagoya Municipal Subway (Nagoya-shiei Chikatetsu)*, sondern innerhalb der Stadtgrenzen auch ein umfangreiches Busnetz. Erste Vorschläge für eine U-Bahn tauchten in den späten 1930er Jahren auf, doch der Bau eines geplanten 6-Linien-Netzes mit einer Gesamtlänge von 49 km begann erst in den 1950er Jahren, der erste Abschnitt wurde 1957 in Betrieb genommen. 1963 beschloss das Unternehmen, sein Straßenbahnnetz, das 1959 mit 108 km seine größte Ausdehnung erreicht hatte, stillzulegen. Daraufhin wurde im Higashiyama Park eine 0,5 km lange Schwebebahn-Teststrecke mit Safege-Technologie errichtet, die von 1964 bis 1974 im Fahrgastbetrieb war. Als Massenverkehrsmittel taugte die Bahn jedoch nicht. Die letzte Tram fuhr in Nagoya 1974, aber ein Wagen ist bis heute in Toyohashi in Betrieb, während drei Wagen im „Nagoya City Tram and Subway Museum" in der Nähe der Station Akaike auf der Tsurumai Line und ein Wagen im

Nagoya Municipal Subway (Nagoya-shiei Chikatetsu) is operated by the City of Nagoya Transportation Bureau (Nagoya-shi Kotsu Kyoku) which also runs an extensive network of bus routes covering central and suburban areas of the city. Proposals for a metro were first considered in the late 1930s but it was not until the 1950s that construction commenced on a planned 49 km six-line network, the first section opening in 1957. In 1963 the undertaking decided to close its tram system which covered 108 km at its greatest extent (1959); a 0.5 km Safege suspended monorail test track was constructed in Higashiyama Park and operated in public service from 1964 to 1974 but the technology was found unsuitable for mainstream application. The last tram ran in 1974 but one former car remains operational in the Toyohashi fleet and others are on static display at the Nagoya City Tram and Subway Museum (3 cars), near Akaike station on the Tsurumai metro line, and the Nagoya Science Museum (1 car).

Nagoya Municipal Subway: 6 Linien | *lines*; 93.3 km; 87 U-Bahnhöfe (100, wenn man sie für jede Linie einzeln zählt) | *87 stations (100 if stations on each line counted separately)*; 782 Wagen | *cars*; 465 900 000 pax/a, 1 277 000 pax/d

„Nagoya Science Museum" ausgestellt sind.

Ein rasches Wirtschaftswachstum beschleunigte den Ausbau der U-Bahn, so dass 1972 sogar ein Netz mit acht Linien und 130 km Streckenlänge vorgeschlagen wurde. Dieser Plan wurde 1992 etwas abgeändert, so dass beispielsweise statt einer Verlängerung der Higashiyama Line die Aonami Line umgesetzt wurde. Wesentliche Projekte jenes Ausbauplans wurden jedoch verwirklicht, wie die Fertigstellung der Meijo-Ringlinie. Der letzte neue Abschnitt der U-Bahn wurde jedoch 2011 eröffnet, derzeit sind keine weiteren U-Bahn-Strecken beschlossen und es scheint unwahrscheinlich, dass die geplanten Linien 5, 7 und 8 in absehbarer Zeit gebaut werden.

Das derzeitige 6-Linien-Netz hat eine Streckenlänge von 93,3 km, wobei die Züge auf dem Netz von *Meitetsu* weitere 58,6 km befahren. Nagoya besitzt Japans einzige echte U-Bahn-Ringlinie (Meijo Line), aber mit der 0,8 km langen Kami-Iida Line auch Japans kürzeste Metro-Linie. Liniennummern wurden bis 1969 verwendet, dann kamen Liniennamen auf; lediglich der Abschnitt Kanayama – Aratama-bashi wurde weiterhin als „Linie 4" bezeichnet, bis er 2004 Teil der heutigen Meijo Line wurde. Die ersten drei (1, 2 und 4) sind Kleinprofillinien und haben Standard-Spurweite (1435 mm) sowie eine seitliche Stromschiene mit 600 V Gleichstrom. Die Tsurumai Line (3) wurde hingegen von Anfang an für den wechselseitigen Betrieb mit *Meitetsu* geplant und weist daher ein größeres Profil, eine Spurweite von 1067 mm und Stromzufuhr über Oberleitung (1500 V DC) auf; die neuere Sakura-dori Line (6) sowie die Kami-Iida Line wurden auch nach diesen Parametern gebaut. Die Fahrzeuge tragen die jeweilige Linienfarbe und es existiert ein Linien- und Stationscodierungssystem. Anders als in Tokyo oder Yokohama gibt es keine *Express*-Züge.

Bei der U-Bahn gilt ein Entfernungstarif, es werden aber auch praktische Tageskarten angeboten: Subway+Bus (850 Yen) oder nur Subway (740 Yen). An Wochenenden, Feiertagen und am 8. Tag jedes Monats (Umwelttag) gibt es eine vergünstigte „Donichi Eco"-Tageskarte für Subway+Bus (600 Yen). Ausländische Touristen (Reisepass erforderlich) können am Central Japan International Airport oder in Touristenbüros eine „Shoryudo"-Tageskarte Subway+Bus für 600 Yen kaufen.

Das Subway-Logo ist eine Darstellung von Gleisen in einem Tunnel, während das Maskottchen des Verkehrsbetriebs, „Hatchii", auf eine mythische Kreatur mit Tigerkopf und Karpfenkörper zurückgeht. Stationszugänge sind wie auch in Tokyo und anderen Städten mit einem Standard-Logo (in der Regel blau und weiß) mit einem Metro-Zug gekennzeichnet (auch die Stationen auf der Spurbustrasse der Yutorito Line). Wochentags gibt es auf der Higashiyama Line ganztägig für Frauen reservierte Wagen, morgens bis 9 Uhr auch auf der Meijo und Meiko Line.

Rapid economic growth spurred on plans for metro expansion and an eight-line network of around 130 km was proposed in 1972. This plan was somewhat modified in 1992 with, for example, the third-sector Aonami Line replacing a projected extension of the Higashiyama Line. Significant elements of these plans have been implemented, such as the completion of the Meijo loop line, but the last new section of metro opened in 2011; no further metro construction is authorised and it seems unlikely that proposed lines 5, 7 and 8 will be built any time soon.

The current six-line network extends to 93.3 km plus through-running over 58.6 km of Meitetsu tracks. It includes Japan's only true metro loop line where trains traverse the complete circle (the Meijo Line) and Japan's shortest metro line, the 0.8 km Kami-Iida Line. Line numbers were used until 1969 when line names were introduced – except that the Kanayama – Aratama-bashi section continued to be known as No. 4 Line until it became part of today's Meijo Line in 2004. The initial three lines (1, 2 and 4) run on standard-gauge (1435 mm) tracks and have 600Vdc third-rail current collection with narrow-profile tunnels and trains. The Tsurumai Line (3) was planned from the outset for through operation with Meitetsu and was constructed to a larger profile with 1067 mm gauge track and 1500Vdc overhead; the more recent Sakura-dori Line (6) and Kami-Iida Line are also built to these standards. Rolling stock is colour-coded by line of operation and there is a line and station numbering system. Unlike Tokyo and Yokohama, there are no express or limited stop services.

Distance-related fares apply and one-day bus/metro (850 Yen) or metro-only (740 Yen) passes are available. A cheaper bus/metro one-day Donichi Eco-pass (600 Yen) is available for weekends, holidays and the 8th day of each month (environment day) and there is also a Shoryudo one-day bus/metro pass (600 Yen) for foreign tourists (passport needed) available from Central Japan International Airport and tourist information centres.

The metro's logo is a representation of tracks in a tunnel and the system's mascot character 'Hatchii' is based on a mythical creature with the head of a tiger and body of a carp. Station entrances have signs featuring the standard metro train symbol (usually blue and white) also used in Tokyo and other cities (and at stations on Nagoya's Yutorito guided-busway). On weekdays, women-only cars operate all-day on the Higashiyama Line and from first train to 09.00 on the Meijo and Meiko Lines.

Hongo – Higashiyama Line N1000-series ► Takabata

Higashiyama Line

Der erste 2,4 km lange Abschnitt der Higashiyama Line wurde 1957 entlang des stark befahrenen Ost-West-Korridors zwischen dem Bahnhof Nagoya und dem traditionellen Stadtzentrum bei Sakae eröffnet. Die Strecke wurde später an beiden Enden in die Vororte verlängert, größtenteils unterirdisch, doch auch mit einem 2,6 km langen Hochbahnabschnitt am östlichen Ende. Bis 1969 war dies die „Linie 1", seither ist sie nach dem Bezirk Higashiyama [östliche Hügel] benannt.

Die Linie hat die höchsten Fahrgastzahlen aller Metro-Linien von Nagoya und gilt nach Osakas Midosuji Line als Japans zweitprofitabelste U-Bahn-Linie. Allerdings ist sie aufgrund des Kleinprofils und ihrer kurzen Züge stets überfüllt; in den 1980er Jahren waren manche Züge zwischen den Stationen Nagoya und Fushimi mit über 250% ihrer eigentlichen Kapazität ausgelastet, was seit Inbetriebnahme

The first 2.4 km section of the Higashiyama Line opened in 1957 along the heavily trafficked east-west corridor between Nagoya station and Sakae, the traditional city centre. The line was subsequently extended at both ends to serve suburban districts, running mainly underground but with a 2.6 km elevated section at its eastern end. It was known as No. 1 Line until 1969 when it was named after the Higashiyama (eastern hills) district.

The line has the highest ridership of Nagoya's metro lines and it is Japan's second most profitable metro line after Osaka's Midosuji Line. However, it suffers from overcrowding due to its narrow-profile construction and short trains; during the 1980s, peak trains on the most crowded section between Nagoya and Fushimi stations were running at over 250% capacity, though this has since been reduced to around 140% with the opening of the

Higashiyama Line (H)

Takabata (H01) – Fujigaoka (H22) (Line 1)
20.6 km, Ⓤ 18 km, 22 Bahnhöfe | stations
1435 mm, 600Vdc ⬇; 487 000 pax/d

15-11-1957: Nagoya – Sakae (2.4 km)
15-06-1960: Sakae – Ikeshita (3.6 km)
01-04-1963: Ikeshita – Higashiyama-Koen (2.5 km)
30-03-1967: Higashiyama-Koen – Hoshigaoka (1.1 km)
01-04-1969: Hoshigaoka – Fujigaoka (4.4 km)
　　　　　　Nagoya – Nakamura-Koen (3.5 km)
21-09-1982: Nakamura-Koen – Takabata (3.1 km)

der parallelen Sakura-dori Line und einer Taktverdichtung auf rund 140% reduziert werden konnte.

Die Züge fahren vom westlichen Endpunkt Takahata erst nach Norden bis Nakamura-Koen, wo einst eine Umsteigemöglichkeit zur Sakura-dori Line geplant war, und dann nach Osten Richtung Bahnhof Nagoya. Dies ist bei weitem die am stärksten frequentierte Station im U-Bahn-Netz mit 60 Mio.

Higashiyama-Koen   RS

Fahrgästen pro Jahr, von denen allein die Higashiyama Line 42 Millionen befördert; um diesen Andrang bewältigen zu können, sind die Haltepositionen am Mittelbahnsteig versetzt angeordnet, Richtung Fujigaoka im südlichen Abschnitt und Richtung Takabata im nördlichen. Gleich südlich des U-Bahnhofs Nagoya liegt eine enge Kurve mit einem Radius von 125 m, danach geht es über Fushimi (Umsteigepunkt zur Tsurumai Line) weiter zum U-Bahnhof Sakae, dem zweitwichtigsten im U-Bahn-Netz und Umsteigepunkt zur in Nord-Süd-Richtung kreuzenden Meijo Line. Von hier aus führt die Strecke weiter unterirdisch nach Osten, bis die Züge hinter Issha den Tunnel verlassen und in Hochlage bis zur Endstation fahren. Jenseits von Fujigaoka gibt es eine zweigleisige Wendeanlage sowie eine Rampe zum ebenerdigen Betriebshof; am westlichen Ende der Linie steht ein zweites oberirdisches Depot zur Verfügung, das über einen Abzweig nördlich von Takahata erreicht wird. Der Hochbahnhof Fujigaoka liegt neben der unterirdischen Endstation der Linimo-Magnetschwebebahn, deren Bau die Pläne für eine östliche Verlängerung der U-Bahn ersetzte. In ähnlicher Weise wurden Pläne für eine Westverlängerung zugunsten des Baus der Aonami Line verworfen.

Bis auf einen zweigleisigen Röhrentunnelabschnitt zwischen Ikeshita und Kakuozan, wo die Linie private Grundstücke unterquert, liegen die Streckentunnel weitgehend flach unter der Straße. Die Stationstiefe reicht von 6,2 m bis 19,7 m.

Der Fahrzeugpark umfasst 48 Sechs-Wagen-Züge der Kleinprofilserien 5050 (seit 1992) und N1000 (seit 2008);

parallel Sakura-dori Line and increased service frequencies.

Commencing at Takahata, the line runs northwards to Nakamura-Koen, a planned but unrealised interchange with the Sakura-dori Line, and then heads for Nagoya station. This is by far the busiest station on the metro network handling 60 million passengers a year of which the Higashiyama Line alone accounts for 42 million; to accommodate these numbers, stopping positions on the single island platform are staggered with Fujigaoka-bound trains using the southern part and Takabata-bound trains the northern part. On leaving Nagoya, the line negotiates a sharp 125 m radius curve before reaching Fushimi (interchange with Tsurumai Line) and then heads for Sakae, the second busiest station on the network and interchange with the north-south Meijo Line. From here the line continues eastwards and emerges from tunnel onto viaduct just beyond Issha. Beyond Fujigaoka station there is a twin-track headshunt for terminating trains and a ramp leading down to the main surface-level depot; there is also a second surface-level depot at the western end of the line reached by a short spur tunnel just north of Takahata terminus. The elevated terminus at Fujigaoka is adjacent to the underground terminus of the Linimo maglev line, the construction of which superseded plans for an eastern extension of the metro. Likewise, plans for an extension at the western end of the line were dropped in favour of building the third-sector Aonami Line.

Tunnel construction is largely shallow cut-and-cover beneath roads, except for a short twin-bore section between Ikeshita and Kakuozan where the line passes beneath private property. Station depth ranges from 6.2 to 19.7 m below ground.

Rolling stock comprises 48 six-car sets of narrow-profile 5050-series (since 1992) and N1000-series (since 2008); all cars are 15.5 m long and 2.5 m wide. A two-car set of original 100-series stock dating from 1957 is on

Nagoya – 5050-series - Frauenwagen | *'Women-Only' car*

Nagoya - Higashiyama Line 5050-series ▷ Takabata

89

Fushimi – Higashiyama Line 5050-series ▶ Takabata (vor Einbau der Bahnsteigtüren | prior to platform gate installation)

alle Wagen sind 15,5 m lang und 2,5 m breit. Eine Zwei-Wagen-Einheit der ursprünglichen Serie 100 von 1957 ist im „City Tram and Subway Museum" ausgestellt, während neuere Wagen in Takamatsu (Kotoden) sowie bei der Metro von Buenos Aires im Einsatz sind. Bis 2016 wurden alle Stationen mit Bahnsteigtüren nachgerüstet, so dass heute auf den äußeren Abschnitten im Ein-Mann-Betrieb mit ATO-Unterstützung gefahren werden kann. Zwischen Kamejima und Ikeshita waren 2016 hingegen noch Zugbegleiter mit an Bord.

Auf der Higashiyama Line herrscht ein dichter Takt mit Zügen alle 2-3 Minuten in den Hauptverkehrszeiten, sonst alle 4-5 Minuten. Alle Züge verkehren stets auf der Gesamtstrecke, wofür sie 40 Minuten benötigen.

display at the City Tram and Subway Museum and more recent retired stock is in use in Takamatsu (Kotoden) and on the Buenos Aires metro. Platform gate installation was completed in 2016 and driver-only ATO was introduced on the outer sections of the line; at the time of writing there were still guards on trains between Kamejima and Ikeshita.

An intensive service is operated with trains every 2-3 minutes in weekday peaks and every 4-5 minutes off-peak. All trains operate over the full length of the line taking 40 minutes.

Sakae   RS

Higashiyama-Koen   RS

Kanayama – Meijo Line 2000-series (im Uhrzeigersinn | *clockwise*)

Meijo & Meiko Lines

Diese beiden Linien haben eine gemeinsame Geschichte und werden auch gemeinsam betrieben. Die „Linie 2" wurde etappenweise zwischen 1965 und 1971 als Nord-Süd-Verbindung durch das Stadtzentrum zwischen Ozone im Norden und Nagoya-ko (Hafen Nagoya) im Süden in Betrieb genommen. An der Station Sakae bestand eine Umsteigemöglichkeit zur in Ost-West-Richtung verlaufenden Higashiyama Line und an den Stationen Ozone und Kanayama zu JR- und *Meitetsu*-Zügen. 1969 wurde daraus die Meijo Line, der Name leitet sich von der Burg Nagoya (zugänglich von der Station Shiyakusho) ab – „Mei" ist eine alternative Lesung für „Na" in Nagoya und „jo" bedeutet „Burg".

Die Idee einer Ringlinie unter Einbeziehung eines Teils der „Linie 2" sowie der neuen „Linie 4" (Ozone – Kanayama) stammte aus einem Bericht des *Urban Transport Council* von 1961. Der erste Abschnitt der „Linie 4" wurde 1974 zwischen Kanayama und Aratama-bashi eröffnet und als Abzweig der Meijo Line betrieben, aber als „Linie 4" bezeichnet. Es dauerte weitere 20 Jahre, bis die Bauarbeiten im Jahr 1994 wieder aufgenommen wurden, so dass die „Linie 4" im Jahr 2004 fertiggestellt werden konnte. Zu diesem Zeitpunkt wurde der Name „Meijo Line" auf die gesamte Ringlinie ausgedehnt, während der Abschnitt der „Linie 2" von Kanayama zum Hafen fortan als „Meiko Line" („Meiko" bedeutet ebenfalls „Hafen von Nagoya") bezeichnet wurde, auch wenn die meisten Züge der Meiko Line weiterhin auf der Meijo Line bis Ozone durchfahren.

These two lines have a shared history and are linked operationally with a common fleet of trains. Line 2 opened in stages between 1965 and 1971 providing a north-south link through the city centre between Ozone in the north and Nagoya-ko (Nagoya Port) in the south. Interchange was available with the east-west Higashi-yama Line at Sakae and with JR and Meitetsu services at both Ozone and Kanayama. In 1969 the Meijo Line name was adopted, meaning Nagoya Castle (accessible from Shiyakusho station) – 'Mei' is an alternative reading for the 'Na' of Nagoya and 'jo' means castle.

The concept of a loop line incorporating part of Line 2 and new Line 4 (Ozone – Kanayama) was recommended in an Urban Transport Council report of 1961 and the first section of Line 4 opened between Kanayama and Aratama-bashi in 1974, operating as a branch of the Meijo Line but known as No. 4 Line. It was then another 20 years before construction recommenced in 1994, with the final completion of Line 4 in 2004. At this point the Meijo Line name was extended to the whole of the loop line and the Kanayama – Nagoya-ko section of Line 2 became the Meiko Line (Meiko meaning Nagoya Port), though most Meiko Line trains continue to run through to Ozone on the Meijo Line.

The western side of the Meijo Line through the city centre is much more intensively used than the eastern side of the loop which serves mainly suburban districts, though including some important traffic generators such

Yagoto – Meijo Line 2000-series (gegen den Uhrzeigersinn | *counterclockwise*)

Der westliche Teil der Meijo Line durch das Stadtzentrum ist viel stärker nachgefragt als der Ostring, der hauptsächlich vorstädtische Gebiete erschließt, obwohl auch hier einige wichtige Einrichtungen wie die Nagoya-Daigaku (Universität) und das Baseball-Stadion Nagoya Dome genügend Nachfrage erzeugen. Das Zugangebot widerspiegelt dieses Ungleichgewicht mit durchlaufenden Zügen der Meiko Line, die die Zugfolge auf dem Westring verdoppeln. Laut Grundfahrplan verkehren die Ringzüge alle 10 Minuten in jeder Richtung; zwischen Ozone und Kanayama hält alle 5 Minuten ein Zug, da auch die Meiko Line von/nach Nagoya-ko alle 10 Minuten verkehrt. Früh morgens und abends pendeln die Meiko Line-Züge zwischen Nagoya-ko und Kanayama, wo unmittelbar Anschluss an die Meiko Line besteht. Auf dem Westteil der Meijo Line werden Spitzenfrequenzen von 2,5-3,5 Minuten erreicht, auf dem Ostteil und auf der Meiko Line von 5-7 Minuten. Für eine Ringfahrt benötigt man ca. 48 Minuten, von Kanayama bis Nagoya-ko 10 Minuten.

as Nagoya-Daigaku (university) and the Nagoya Dome baseball stadium. The service pattern reflects this imbalance with through-running Meiko Line trains doubling the frequency on the western side of the loop. The base off-peak timetable sees trains operating each way around the complete loop every 10 minutes, supplemented on the western side by an additional 10-minute through service between Ozone, Kanayama and Nagoya-ko on the Meiko Line. In the early mornings and evenings, Meiko Line trains operate a shuttle service between Nagoya-ko and Kanayama connecting with Meiko Line trains. Peak frequencies are enhanced up to 2.5-3.5 minutes on the Meijo Line (west) and 5.0-7.0 minutes on the Meijo Line (east) and Meiko Line. Services take 48 minutes around the loop and 10 minutes from Kanayama to Nagoya-ko.

These lines have the same narrow-profile tunnels, 1435 mm track gauge and third-rail electrification as the Higashiyama Line and the older sections (the western side of the loop from Ozone to Aratama-bashi and the

Meijo (M) & Meiko (E) Lines

Meijo Line (Line 2/4): Kanayama (M01) – Kanayama (M01) (Ring | *loop*)
26.4 km Ⓤ, 28 Bahnhöfe | *stations*

Meiko Line (Line 2): Kanayama (E01) – Nagoya-ko (E07)
6.0 km Ⓤ, 7 Bahnhöfe | *stations*

Meijo & Meiko Lines: 1435 mm, 600Vdc Ⓓ; 387 000 pax/d

15-10-1965: Sakae – Shiyakusho (1.3 km)
30-03-1967: Sakae – Kanayama (3 km)
29-03-1971: Kanayama – Nagoya-ko (6 km)
20-12-1971: Shiyakusho – Ozone (4.6 km)
30-03-1974: Kanayama – Aratama-bashi (5.7 km)
19-01-2000: Ozone – Sunada-bashi (1.7 km)
13-12-2003: Sunada-bashi – Nagoya-Daigaku (6.2 km)
06-10-2004: Nagoya-Daigaku – Aratama-bashi (5.1 km)

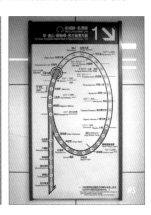

Nagoya-ko (Meiko Line)   RS

Diese Linien haben wie die Higashiyama Line das kleinere Tunnelprofil, 1435-mm-Spurweite und eine seitliche Stromschiene. Die älteren Abschnitte (Westring von Ozone bis Aratama-bashi und die Meiko Line) wurden überwiegend in offener Bauweise mit kurzen Abschnitten im Schildvortrieb erstellt. Der neuere Ostabschnitt wurde zwischen Ozone und Sunada-bashi offen und zwischen Sunada-bashi und Aratama-bashi im Schildvortrieb errichtet. Der östliche Abschnitt hat tiefere Stationen, die tiefste ist Motoyama mit 24 m.

Im Einsatz ist eine einheitliche Flotte von 36 Sechs-Wagen-Zügen der Serie 2000 von Nippon Sharyo von 1989-2004. Sie sind mit ATC ausgerüstet. Es gibt zwei Betriebshöfe – eine unterirdische Anlage in Daiko (zwischen Nagoya Dome-mae Yada und Sunada-bashi) für 186 Wagen und eine oberirdische für 54 Wagen, die über einen Abzweig der Meiko Line zwischen Tsukiji-guchi und Nagoya-ko erreicht wird.

Meiko Line) are predominantly cut-and-cover construction with short sections of twin-bore tunnel. The more recently built eastern section of the loop is cut-and-cover between Ozone and Sunada-bashi and shield construction between Sunada-bashi and Aratama-bashi. The eastern section has deeper stations, the deepest being Motoyama at 24 m below ground.

Services are provided by a unified fleet of 36 six-car 2000-series trains built by Nippon Sharyo in 1989-2004. Trains are two-person operated with ATC. There are two depots – an underground facility at Daiko (between Nagoya Dome-mae Yada and Sunada-bashi) with capacity for 186 cars and a 54-car surface-level facility accessed by a spur off the Meiko Line between Tsukiji-guchi and Nagoya-ko stations.

Shiyakusho

Meijo/Meiko Line 2000-series   RS

Yagoto – Tsurumai Line N3000-series ▶ Kami-Otai

Tsurumai Line

Nagoyas dritte Metro-Linie war von Anfang an für den wechselseitigen Betrieb ausgelegt und wurde demnach mit größerem Tunnelprofil, 1067-mm-Spurweite und 1500 V Gleichstrom über Oberleitung errichtet. Die Linie führt vom Norden Richtung Südosten, von Kami-Otai an der Inuyama Line von *Meitetsu* über die Innenstadt nach Akaike direkt hinter der Stadtgrenze, wo sie mit der Toyota Line von *Meitetsu* verknüpft ist. Die Toyota Line wurde gleichzeitig mit der Tsurumai Line geplant und gebaut, so dass bereits 1979 eine direkte Verbindung zwischen Nagoya und Toyota-shi (Stadt), der Heimat des Toyota-Konzerns, in Betrieb genommen werden konnte; alle Züge der Toyota Line werden auf die U-Bahn durchgebunden. Am anderen Ende der Strecke wurde die 1,4 km lange Verbindung zur Inuyama Line, was den Bau einer neuen Station in Kami-Otai erforderte, erst 1993 vollendet.

Nagoya's third metro line was designed from the outset for through running with wider-profile tunnels, 1067 mm track gauge and 1500Vdc electrification. The line runs north to south-east from Kami-Otai on Meitetsu's Inuyama Line via the central area to Akaike, just beyond the city boundary, where it connects with Meitetsu's Toyota Line. The Toyota Line was planned and built at the same time as the Tsurumai Line, opening in 1979 to provide a direct link between Nagoya and Toyota-shi (city), home of the Toyota motor company; all Toyota Line trains run through to the metro. At the other end of the line, the final 1.4 km connection into Meitetsu's Inuyama Line, which involved the construction of a new station at Kami-Otai, was not completed until 1993.

The line is mainly underground except, for a 0.5 km ramp section approaching the elevated northern ter-

Tsurumai Line (T)

Kami-Otai (T01) – Akaike (T20) (Line 3)
20.4 km, Ⓤ 19.9 km, 20 Bahnhöfe | *stations*
1067 mm; 1500Vdc ⊕; 194 000 pax/d
Tsurumai Line ⇔ Meitetsu's Toyota, Mikawa & Inuyama Lines

18-03-1977: Fushimi – Yagoto (8.0 km)
01-10-1978: Yagoto – Akaike (5.4 km)
27-11-1981: Fushimi – Joshin (2.9 km)
06-09-1984: Joshin – Shonai-Ryokuchi-Koen (2.7 km)
12-08-1993: Shonai-Ryokuchi-Koen – Kami-Otai (1.4 km)

Kami-Otai – Tsurumai Line 3000-series (Zug endet hier | *terminating*)

Die Tsurumai Line ist größtenteils unterirdisch, lediglich der 0,5 km lange Rampenabschnitt mit Anschluss an den Hochbahnhof Kami-Otai liegt im Freien. Die Tunnelabschnitte wurden vorwiegend in offener Bauweise unter breiten Straßen (etwa 60%) errichtet, doch an fünf separaten Abschnitten unter privaten Grundstücken oder Flüssen wurden eingleisige Röhren im Schildvortrieb aufgefahren.

Die Station Kami-Otai hat zwei Mittelbahnsteige, wobei die inneren Gleise von der Tsurumai Line und die äußeren von der Inuyama Line vom/zum Bahnhof Meitetsu-Nagoya befahren werden. Die Endstation Akaike hat auch zwei Mittelbahnsteige, jedoch mittig nur ein Gleis für hier endende Züge und als Zufahrt zum Depot Nisshin, das man über einen Abzweig östlich der Station erreicht. Innerhalb des Betriebshofsgeländes liegt das „City Tram and Subway Museum". Die Zwischenstationen haben entweder Seiten- oder Mittelbahnsteige, alle mit 170 m Länge für 8-Wagen-Züge ausgelegt, auch wenn bis 1993 nur 4-Wagen-Züge und heute nur 6-Wagen-Züge eingesetzt werden und eine Verlängerung der Züge momentan nicht geplant ist.

Die Tsurumai Line verkehrt in der Morgenspitze alle 4 Minuten, in der Abendspitze alle 5 Minuten und sonst alle 7½ Minuten, wobei eine Fahrt von Kami-Otai bis Akaike 35 Minuten dauert. In Akaike endet tagsüber jeder zweite Zug, der andere fährt weiter über *Meitetsus* Toyota und Mikawa Line bis Toyota-shi (16,6 km ab Akaike); während der Hauptverkehrszeiten enden mehr Züge in Akaike. Im Westen endet die Fahrt für die meisten Züge in Kami-Otai, typischerweise fahren tagsüber nur ein oder zwei Züge pro Stunde weiter nach Inuyama

minus at Kami-Otai. The tunnelled sections are mainly cut-and-cover construction beneath roads (about 60%) with five separate sections of twin-bore tunnels where the line passes beneath private property and rivers.

Kami-Otai station has two island platforms with two centre tracks used by Tsurumai Line services and two outer tracks used by Inuyama Line trains heading to/from Meitetsu-Nagoya station. The Akaike terminus also has two island platforms but only three tracks (two outer and one centre) to facilitate terminating trains and access to Nisshin depot, reached via a spur tunnel to the east of the station. Akaike is the nearest station to the City Tram and Subway Museum which is within the depot complex. Intermediate stations have either side or single island platforms and all platforms are 170 m long to handle 8-car trains, though services ran with 4-car trains until 1993 and there do not appear to be any immediate plans to lengthen the current 6-car formations.

Tsurumai Line trains run every 4 minutes in the morning peak, every 5 minutes in the evening peak and every 7.5 minutes off-peak taking 35 minutes from Kami-Otai to Akaike. At the eastern end of the line, half the off-peak service terminates at Akaike and the other half continues via Meitetsu's Toyota and Mikawa Lines to Toyota-shi (16.6 km from Akaike); during the peaks a higher proportion terminates at Akaike. At the other end of the line the majority of trains terminate at Kami-Otai with typically only 1 or 2 tph (off-peak) continuing to Inuyama (21.4 km from Kami-Otai) or other Inuyama Line destinations. However, up to 6tph run through in the morning peak.

Akaike – Meitetsu 100-series durchgebunden | *through-running* ▶ Iwakura (Meitetsu Inuyama Line)   RS

(21,4 km ab Kami-Otai) oder zu anderen Zielen auf der Inuyama Line, in der Morgenspitze jedoch bis zu sechs Züge pro Stunde.

Auf der Tsurumai Line ist eine Flotte von 25 Sechs-Wagen-Zügen der U-Bahn im Einsatz: drei Serien – 3000 (seit 1977; 1993 von 4- auf 6-Wagen-Einheiten verlängert), 3050 (seit 1993) und N3000 (seit 2012). Dazu kommen 11 Züge von *Meitetsu* der Serie 100/200 von 1978-94, die auch 1993 von 4- auf 6-Wagen-Einheiten verlängert wurden. Die Züge werden mit zwei Personen betrieben und sind mit ATC bzw. *Meitetsus* ATS ausgerüstet.

Services are operated by a fleet of 25 six-car metro trains in three series – 3000-series (since 1977, reformed from 4 to 6-car sets in 1993), 3050-series (since 1993) and N3000-series (since 2012). These are supplemented by 11 sets of Meitetsu 100/200-series stock dating from 1978-94 which again were reformed from 4 to 6-car sets in 1993. Trains are two-person operated and fitted with ATC and Meitetsu ATS.

Fushimi   RS

Fushimi – Tsurumai Line 3050-series ▶ Akaike

Imaike

RS

Sakura-dori Line

Diese Linie wurde errichtet, um die Higashiyama Line auf ihrem überfüllten zentralen Abschnitt zu entlasten und um Vorstadtbezirke zu erreichen, die bis dahin noch keinerlei Bahnanschluss hatten. Die Linie beginnt an der Station Nakamura-Kuyakusho [Bezirksrathaus] und verläuft zwischen dem Bahnhof Nagoya und Imaike parallel etwa 400 m nördlich der Higashiyama Line. Dieser Abschnitt liegt unter dem Boulevard Sakura-dori, von dem sich der Linienname ableitet. Bei Imaike biegt die Sakura-dori Line nach Süden, fährt dann 8,6 km unter der Ringstraße bis Nonami und erreicht schließlich Tokushige in den äußeren Vororten.

Die Sakura-dori Line wurde tiefer als die älteren U-Bahn-Linien mit Stationen in einer durchschnittlichen Tiefe von 19 m errichtet. Die Streckentunnel sind überwiegend eingleisige Röhren, doch drei kurze Abschnitte (Nagoya bis Kokusai-Center, Imaike bis Fukiage und Sakurayama bis Aratama-bashi) wurden offen gebaut und ein Abschnitt als zweigleisige Röhre unterhalb eines Flusses zwischen Tsurusato und Nonami im Schildvortrieb aufgefahren.

This line was built to provide additional east-west capacity to relieve the overcrowded central section of the Higashiyama Line and to provide a metro link for suburban areas not served by other rail lines. The line commences at Nakamura-Kuyakusho (ward office) and runs parallel and approximately 400 m to the north of the Higashiyama Line between Nagoya station and Imaike. This section lies beneath Sakura-dori (avenue) from which the line takes its name. At Imaike, the Sakura-dori Line turns south and runs 8.6 km to Nonami beneath the Loop Route (ring road) and then heads east to Tokushige in the outer suburbs.

The Sakura-dori Line was built at a deeper level than the earlier metro lines with stations at an average depth of 19 m below ground. Tunnels are predominantly

Sakura-dori Line (S)

Nakamura-Kuyakusho (S01) – Tokushige (S21) (Line 6)
19.1 km Ⓤ, 21 Bahnhöfe | *stations*
1067 mm, 1500Vdc ⬆; 188 000 pax/d

10-09-1989: Nakamura-Kuyakusho – Imaike (6.3 km)
30-03-1994: Imaike – Nonami (8.6 km)
27-03-2011: Nonami – Tokushige (4.2 km)

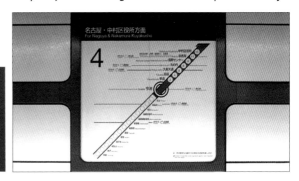

Aratama-bashi – Sakura-dori Line 6000-series ▶ Nakamura-Kuyakusho

Tagsüber verkehrt die Sakura-dori Line alle 7½ Minuten, in den Spitzenzeiten alle 4-5 Minuten. Fast alle Züge fahren über die gesamte Strecke und benötigen dafür 37 Minuten.

Die Sakura-dori Line wird mit 24 Fünf-Wagen-Zügen der Serien 6000 (gebaut 1987-93) und 6050 (2010) von Nippon Sharyo betrieben. Die 6000er-Serie wurde ursprünglich als 4-Wagen-Einheiten mit Fahrer und Zugbegleiter eingesetzt, doch 1994, vor der Eröffnung der Nonami-Verlängerung, wurde ein fünfter Wagen eingefügt und der Ein-Mann-Betrieb eingeführt. Das Depot befindet sich in Tokushige, aber größere Instandhaltungsarbeiten werden im Betriebshof Nisshin auf der Tsurumai Line durchgeführt, weshalb die beiden Linien im Bereich Maru-nouchi miteinander verbunden sind.

twin-bore shield-driven, though there are three short cut-and-cover sections (Nagoya to Kokusai-Center, Imaike to Fukiage and Sakurayama to Aratama-bashi) and one section of single-bore twin-track tunnel beneath a river between Tsurusato and Nonami.

The base off-peak service operates every 7.5 minutes increasing to every 4-5 minutes during the peaks. Almost all trains operate over the whole line taking 37 minutes.

The train fleet comprises 24 five-car sets of Nippon Sharyo 6000-series (built 1987-93) and 6050-series (2010). The 6000-series originally operated as 4-car crew-operated sets but were reformed as 5-car units and converted to driver-only operation with ATO in 1994 prior to the opening of the Nonami extension. The depot is situated at Tokushige but heavy maintenance is handled at Nisshin

Nagoya   RS

Takaoka   RS

Marunouchi

Als Ausdruck des Wirtschaftsaufschwungs in jener Zeit wurden die Stationen der ersten beiden Phasen der Strecke großzügig mit breiten, für 8-Wagen-Züge ausgelegten 170 m langen Bahnsteigen errichtet. Dabei wurden hochwertige Materialien verwendet und von privaten Unternehmen gesponserte Wandbilder angebracht. In der dritten Phase war jedoch klar, dass die Fahrgastprognosen zu hoch angesetzt worden waren, weshalb die Stationen auf der Tokushige-Verlängerung kleiner ausfielen und engere, 125 m lange Bahnsteige für 6-Wagen-Züge aufweisen. Alle U-Bahnhöfe haben Mittelbahnsteige mit halbhohen Bahnsteigtüren für 5-Wagen-Züge. Jede Station ist in einer anderen Farbe gehalten, die sich an den Bahnsteigtüren und anderen Flächen widerspiegelt. Derzeit gibt es keine Pläne, die Linie zu verlängern, weder im Westen noch im Osten.

depot on the Tsurumai Line which is accessed via a connecting line near Marunouchi station.

Reflecting the buoyant economy of the time, stations on the first two phases of the line are generously proportioned with wide 170 m long platforms designed for 8-car trains. They also feature high-quality materials and murals sponsored by private businesses. However, by the third phase it was clear that ridership projections would not be met and stations on the Tokushige extension were built with lower specification finishes and narrow 125 m long platforms suitable only for 6-car operation. All stations have single island platforms with platform gates designed for the current 5-car trains. Each station has a different design colour which is used on platform gates and other features. Plans to extend the line at both ends are in abeyance.

Sakura-dori Line

Takaoka

Heian-dori (Kami-Iida Line) – Meitetsu 300-series - *Local* ► Inuyama

Kami-Iida Line

Japans kürzeste Metro-Linie ist eigentlich Teil der etwas längeren „Kami-Iida Link Line", einer 3,1 km langen unterirdischen Strecke, die gebaut wurde, um an der Station Heian-dori eine Umsteigemöglichkeit von der isolierten Komaki Line von *Meitetsu* zur Meijo-Metrolinie zu schaffen. Die *Kami-Iida Link Line Company* (Eigentum der Präfektur Aichi, der Stadt Nagoya und anderen Kommunen entlang der Komaki Line sowie von *Meitetsu*) besitzt die gesamte Strecke, aber mit dem Betrieb wurden *Meitetsu* (Ajima – Kami-Iida) und *Nagoya Municipal Subway* (Kami-Iida – Heian-dori) beauftragt, die ihre jeweiligen Abschnitte als Bestandteile ihrer eigenen Netze darstellen.

Die Straßenbahnverbindung zur Endstation Kami-Iida von *Meitetsus* Komaki Line wurde 1971 stillgelegt, stattdessen sollte laut Plänen des *Urban Transport Council* von 1972 die neue U-Bahn-Linie 7 eine Verbindung ins Zentrum von Nagoya herstellen. Da bei diesem Projekt keine Fortschritte zu erkennen waren, wurde 1992 ein überarbeiteter Plan mit einer kürzeren Verbindung bis Heian-dori verabschiedet.

Die Kami-Iida Link Line wurde im Jahr 2003 eröffnet und ersetzte die vormals aufgeständerte Trasse der

Japan's shortest metro line is actually part of the somewhat longer Kami-Iida Link Line, a 3.1 km underground line that was built to provide interchange between Meitetsu's isolated Komaki Line and the Meijo metro line at Heian-dori. The third-sector Kami-Iida Link Line Company (mainly owned by Aichi Prefecture, Nagoya City, Meitetsu and other Komaki Line local authorities) owns the whole line but operations are contracted out to Meitetsu (Ajima — Kami-Iida) and Nagoya Municipal Subway (Kami-Iida — Heian-dori) who publicise the respective sections as integral parts of their own networks.

The tram link to Meitetsu's Komaki Line terminus at Kami-Iida closed in 1971 and plans were put forward by the Urban Transport Council in 1972 for new metro line 7 to provide an alternative link into central Nagoya. However, no progress was made on this and a revised plan was adopted in 1992 giving priority to the construction of a shorter link to Heian-dori only.

The Kami-Iida Link Line opened in 2003 replacing the previous elevated section of the Komaki Line between Ajima and Kami-Iida with twin-bore tunnels. Two of the stations - Kami-Iida and Heian-dori - are underground

Kami-Iida Line (K)

Kami-Iida (K01) – Heian-dori (K02)
0.8 km Ⓤ, 2 Bahnhöfe | *stations*;
1067 mm gauge, 1500Vdc ⬆; 17 000 pax/d
Kami-Iida Line ⇔ Meitetsu's Komaki Line

27-03-2003: Kami-Iida (K01) — Heian-dori (K02) (0.8 km)

Ajiyoshi (Meitetsu Komaki Line) – Meitetsu 300-series - *Local* ▶ Heian-dori   RS

Komaki Line zwischen Ajima und Kami-Iida durch zwei Tunnelröhren. Zwei der Stationen, Kami-Iida und Heian-dori, sind unterirdisch, die dritte, Ajima, befindet sich in Hochlage. Alle Bahnsteige sind vorsorglich 130 m lang, falls eine Südverlängerung in die Innenstadt von Nagoya eines Tages doch verwirklicht wird. Nur die beiden U-Bahnhöfe verfügen über Bahnsteigtüren, nicht jedoch Ajima oder die anderen Stationen der Komaki Line.

Im Einsatz sind 4-Wagen-Züge mit ATC-Unterstützung ohne Zugbegleiter: zwei Einheiten der Serie 7000 der *Nagoya Municipal Subway* und acht der Serie 300 von *Meitetsu*. *Meitetsu* wartet auch die *Subway*-Einheiten und stellt seit 2007 das gesamte Fahrpersonal.

Abgesehen von einer täglichen Fahrt zwischen Kami-Iida und Heian-dori verkehren die Züge zwischen Heian-dori und Komaki (10,6 km) bzw. Inuyama (21,4 km) auf der Komaki Line, in der Hauptverkehrszeit alle 7½-10 Minuten, sonst alle 15 Minuten.

and the third – Ajima – is elevated; all have 130 m long platforms to cater for longer trains which may be needed if a planned southern extension to central Nagoya eventually materialises. The two underground stations have platform gates, though Ajima and the other Komaki Line stations are not similarly equipped.

Services are provided by 4-car, driver-only trains with ATC; two 7000-series Nagoya Municipal Subway sets and eight 300-series Meitetsu sets. Meitetsu maintains the metro sets and since 2007 has staffed all trains over the entire line.

Apart from one daily journey each way between Kami-Iida and Heian-dori, trains operate between Heian-dori and either Komaki (10.6 km) or Inuyama (21.4 km) on the Komaki Line at a frequency of every 7.5-10 minutes (peaks) and 15 minutes (off-peak).

Kasugai (Meitetsu Komaki Line) – Nagoya Municipal Subway 7000-series ▶ Inuyama

Meitetsu Komaki Line 300-series   RS

Nakajima – Aonami Line, 1000-series ▶ Kinjo-Futo   RS

AONAMI LINE

Die Aonami [Blaue Welle] Line wird von der *Nagoya Sea-side Rapid Railway* (*Nagoya Rinkai Kosoku Tetsudo*) betrieben, an der mehrheitlich die Stadt Nagoya und die Präfektur Aichi beteiligt sind. Das Unternehmen wurde gegründet, um die 12 km lange Nishi-Nagoya-ko [Westhafen]-Güterbahn von *JR Central* für den Personenverkehr umzubauen. Auf dem 5,1 km langen Abschnitt zwischen dem Bahnhof Nagoya und dem Frachtterminal wurden neue Bahnhöfe errichtet, doch verkehren hier weiterhin auch Güterzüge. Die eingleisige Strecke hinter dem Frachtterminal wurde 2001 geschlossen, durch eine neue zweigleisige Hochbahn ersetzt und etwa 4 km über die ehemalige Westhafen-Endstation hinaus verlängert, um Entwicklungsgebiete auf künstlichen Inseln zu erschließen; bei Kinjo-Futo liegen u.a. die „Portmesse Nagoya", Legoland und der „SCMAGLEV and Railway Park".

The Aonami (Blue Wave) Line is operated by the third-sector Nagoya Seaside Rapid Railway (Nagoya Rinkai Kosoku Tetsudo) which is mainly owned by Nagoya City and Aichi Prefecture. The company was formed to convert the 12 km JR Central Nishi-Nagoya-ko (West Nagoya Port) freight line for passenger use. The initial 5.1 km section between Nagoya station and Nagoya Freight Terminal was upgraded with new stations and is still used by freight trains as well as passenger trains; the single-track line beyond the freight terminal was closed in 2001 and replaced by a new double-track elevated line which extends approximately 4 km beyond the former West Port terminus to serve development areas on reclaimed land, including the Nagoya International Exhibition Hall, Legoland and the SCMAGLEV and Railway Park at Kinjo-Futo.

RS   Nakajima – 1000-series ▶ Nagoya

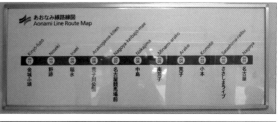

Aonami Line (AN)

Nagoya (AN01) – Kinjo-Futo (AN11)
15.2 km, 11 Bahnhöfe | *stations*, 1067 mm, 1500Vdc ⊕

06-10-2004: Nagoya – Kinjo-Futo (15.2 km)

Sasashima-Raibu – Aonami Line 1000-series ▶ Nagoya

Am Bahnhof Nagoya hat die Aonami Line einen eigenen Mittelbahnsteig zwischen denen des Shinkansen und den konventionellen Gleisen von *JR Central*. Alle Stationen haben wellenförmige Dächer und halbhohe Bahnsteigtüren, lediglich Kinjo-Futo besitzt Bahnsteigtüren in voller Höhe. Die Bahnsteige wären lang genug für 6-Wagen-Züge, doch derzeit werden nur acht 4-Wagen-Züge der Baureihe 1000 im Ein-Mann-Betrieb eingesetzt. Diesen steht auf dem Gelände des ehemaligen Westhafen-Frachtterminals ein Depot zur Verfügung.

Die Aonami Line verkehrt zu Spitzenzeiten alle 10 Minuten, sonst alle 15 Minuten; eine Fahrt dauert 24 Minuten. Die Fahrgastprognosen erwiesen sich als zu optimistisch, zwei Jahre nach Inbetriebnahme beförderte die Bahn nur 24.000 Fahrgäste pro Tag – ein Drittel der Prognose. Das Unternehmen wurde 2010 umstrukturiert, die öffentliche Beteiligung stieg auf rund 90%. Heute werden rund 30.000 Fahrgäste pro Tag gezählt.

At Nagoya station the Aonami Line has a dedicated island platform situated between JR Central's Shinkansen and conventional tracks. Stations have wave-like roofs and platform gates, apart from Kinjo-Futo which has full height screen doors. Platforms are long enough for eventual operation of 6-car trains but services are currently run by eight 4-car 1000-series driver-only operated EMUs. These are housed in a depot on the site of the former West Port freight terminus.

Trains operate every 10 minutes at peak times and every 15 minutes off-peak taking 24 minutes. Passenger forecasts proved to be over-optimistic with the line carrying only 24,000 passengers/day two years after opening - one third of the forecast. The company was restructured in 2010 to avoid bankruptcy with the public-sector shareholdings being increased to around 90%. Ridership has since risen to around 30,000 passengers/day.

Aonami Line 1000-series

Nagoya

Yakusa > Toji-Shiryokan-Minami – Linimo 06 ▶ Fujigaoka

LINIMO

Linimo, offiziell die „Tobu Kuryo Line", ist eine Magnet-schwebebahn mit Linearmotoren (daher der Name), die anlässlich der Expo 2005 errichtet wurde und auch die Entwicklung der Gebiete östlich von Nagoya unterstützen sollte. Die Linie beginnt an der Station Fujigaoka, End-station der Higashiyama-Metrolinie, und endet an der tangentialen Aichi Loop Line. Eigentümer und Betreiber ist *Aichi Rapid Transit* (*Aichi Kosoku Kotsu*). Linimo war die erste kommerzielle Anwendung der von *Japan Airlines* in den 1970er Jahren entwickelten HSST (High-Speed Surface Transport)-Technologie.

Die doppelspurige Linimo verläuft ab Fujigaoka 1,3 km im Tunnel und erklimmt dann eine Hochbahnstrecke über oder neben öffentlichen Straßen. Die Trasse durchquert hügeliges Gelände und erreicht an der Station Toji-Shiryo-kan-Minami den höchsten Punkt, bevor es bergab zur Endstation Yakusa geht; die maximale Steigung beträgt 6% auf einem 1 km langen Abschnitt, was mit ein Grund für die Wahl der HSST-Technologie war.

Die Stationen sind nicht nur nummeriert, sondern wer-den auch durch Symbole und Farben unterschieden. Alle verfügen über Bahnsteigtüren in voller Höhe. Die Station Ai-Chikyuhaku-Kinen-Koen [Expo-Gedenkpark] hat zwei Mittelbahnsteige mit einer dritten mittigen Fahrspur, die

Linimo, officially the Tobu Kyuryo Line, is a maglev line with linear motor driven trains which was built to serve the 2005 Expo site and developing suburbs to the east of Nagoya. The line connects with the Fujigaoka terminus of the Higashiyama metro line at one end and with the outer orbital Aichi Loop Line at the other. It is owned and operated by third-sector Aichi Rapid Transit (Aichi Kosoku Kotsu) and is the first commercial application of HSST (high-speed surface transport) technology originally pioneered by Japan Airlines in the 1970s.

The double-track line runs in tunnel for 1.3 km from Fujigaoka and then ascends onto an elevated guideway built over and alongside public roads. It climbs through hilly terrain towards Toji-Shiryokan-Minami station, the highest point on the route, before descending to the terminus at Yakusa; the maximum gradient is 6%, for a distance of 1.0 km, one of the reasons cited for the choice of HSST technology.

Stations are numbered and have differently shaped and coloured identifying symbols. All have full-height platform screen doors. Ai-Chikyuhaku-Kinen-Koen sta-tion ("Expo Memorial Park") has two island platforms with a third centre track which descends to the ground level depot; other stations have single island platforms

Linimo (L)

Fujigaoka (L01) – Yakusa (L09)
8.9 km, Ⓤ 1.3 km, 9 Bahnhöfe | *stations*
Maglev, 1500Vdc (seitliche Stromschienen | *trackside conductor rails*)

06-03-2005: Fujigaoka – Yakusa (8.9 km)

Nagakute-Kosenjo – Linimo 01 ▶ Fujigaoka
- Toyota Automobile Museum im Hintergrund | *in the background*

zum ebenerdigen Depot hinunterführt; alle anderen Stationen haben einfache Mittelbahnsteige, nur Hanamizuki-dori hat Seitenbahnsteige.

Der fahrerlose Betrieb im ATO-Modus wird mit acht 3-Wagen-Zügen der Serie 100 abgewickelt. Jeder Wagen hat fünf magnetische „Drehgestelle", die 8 mm über der Fahrbahn schweben, wenn der Zug in Bewegung ist; die Fahrt verläuft ruhig und sanft. Manche Züge haben Fahrgastbetreuer an Bord. Normalerweise herrscht ein 10-Minuten-Takt, der in den Hauptverkehrszeiten etwas verdichtet wird. Die Gesamtfahrzeit beträgt 17 Minuten.

Während der Expo 2005 war die Linie stark überlastet, doch seither liegen die Passagierzahlen unter den Erwartungen, so dass die Bahn erhebliche Verluste einfährt. Eine Linimo-Tageskarte kostet 800 Yen.

except for Hanamizuki-dori which has two side platforms.

Services are provided by a fleet of eight 3-car 100-series trains. Each car has five magnetic 'bogies' which float 8 mm above the track when in motion providing a quiet smooth ride. Trains operate in ATO mode without drivers but some have attendants on board. Service frequency is every 10 minutes with a slightly enhanced peak service. Journey time is 17 minutes end to end.

The line experienced severe overcrowding during Expo 2005, but since then passenger numbers have not met expectations and the line operates at a significant loss. A one-day unlimited trip ticket is available (800 Yen).

Linimo 100-series

Ai-Chikyuhaku-Kinen-Koen – Linimo 05 ▶ Fujigaoka

Irigaike-Koen (Linimo)

RS

Peachliner   Tokadai New Transit (Tokadai Shin Kotsu)

Der kurzlebige Peachliner (1991-2006) war einer von zwei in Japan gebauten VONA-Bahnen (*Vehicles of New Age* – ein gummibereifter Peoplemover mit mittlerer Führungsschiene); nur die Yukarigaoka-Line in der Präfektur Chiba ist noch in Betrieb (siehe Band 1). Die 7,4 km lange, vorwiegend aufgeständerte Linie mit sieben Stationen und einer Flotte von fünf 4-Wagen-Zügen verband Komaki auf der Komaki Line von *Meitetsu* mit der Planstadt Tokadai; eine geplante Verlängerung von Tokadai bis Kozoji auf der JR Chuo Line wurde nie gebaut. Da die Planstadt schließlich in kleinerer Form umgesetzt wurde, wählte man für die Bahn aus Kostengründen manuellen statt fahrerlosen Betrieb. An beiden Enden der Strecke wurden Wendeschleifen errichtet, damit Einrichtungszüge mit Türen nur auf einer Seite angeschafft werden konnten. Die prognostizierten Fahrgastzahlen blieben weit hinter den Erwartungen zurück, so dass das angehäufte Defizit schließlich zur Stilllegung zwang; ein Umbau auf Spurbusbetrieb wurde abgelehnt. Das Depot-Gelände wurde geräumt, doch die Hochtrasse mitsamt Stationen stehen bis heute; ein geplanter Abriss wartet auf die nötige Finanzierung.

Peachliner 100-series

This short-lived third-sector line (1991-2006) was one of two VONA systems (Vehicles of New Age - rubber-tyred people-movers with centre-rail guidance) built in Japan; the Yukarigaoka Line in Chiba Prefecture still operates (see Volume 1). The 7.4 km mainly elevated line, with seven stations and a fleet of five 4-car trains, connected Komaki on Meitetsu's Komaki Line with Tokadai New Town; a planned second phase between the New Town and Kozoji on the JR Chuo Line was never built. Reductions in the planned size of the New Town led to the adoption of manual rather than fully-automated operation and the double-track line was constructed with loops at either end allowing the operation of single-ended trains with doors on only one side. However, the line only ever carried a fraction of the original traffic projections and a mounting deficit eventually forced closure, the option of converting the line to guided-bus technology having been rejected. The depot site has been cleared but most of the guideway and stations were still standing at the time of writing; plans exist for their demolition subject to the availability of funding.

Ozone

RS

YUTORITO LINE

Bei der Yutorito Line handelt es sich um eine aufgeständerte Spurbustrasse über öffentlichen Straßen; rechtlich hat diese Linie einen ähnlichen Status wie andere spurgeführte Bahnen, etwa Monorails oder neuartige Transit-Systeme. Sie verläuft vom Knoten Ozone (U-Bahn, JR, *Meitetsu*) nach Nordosten bis Obata-Ryokuchi, wo die Trasse auf Straßenebene abfällt und einige Busse auf gewöhnlichen Straßen weiter in äußere Stadtbezirke fahren. Die Trasse und Busse sind Eigentum der *Nagoya Guideway Bus Company*, aber *Nagoya City Transportation* wurde mit dem Busbetrieb beauftragt. Auf der Spurbustrasse fahren vier Linien und bieten in Spitzenzeiten einen kombinierten 2 bis 3-Minuten-Takt, sonst einen 10-Minuten-Takt. Auf dem Spurbusabschnitt gilt ein Entfernungstarif, auf den äußeren Abschnitten hingegen der übliche Einheitstarif für städtische Busse. Der Fahrpreis wird beim Aussteigen gezahlt, nur an der Station Ozone gibt es Zu- und Ausgangssperren, die zu Spitzenzeiten aktiviert werden. Die Busflotte umfasst 25 Diesel-Hybridfahrzeuge von Hino aus den Jahren 2013-14.

The Yutorito Line is an elevated guided busway with track and stations built mainly above existing roads; it has a similar legal status to other guided systems such as monorails and new transit systems. It runs north-east from Ozone, an interchange with metro, JR and Meitetsu services, to Obata-Ryokuchi where the guideway descends to ground level and some buses continue into outer suburban areas on the ordinary road network. The guideway and buses are owned by the third-sector Nagoya Guideway Bus Company but Nagoya City Transportation is contracted to operate the service. Four routes provide a combined 2-3 minute peak and 10 minute off-peak frequency on the guideway section. Distance-related fares apply on the guideway but the standard city bus flat fare applies on the outer surface-level sections; most ticket checking and fare collection occurs as passengers exit the buses but Ozone terminus has facilities for off-bus fare collection at peak times. The bus fleet comprises 25 Hino diesel hybrid vehicles dating from 2013-14.

砂田橋駅 Sunada-bashi Sta. 1 出入口 Entrance

Yutorito Line (Y)

Spurbus | *Guided busway*: Ozone (Y01) – Obata-Ryokuchi (Y09)
6.5 km, 9 Haltestellen | *stops*

23-03-2001: Ozone – Obata-Ryokuchi (6.5 km)

Sunada-bashi

RS

Futatsu-Iri – Meitetsu 'Panorama Super' 1000-series - *Limited Express* ▶ Toyohashi *(Photo Oliver Mayer)*

S-BAHN-VERKEHR

SUBURBAN RAIL

Nagoya Railway (Meltetsu), das drittgrößte private Eisenbahnunternehmen in Japan nach Kintetsu und Tobu in der Region Tokyo, ist im Großraum von Nagoya der dominierende Betreiber im S-Bahn-Verkehr mit einem 20 Linien umfassenden Netz mit einer Gesamtstreckenlänge von 444,2 km. *JR Central (JR Tokai)* betreibt auf ihren drei Hauptlinien (Tokaido, Chuo und Kansai) vom Bahnhof Nagoya ausgehend ebenfalls Regionalzüge, genauso wie *Kintetsu* auf ihrer Nagoya Line. *Meitetsu* und JR-Strecken haben eine Spurweite von 1067 mm, *Kintetsu* hingegen 1435 mm; alle drei Bahngesellschaften nutzen Oberleitung mit 1500 V Gleichstrom.

Nagoya Railway (Meitetsu), the third largest private railway in Japan after Kintetsu and Tokyo's Tobu, is the dominant operator of suburban and interurban rail services in Greater Nagoya with its extensive network of 20 lines covering 444.2 km. JR Central (JR Tokai) also operates suburban/interurban services on its three main lines (Tokaido, Chuo and Kansai) which radiate from Nagoya station, as does Kintetsu on its Nagoya Line. Meitetsu/JR are 1067 mm gauge, Kintetsu is 1435 mm: all three are electrified at 1500Vdc overhead.

Nagoya – JR Central 211-series RS

Kintetsu-Nagoya – *Limited Express* ▶ Toba RS

Ozone – Meitetsu Seto Line 4000-series ► Sakaemachi (Yutorito Line im Hintergrund | *in background*)

Meitetsu

Die Hauptstrecke des *Meitetsu*-Netzes ist die **Nagoya Line**, die parallel zur Tokaido Main Line von *JR Central* zwischen Gifu, Nagoya und Toyohashi (99,8 km) verläuft. Die Nagoya Line, von der zahlreiche Zweigstrecken mit durchgehenden Zügen abgehen, ist größtenteils zweigleisig und enthält eine intensiv genutzte 1,5 km lange Tunnelstrecke in der Innenstadt von Nagoya. Der unterirdische Bahnhof Meitetsu-Nagoya hat nur zwei Gleise (mit vier Bahnsteigkanten) und bewältigt 26 Züge pro Stunde und Richtung; um die Aufenthaltszeiten zu minimieren, halten die Züge je nach Fahrtziel an unterschiedlichen Punkten entlang des Bahnsteigs, wobei in der Regel von den Seitenbahnsteigen eingestiegen wird, der Mittelbahnsteig hingegen zum Aussteigen dient. Es wird eine Vielzahl von Zuggattungen angeboten, von *Local* bis *Limited Express*, und genauso vielfältig ist der Fahrzeugpark, von metroähnlichen Pendlerwagen bis zu hochklassigen „Panorama Super"-Fahrzeugen, die als *Limited Express* oder *Rapid Limited Express* eingesetzt werden. *Meitetsu* bedient auch den „Central Japan International Airport" (Centrair), 35 km südlich von Nagoya auf einer künstlichen Insel gelegen, unter anderem mit dem nur 1. Klasse führenden *µSKY Limited Express*, der ab Meitetsu-Nagoya 28 Minuten benötigt.

Neben der Nagoya Line und ihren Zweiglinien betreibt *Meitetsu* auch drei separate metroartige S-Bahn-Linien. Die Toyota und die Komaki Line verkehren in wechselseitigem Betrieb mit der U-Bahn, während die Seto Line auf ihrer eigenen unterirdischen Strecke das Zentrum von Nagoya erreicht. Die 15,2 km lange **Toyota Line** wurde 1979 als Verlängerung der Tsurumai-Metrolinie eröffnet, der Mischbetrieb geht über die Toyota Line bis Toyota-shi auf

Meitetsu

The core of the Meitetsu network is its **Nagoya Line** which parallels and competes with JR Central's Tokaido Main Line between Gifu, Nagoya and Toyohashi (99.8 km). The Nagoya Line, which has many branches with through services, is mainly double-track including the intensively used 1.5 km underground section in central Nagoya. Meitetsu-Nagoya station's two tracks (with four platform faces) handle 26tph in each direction; to minimise dwell times, trains for different destinations stop at slightly different platform positions and most unload onto the centre island platform and load from the two side platforms. A wide variety of train types is operated ranging from Local to Limited Express and the train fleet is also varied with both high-capacity commuter stock and superior-standard Panorama Super cars used on Limited Express and Rapid Limited Express services. Meitetsu operates a range of services to Central Japan International Airport (Centrair), situated on an artificial island 35 km south of Nagoya, including the all first class µSKY Limited Express which takes 28 minutes from Meitetsu-Nagoya using tilting 2000-series EMUs.

Apart from its main Nagoya Line network, Meitetsu also operates three separate metro-style commuter routes into Nagoya; the Toyota and Komaki Lines which operate reciprocal through services with the metro and the Seto Line which runs underground to its own central Nagoya terminus. The 15.2 km **Toyota Line** opened in 1979 as an extension of the Tsurumai metro line - joint services run through from the metro via the Toyota Line to Toyota-shi on Meitetsu's Mikawa Line. The 20.6 km **Komaki Line** opened between Inuyama and Kami-Iida (Nagoya) in 1931 and in 2003 was connected via a new

Meitetsu-Nagoya – Local ▶ Higashi-Okazaki
(Ausstieg am Mittelbahnsteig, Einstieg am Seitenbahnsteig | *alighting to island platform, boarding from side platform*)

Meitetsus Mikawa Line. Die 20,6 km lange **Komaki Line** wurde zwischen Inuyama und Kami-Iida (Nagoya) im Jahr 1931 in Betrieb genommen und 2003 über einen neuen 2,6 km langen Tunnelabschnitt mit der Kami-Iida Line der U-Bahn an der neuen Endstation Heian-dori verbunden. Die 20,6 km lange **Seto Line** verbindet Sakaemachi im Zentrum von Nagoya mit Owari-Seto östlich der Stadt. Die Linie wurde von *Meitetsu* 1939 erworben, 1976 wurde die ursprüngliche Endstation Horikawa geschlossen und 1978 durch einen 1,7 km langen Tunnel bis Sakaemachi im zentralen Geschäftsviertel ersetzt, wo außerdem zu zwei U-Bahn-Linien umgestiegen werden kann. Gleichzeitig wurde die Spannung von 600 V DC auf 1500 V DC hochgesetzt; die Seto Line hat keine Gleisverbindung mit irgendwelchen anderen Linien.

Das „Meitetsu Free Ticket" (1 Tag - 3.100 Yen, 2 Tage - 4.000 Yen) ist an mit Personal besetzten Stationen erhältlich und erlaubt von 10 bis 16 Uhr die Nutzung der 1. Klasse.

2.6 km tunnelled section to the Kami-Iida Line of the metro with through running to a new terminus at Heian-dori. The 20.6 km Seto Line links Sakaemachi in central Nagoya with Owari-Seto to the east of the city. The line was acquired by Meitetsu in 1939; its Nagoya terminus Horikawa was closed in 1976 and replaced in 1978 by a 1.7 km underground link to Sakaemachi, providing more convenient access to the main central business district and interchange with Sakae station on the metro network. The line was converted from 600Vdc to 1500Vdc at the same time; it has no track connection to any other lines.

The Meitetsu Free Ticket (1 day - 3,100 Yen, 2 days - 4,000 Yen), available from stations with attendants, includes first-class travel between 10.00 and 16.00.

Sakaemachi (Seto Line)

Toyota-shi – Nagoya Subway 3050-series
▶ Kami-Otai (via Toyota Line and Tsurumai Line)
& Meitetsu Mikawa Line 6000-series ▶ Chiryu

Tsurumai (JR Chuo Main Line) – 313-series ► Nagoya

JR Central

Der Vorortverkehr von *JR Central* im Großraum von Nago-ya ist nicht vergleichbar mit den JR-Netzen in Tokyo oder Osaka, da weniger Strecken vorhanden sind und kürzere Züge weniger oft verkehren. Auf allen drei JR-Linien gibt es sowohl *Local*-Züge als auch verschiedene Express-Züge (*Semi-Rapid*, *Rapid*, *New Rapid* usw.) mit unterschiedli-chen Halten. Auf der **Tokaido Main Line** fahren tagsüber 8 Züge pro Stunde (4 als *Local*, 4 als *Rapid*/*New Rapid*), die meisten davon zwischen Gifu und Toyohashi über Nagoya (102,7 km). In der Hauptverkehrszeit verkehren bis zu 12 Züge/Std. mit zusätzlichen *Semi Rapid* und *Special Rapid*. Die **Chuo Main Line** bietet tagsüber auch 8 Züge/Std. (5 als *Local*, 3 als *Rapid*); alle Züge starten in Nagoya, *Local*-Züge verkehren bis Tajimi (36,2 km) und *Rapid* bis Nakatsugawa (79,9 Kilometer), aber mit einzelnen Kurzläu-fern. Auf der **Kansai Main Line**, die parallel zu *Kintetsus* Nagoya Line verläuft, herrscht ein weniger dichter Takt, meist 4-5 Züge pro Stunde (2-3 als *Local*, 2 als *Rapid*), davon einige bis Kameyama (59,9 km), aber viele beenden ihre Fahrt schon früher. Bei den *JR Central*-Zügen ist der Zwei-Mann-Betrieb vorherrschend, nur einige Züge der Kansai Main Line sind außerhalb der Spitzenzeiten nur mit Fahrer unterwegs.

JR Central

JR Central's Nagoya operations are not on the same scale as the JR networks in Tokyo or Osaka, with fewer routes and generally lower frequencies and shorter trains. All three JR lines have a mix of all stations (Local) trains and a variety of limited-stop (Semi-Rapid, Rapid, New Rapid etc.) services with different stopping patterns. The **Tokaido Main Line** *has an off-peak 8tph service (4tph Local, 4tph Rapid/New Rapid) which mostly oper-ates between Gifu and Toyohashi via Nagoya (102.7 km). The peak service is enhanced up to 12tph with additional Semi-Rapid and Special Rapid services. The* **Chuo Main Line** *also has an 8tph off-peak service (5tph Local, 3tph Rapid); all these trains start/finish at Nagoya with Locals running as far as Tajimi (36.2 km) and Rapids as far as Nakatsugawa (79.9 km) though with some short-workings. The* **Kansai Main Line**, *which parallels Kintetsu's Nagoya Line, has a lower frequency service with generally 4-5tph off-peak (2-3 Local, 2 Rapid), some running as far as Kameyama (59.9 km) but many termi-nating at intermediate stations. Most JR Central trains are two-person operated but some off-peak Kansai Main Line trains are driver-only operated.*

Biwajima (JR Tokaido Line) – 313-series Local ► Gifu

JR Nagoya

Kintetsu-Nagoya – Kintetsu 1259-series - *Local* ▶ Shiratsuka

Kintetsu

Kintetsu ist in Nagoya nur mit einer einzigen Linie präsent, nämlich der Nagoya Line, die ab Kintetsu-Nagoya, einem fünfgleisigen unterirdischen Kopfbahnhof, nach Südwesten bis Ise-Nakagawa (78,8 km) verkehrt. Auf der Nagoya Line gibt es sowohl *Express*-Züge auf längeren Strecken (bis Osaka und zur Halbinsel Ise) als auch Vorortzüge als *Local*; letztere fahren dreimal pro Stunde bis Tomiyoshi (12,1 km), manche Züge erreichen auch Ise-Nakagawa oder Stationen dazwischen.
[Mehr zu *Kintetsu* im Band 3 dieser Serie]

Johoku Line

Das Besondere an dieser 11,2 km langen Tangentialstrecke ist der Gegensatz zwischen der aufwändig errichteten Infrastruktur und dem Einsatz von Dieseltriebwagen bei relativ schlechtem Takt. Die nicht elektrifizierte Strecke mit einer Spurweite von 1067 mm verdankt ihre Existenz Plänen von JNR (Vorgänger von JR), um Nagoya eine Güterumgehungsbahn zu errichten, die jedoch nur teilweise umgesetzt wurden, da einerseits die Baukosten explodiert waren, andererseits der Güterverkehr stark abgenommen hatte. *JR Central* erbte die unvollständige Strecke und gründete TKJ (*Tokai Kotsu Jigyo* – Tokai Transport Service Company) als hundertprozentige Tochtergesellschaft, um die Strecke für den Personenverkehr nutzbar zu machen. Die Linie beginnt in Biwajima an der JR Tokaido Main Line und führt durch Nagoyas nördliche Vorstädte bis Kachigawa, wo sie stumpf etwas ungünstig in 500 m Entfernung vom Bahnhof Kachigawa an der JR Chuo Main Line endet. Während der größte Teil der Strecke von Kachigawa bis Owari-Hoshinomiya (9,3 km) am 1. Dezember 1991 eröffnet wurde, wurde die restliche Strecke bis Biwajima erst am 18. März 1993 fertiggestellt. An den Endstationen Biwajima und Kachigawa gibt es jeweils kurze eingleisige Abschnitte, sonst ist die Linie zweigleisig auf einem hohen Beton-Viadukt, der meist neben Nagoyas 2. Ringstraße entlangläuft. Abgesehen von Biwajima sind die Stationen unbesetzt und liegen hoch über der Straßenebene (Otai z. B. 17 m), zugänglich mit

Kintetsu

Kintetsu's presence in the city is limited to a single line, the Nagoya Line which runs south-west to Ise-Nakagawa (78.8 km) from Kintetsu-Nagoya, a five-track underground terminus built in 1938. Nagoya Line services comprise both long-distance expresses (to Osaka and the Ise peninsula) and local commuter services; the latter provide a 3tph off-peak service to Tomiyoshi (12.1 km) with some trains continuing further to Ise-Nakagawa or other intermediate stations.
[More about Kintetsu in Vol. 3 of this series]

Johoku Line

The striking thing about this 11.2 km line is the mismatch between its heavily-engineered infrastructure and its low-frequency diesel railcar service. The un-electrified 1067 mm line owes its existence to JNR (JR's predecessor) plans for an orbital freight line around Nagoya which was partially completed but then abandoned due to a downturn in freight traffic and spiralling construction costs. JR Central inherited and completed the unfinished line and established TKJ (Tokai Kotsu Jigyo), Tokai Transport Service Company, as a fully-owned subsidiary to run a passenger service. The line commences at Biwajima on the JR Tokaido Main Line and runs through Nagoya's northern suburbs to Kachigawa, where its stub terminus is inconveniently sited 500 m from Kachigawa station on the JR Chuo Main Line. While most of the route from Kachigawa to Owari-Hoshinomiya (9.3 km) was opened on 1 Dec 1991, the remaining stretch to Biwajima was only completed on 18 March 1993. There are short single-track sections at Biwajima and Kachigawa termini but the rest of the line is double-track on high-level concrete viaduct, much of it running alongside Nagoya Loop Road No 2. Apart from Biwajima, stations are unmanned and at high level with lift and stair access

Kachigawa – TKJ Johoku Line Kiha-11 (Diesel) ▶ Biwajima

Aufzügen und festen Treppen. Die Flotte besteht aus zwei Kiha-11 Dieseltriebwagen von *JR Central* aus dem Jahr 1999, die mit Zahlboxen für den Ein-Mann-Betrieb ausgestattet sind. Beide Wagen sind in der Hauptverkehrszeit im Einsatz, wenn 2-3 Mal pro Stunde gefahren wird. Sonst reicht ein Wagen für eine Fahrt pro Stunde. Wenn ein Wagen in Wartung ist, überlässt *JR Central* einen Ersatz-Triebwagen. Das Depot befindet sich auf dem Viadukt hinter dem Bahnhof Kachigawa. Die Auslastung ist niedrig und liegt bei etwa 450-500 Passagieren pro Tag. IC Cards werden nicht akzeptiert; eine Tageskarte, das „Holiday Free Ticket", gibt es nur samstags, sonntags und an Feiertagen (720 Yen).

Aichi Loop Line

Die *Aichi Loop Railway* (*Aichi Kanjo Tetsudo* – „Aikan") ist eine 45,3 km lange Nord-Süd-Linie, die Toyota City und Vorstädte östlich von Nagoya tangential miteinander verbindet. Wie die Johoku Line geht sie auf eine nicht vollendete Güterumgehungsbahn zurück. Die teils eingleisige Strecke (1067 mm, 1500 V DC, 23 Stationen) verläuft von Okazaki (01) an der JR Tokaido Main Line bis Kozoji (23) an der JR Chuo Main Line; zur Seto Line von *Meitetsu* kann an der Station Setoshi umgestiegen werden, zur Linimo an der Station Yakusa und zur Nagoya Line von *Meitetsu* an der Station Naka-Okazaki. Normalerweise fahren vier Züge pro Stunde mit Halt an allen Stationen, wofür sie 67 Minuten benötigen. Zu Spitzenzeiten kommen Shuttle-Züge zwischen Shin-Toyota und Mikawa-Toyota für Pendler der Toyota-Werke hinzu, außerdem gibt es durchgehende Züge von Nagoya bis Setoguchi über die JR Chuo Main Line. Der Betrieb wird mit 20 Zwei-Wagen-Einheiten der Baureihe 2000 (Baujahr 2002-2009) abgewickelt.

to platforms; Otai station, for example, is 17 m above ground. The fleet comprises two ex-JR Central Kiha-11 diesel railcars dating from 1999 equipped with fareboxes for one-person operation. Both cars are required for the 2-3tph peak service but only one is needed for the 1tph off-peak service; JR Central supplies replacement railcars when needed for maintenance cover. The depot is on the viaduct beyond Kachigawa station. Passenger loadings are low, running at around 450-500 per day. IC cards are not accepted though an unlimited-ride Holiday Free Ticket is available (Sat/Sun/Hols - 720 Yen).

Aichi Loop Line

The third-sector Aichi Loop Railway (Aichi Kanjo Tetsudo - 'Aikan') is a 45.3 km north-south line serving Toyota City and outer suburban districts to the east of Nagoya. As with the Johoku Line, it has its origins in abandoned plans for a freight loop line around Nagoya. The part-single/part-double-track line (1067 mm gauge, 1500Vdc; 23 stations) runs from Okazaki (01) on the JR Tokaido Main Line to Kozoji (23) on the JR Chuo Main Line; interchange is available with Meitetsu's Seto Line at Setoshi, Linimo at Yakusa and Meitetsu's Nagoya Line at Naka-Okazaki. The standard 4tph all-stations service takes 67 minutes from end to end; this is supplemented at peak times by a Shin-Toyota – Mikawa-Toyota shuttle service to cater for commuters to Toyota Motor factories and by through-running JR Central Chuo Main Line services between Nagoya and Setoguchi. Rolling stock comprises 20 two-car 2000-series EMUs (built 2002-09).

Yakusa – Aichi Loop Railway 2000-series ▶ Kozoji (links | *left*) & Okazaki (rechts | *right*)

Ekimae – Toyotetsu #T1001 ► Akaiwaguchi

TOYOHASHI

Toyohashi ist eine mittelgroße Stadt mit 383.691 Einwohnern auf einer Fläche von 261,26 km² im Südosten der
Präfektur Aichi, 68 km von Nagoya und 274 km von Tokyo
entfernt. Die Stadt gehört zur Metropolregion Chukyo
(Großraum Nagoya) und ist durch den *Tokaido Shinkansen*
und die konventionelle JR Tokaido Main Line mit Nagoya
verbunden. Mit letzterer konkurriert die private *Nagoya
Railway* (*Meitetsu*) mit einem dichten S-Bahn-Verkehr auf
ihrer Nagoya Line. Der Stadtverkehr wird vorwiegend mit
Bussen abgewickelt, doch *Toyohashi Railway* betreibt auch
eine kurze städtische Straßenbahn sowie eine S-Bahn-
Linie.

*Toyohashi is a medium-sized city with a population of
383,691 in an area of 261.26 km². It is situated in south-
eastern Aichi Prefecture, 68 km from Nagoya and 274 km
from Tokyo. The city is within the Chukyo (Greater
Nagoya) metropolitan area and is connected to Nagoya
by the Tokaido Shinkansen and the conventional Tokaido
Main Line, both operated by JR Central. The private
Nagoya Railway (Meitetsu) also competes for traffic between the two cities with frequent services on its Nagoya
Line. City transport is primarily bus-based but Toyohashi
Railway operates a short city tramway and a suburban
railway line.*

Shinai Line (City Line)
Tram: Ekimae (1) – Akaiwaguchi (13) / Undo-Koen-mae (14)
5.4 km, 14 Haltestellen | *stops*; 1067 mm, 600Vdc ⊕

1925: Ekimae – Azumada-Sakaue (2.9 km)
1950: Ekimae – Shiyakusho-mae
    (Neutrassierung | *tracks relocated to new road system*)
1950: Azumada-Sakaue – Keirinjo-mae (0.7 km)
01-06-1960: Keirinjo-mae – Akaiwaguchi (1.2 km)
31-01-1982: Ihara – Undo-Koen-mae (Athletics Park) (0.6 km)
1998: Ekimae unter Fußgängerbrücke verlegt
                    relocated beneath pedestrian deck

[Stillgelegte Strecken nicht aufgelistet | *closed sections not listed*]

Atsumi Line
Vorortbahn | *Suburban Rail*: Shin-Toyohashi – Mikawa-Tahara
18.0 km, 16 Haltestellen | *stations*; 1067 mm, 1500Vdc ⊕

Ihara – #782 ► Undo-Koen-mae (Verzweigung | *line junction*)

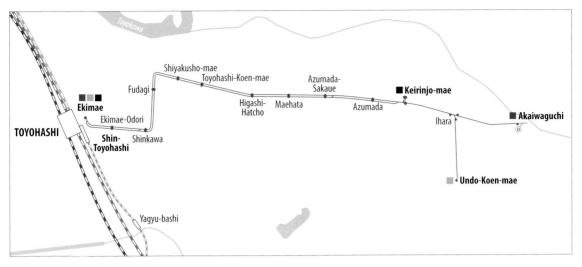

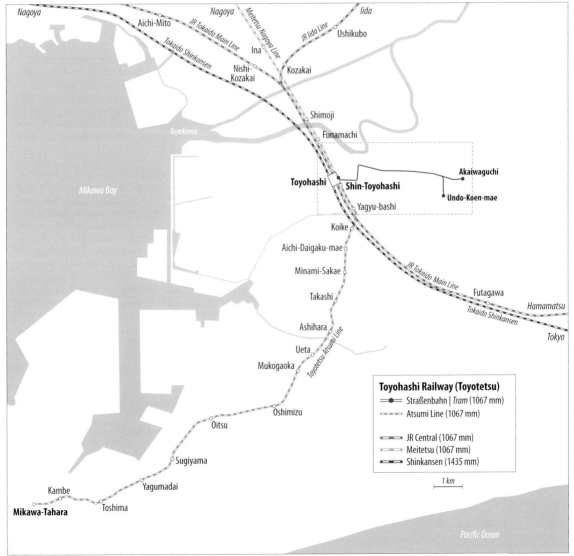

Toyohashi Railway (Toyotetsu)

- Straßenbahn | *Tram* (1067 mm)
- Atsumi Line (1067 mm)

- JR Central (1067 mm)
- Meitetsu (1067 mm)
- Shinkansen (1435 mm)

1 km

TOYOHASHI

Shiyakusho-mae - 780-series
► Akaiwaguchi (links | *left*) & ► Ekimae (rechts | right)

Keirinjo-mae – ex-Meitetsu #3201 (1956) & #786 (1998)

TOYOHASHI RAILWAY   Toyohashi Tetsudo, 'Toyotetsu'

Straßenbahn

Toyohashi Railway, bekannt als *Toyotetsu*, ist eine Tochter-gesellschaft der *Meitetsu*-Gruppe. Die städtische Straßen-bahn wurde 1925 zwischen dem Bahnhof Toyohashi (Eki-mae) und Azumada (3.1 km) zusammen mit einem 1.1 km langen Abzweig nach Yagyubashi eröffnet. Ihr offizieller Name ist „Azumada Main Line", doch sie wird allgemein als die **Shinai Line** [Stadt-Linie] bezeichnet. Bei Luftangriffen wurden 1945 rund 60% der Stadt zerstört, beim Wieder-aufbau wurde ein Großteil der Straßenbahnstrecken im zentralen Bereich auf neue breitere Straßen verlegt. 1950 wurde der Abschnitt zwischen Azumada-Sakaue und dem ursprünglichen Endpunkt Azumada stillgelegt und die Strecke stattdessen bis Keirinjo-mae (Rennbahn) verlän-gert. 1952 wurde eine kurze Erweiterung von Ekimae bis Shimin-Byoin-mae als erste Stufe einer Innenstadtringlinie gebaut, doch diese wurde nie vollendet, so dass die Tram 1969 wieder zum Bahnhof zurückgenommen wurde. 1960 erreichte die Hauptlinie ihre heutige Endstelle Akaiwaguchi, wo ein neues Depot gebaut wurde. 1982 folgte schließ-lich ein kurzer Abzweig zu einem Sportstadion an der Haltestelle Undo-Koen-mae. Der Yagyubashi-Ast, der ab Shinkawa als Shuttle betrieben wurde, ist seit 1976 außer Betrieb. Die jüngste Erweiterung gab es 1998, als die Linie um 150 m zu einer neuen Endstation Ekimae unter einer

Tramway

Toyohashi Railway, known as *Toyotetsu*, is a subsidi-ary of the Meitetsu Group. The city tramway opened in 1925 between Toyohashi station (Ekimae) and Azumada (3.1 km) together with a 1.1 km branch to Yagyubashi. Its official name is the Azumada Main Line but it is com-monly referred to as the **Shinai Line** (City Line). The Toyohashi air-raid of 1945 destroyed around 60% of the city and post-war reconstruction involved the reloca-tion of much of the central area tramway to new wider streets. In 1950, the line was closed between Azumada-Sakaue and its original Azumada terminus and extended instead to Keirinjo-mae (cycle racing track). A short extension opened from Ekimae to Shimin-Byoin-mae in 1952 as the first stage of a central area loop line but this was not completed and the line was cut back to Ekimae again in 1969. By 1960 the main line had reached its current terminus, Akaiwaguchi, where a new depot was constructed, and in 1982 a short branch line opened to Undo-Koen-mae to serve a sports stadium. The Yagyu-bashi branch which operated as a shuttle service to/from Shinkawa closed in 1976. The most recent extension oc-curred in 1998 when the line was re-extended 150 m to a new Ekimae terminus beneath a pedestrian deck leading to Toyohashi station.

Keirinjo-mae – #784 (ex-Meitetsu) ► Ekimae
- mit Klappstufe | *with retractable step*

Ihara > Akaiwaguchi – #3502 (ex-Tokyo) ► Ekimae

Fußgängerbrücke, die zum Bahnhof Toyohashi führt, verlängert wurde.

Die Straßenbahn verkehrt in der Regel alle 7 Minuten abwechselnd nach Akaiwaguchi oder Undo-Koen-mae, die Fahrt dauert ab Ekimae jeweils 22 Minuten. Einzelne Fahrten beginnen bzw. enden in Keirinjo-mae, wo es ein Straßenbahn-Verwaltungsgebäude und zwei kurze Stumpfgleise gibt. Etwa 3 km von Ekimae bis Higashi-Hatcho verläuft die Straßenbahn meist vom Autoverkehr getrennt in Mittellage breiter, moderner Straßen mit mittigen Oberleitungsmasten. Ab Higashi-Hatcho hat die Strecke noch eher das Flair einer alten Straßenbahn auf schmaleren Straßen und mit eingepflasterten Gleisen, bis Keirinjo-mae zweigleisig, dann jeweils eingleisig bis zu den beiden Endstellen.

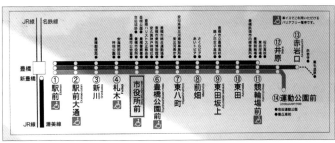

Die Straßenbahn von Toyohashi war traditionell auf gebrauchte Fahrzeuge angewiesen, doch im Jahr 2008 erwarb sie einen neuen dreiteiligen Niederflurgelenkwagen vom Typ T1000 „Hottram" von Alna Sharyo (16,2 m). Die übrigen 16 Wagen umfassen elf aus Gifu (*Meitetsu*) (gebaut 1955/56/97/98/2000), einen aus Nagoya (1943) und vier aus Tokyo (1955/56, mit neuem Wagenkasten von 1977).

Der Fahrpreis für die Straßenbahn beträgt 150 Yen, ein „One Day Free Pass" kostet 400 Yen (nur Straßenbahn). *Toyotetsu* ist an der aufladbaren „manaca" IC Card der Region Nagoya beteiligt.

S-Bahn

Die **Atsumi Line** wurde 1924-25 von der *Atsumi Electric Railway* eröffnet, welche 1940 Teil der *Nagoya Railway* wurde und dann 1954 von der *Toyohashi Railway* übernommen wurde. Die eingleisige Strecke beginnt an der Station Shin-Toyohashi, die neben dem JR-Bahnhof Toyohashi liegt, und erschließt Vororte und Dörfer auf der Halbinsel Atsumi. Die Züge verkehren alle 15 Minuten mit Halt an allen Stationen. Dabei werden 10 von Tokyu erworbene Drei-Wagen-Einheiten, jeweils in einer anderen Farbe mit Blumenmotiv, eingesetzt. Es gilt ein Entfernungstarif; ein „Colourful Train 1-Day Free Pass" (nur S-Bahn-Linie) ist für 1.100 Yen erhältlich.

Services generally operate every 7 minutes with alternate trams serving either Akaiwaguchi or Undo-Koen-mae, both of which take 22 minutes from Ekimae. A few services operate to/from Keirinjo-mae where there is a tramway office and two short sidings. For approximately 3.0 km from Ekimae to Higashi-Hatcho the tramway runs along the centre of wide modern streets with centre-pole catenary, mostly segregated from other traffic; from here on, the line has more of the atmosphere of an old-style tramway with narrower streets, stone-paved double track as far as Keirinjo-mae and single track beyond Keirinjo-mae to the two termini.

Toyohashi has traditionally relied on second-hand trams but in 2008 acquired a new Alna Sharyo T1000-series 3-section low-floor 16.2 m articulated car, which is marketed as 'Hottram'. The other 16 cars in the fleet comprise eleven ex-Gifu (Meitetsu) (built 1955/56/97/ 98/2000), one ex-Nagoya (built 1943) and four ex-Tokyo (1955/56 re-bodied 1977).

The tram flat fare is 150 Yen and there is a One Day Free Pass for 400 Yen (tram only). Toyotetsu also participates in the Nagoya area 'manaca' rechargeable IC card.

Suburban Rail

The **Atsumi Line** was opened by the Atsumi Electric Railway in 1924-25, becoming part of the Nagoya Railway in 1940 and then transferring to the Toyohashi Railway in 1954. The single-track line runs from Shin-Toyohashi, adjacent to JR Toyohashi station, serving suburban and rural settlements on the Atsumi peninsula. Services operate every 15 minutes calling at all stations. The fleet consists of 10 three-car sets of ex-Tokyu stock, each in a different coloured flower-themed livery. Fares are distance-related; a Colourful Train 1-Day Free Pass (rail only) costs 1,100 Yen.

Shin-Toyohashi – Toyotetsu Atsumi Line 1800-series (ex-Tokyu)

Toyotetsu Atsumi Line 1800-series

Shin-Shimizu > Irieoka – Shizutetsu 'Rainbow Train' A3000-series ► Shin-Shizuoka

SHIZUOKA

Shizuoka liegt etwa auf halber Strecke zwischen Tokyo und Nagoya, mit der Suruga Bay im Süden und dem Akaishi-Gebirge (Südalpen) im Norden. Shizuoka ist die Hauptstadt der gleichnamigen Präfektur und hat heute 715.000 Einwohner, nachdem im Jahr 2003 das benachbarte Shimizu eingemeindet wurde. Das Geschäfts- und Verwaltungszentrum der Stadt liegt rund um den JR-Bahnhof Shizuoka, während Shimizu ein wichtiger Container- und Fischereihafen ist. Zwischen den beiden vormals eigenständigen Städten ist die typische Vorortbebauung durchgehend.

Drei Eisenbahnlinien verlaufen parallel zueinander vom Südwesten Richtung Nordosten durch die Stadt; *Shizutetsus* S-Bahn-Linie verbindet Shizuoka und Shimizu, daneben verkehren die konventionelle Tokaido Main Line sowie der *Tokaido Shinkansen* von *JR Central*. Eine Luftseilbahn führt auf den innerhalb der Stadtgrenzen gelegenen Mount Kuno.

Shizuoka is situated approximately half way between Tokyo and Nagoya facing Suruga Bay to the south, with the Southern Alps immediately to the north. It is the capital city of Shizuoka Prefecture and, since merging with adjoining Shimizu in 2003, has a population of 715,000. The city's main commercial, administrative and retail centre is adjacent to JR Shizuoka station; and, Shimizu is home to an extensive commercial container and fishing port. The two formerly separate cities are linked by continuously built-up suburban development.

Three railway lines run broadly parallel to each other through the city in a north-east to south-west direction; Shizutetsu's suburban line linking Shizuoka and Shimizu, JR Central's conventional Tokaido Main Line and the Tokaido Shinkansen. An aerial ropeway serves Mt Kuno, situated within the city boundary.

SHIZUOKA RAILWAY   Shizuoka Tetsudo – 'Shizutetsu'

Diese S-Bahn-Linie wurde ursprünglich mit 762-mm-Spurweite von Shizuoka zu den Hafenanlagen von Shimizu (12,2 km) eröffnet, hauptsächlich um den Export von grünem Tee zu ermöglichen, für den die Region Shizuoka berühmt ist. Die Strecke wurde im Jahr 1920 umgespurt und elektrifiziert und zwischen 1925 und 1930 bis auf einen 1,2 km langen Hafenabschnitt, der 1945 geschlossen wurde, zweigleisig ausgebaut. Das Unternehmen betrieb auch kurze Straßenbahnen in Shizuoka (2,0 km) und Shimizu (4,7 km), die 1920 eröffnet und 1962 bzw. 1975 stillgelegt wurden.

This line opened as a 762 mm gauge line linking Shizuoka with wharves at Shimizu (12.2 km), primarily to facilitate the export of green tea, for which the Shizuoka region is renowned. The line was re-gauged and electrified in 1920 and double-tracked between 1925 and 1930,

Shizuoka-Shimizu Line
Shin-Shizuoka (S01) – Shin-Shimizu (S15)
11.0 km, 15 Haltestellen | *stations*; 1067 mm; 600Vdc ⊕

09-12-1908: Shin-Shizuoka – Shin-Shimizu (11.0 km)
25-03-1986: + Kenritsu-Bijutsukan-mae

Heute gilt *Shizutetsu* als eine von Japans gewinnbringenderen kleinen Privatbahnen; ihre S-Bahn verkehrt relativ häufig, allerdings nur mit 2-Wagen-Zügen. Die Stationen wurden mit Zugangssperren ausgestattet, die IC Cards akzeptieren. Außerdem wurde damit begonnen, die Fahrzeugflotte zu erneuern, wobei wie bereits früher völlig neue Züge angeschafft werden, anstatt auf Gebrauchtfahrzeuge zurückzugreifen, wie das häufig bei kleineren Unternehmen der Fall ist.

Die Endstelle Shin-Shizuoka liegt ebenerdig etwa 650 m von JR-Bahnhof Shizuoka entfernt, darüber errichtete die Bahn ihr eigenes Einkaufszentrum Cenova; im Gebäudekomplex ist auch der Busbahnhof Shin-Shizuoka untergebracht. Der dreigleisige Kopfbahnhof hat zwei Mittelbahnsteige. Alle anderen Stationen sind zweigleisig, eine Ausnahme bilden Ken-Sogo-Undojo (Prefectural Sports Park) mit vier Gleisen und zwei Mittelbahnsteigen für den Express-Betrieb sowie Naganuma mit drei Gleisen, eins davon als Zufahrtsgleis zum Betriebshof. Die Strecke führt durch flache Vorstadtbezirke mit zahlreichen Bahnübergängen. Die teilweise parallele Tokaido Main Line sowie der Tokaido Shinkansen werden in der Nähe von Ken-Sogo-Undojo auf einer Brücke gekreuzt, eine weitere Brücke führt die S-Bahn über einen Kanal kurz vor Shin-Shimizu. Die Station Kusanagi erschließt die Universität von Shizuoka, während die Station Kenritsu-Bijutsukan-mae 1986 eingefügt wurde, um das dorthin umgezogene Kunstmuseum der Präfektur Shizuoka erreichbar zu machen.

Tagsüber verkehren *Local*-Züge alle 6-7 Minuten mit Halt an allen Stationen, wofür sie 21-22 Minuten benötigen. In der Morgenspitze steigt die Anzahl der Züge durch Express-Fahrten und Kurzläufer auf bis zu 15 Abfahrten pro Stunde in Shin-Shizuoka, wobei Richtung Westen an anderen Stationen gehalten wird als Richtung Osten; die Kurzläufer zwischen Shin-Shizuoka und Ken-Sogo-Undojo halten überall.

30 Jahre lang war die S-Bahn-Flotte einheitlich mit zwölf 2-Wagen-Einheiten der Baureihe 1000, die zwischen 1973 und 1986 von Tokyu Car für *Shizutetsu* produziert wurden. Diese Einheiten haben unlackierte Edelstahl-

1st color 2016.3.24 debut.

except for the 1.2 km section serving Shimizu wharves which closed in 1945. The company also ran short tramways in Shizuoka (2.0 km) and Shimizu (4.7 km) which opened in 1920 and closed respectively in 1962 and 1975.

Today, *Shizutetsu* appears to be one of Japan's more prosperous small private railways, operating a relatively high-frequency metro-style suburban service, albeit with 2-car trains. The company has equipped its stations with gates which accept IC cards and has commenced replacement of its fleet, continuing its policy of acquiring new trains rather than relying on second-hand vehicles, as is often the case with smaller companies.

Shin-Shizuoka terminus is about 650 m from JR Shizuoka station on the ground floor of the company's Cenova shopping complex which also houses Shin-Shizuoka bus terminal. This three-track station has two bay platforms; all other stations are double-tracked except for Ken-Sogo-Undojo (Prefectural Sports Park) which has four tracks and two island platforms to allow express operation and Naganuma, location of the depot, which has a third track. The line serves flat suburban districts, with many level crossings, running in part alongside the Tokaido Main Line, but is carried on a bridge over the Shinkansen and Tokaido Main Line near Ken-Sogo-Undojo and another bridge over a waterway on the approach to Shin-Shimizu. Kusanagi serves the University of Shizuoka and Kenritsu-Bijutsukan-mae opened in 1986 to serve Shizuoka Prefectural Art Museum which was relocated nearby.

During the midday period an all-stations 'Local' service operates every 6-7 minutes (9tph) taking 21-22 minutes end-to-end. In the morning peak only, limited-

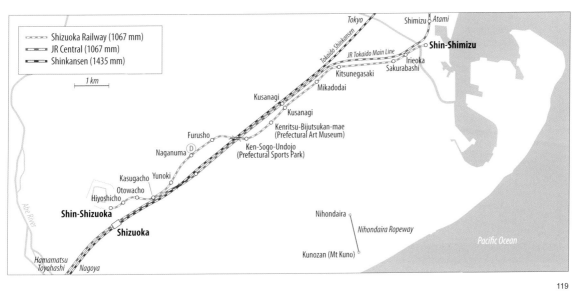

Hiyoshicho – Shizutetsu 1000-series ▶ Ken-Sogo-Undojo

wagenkästen (einige sind mit Vollwerbung beklebt) und Sitze in Längsanordnung. Sie verkehren im Ein-Mann-Betrieb. Im März 2016 wurde der erste Zug der Baureihe A3000 von J-TREC (Nachfolger von Tokyu Car) in Dienst gestellt. Diese Baureihe gehört zu den Edelstahl-Zügen der Produktfamilie „Sustina". Verteilt über acht Jahre werden insgesamt zwölf Züge ausgeliefert; sieben davon als „Shizuoka Rainbow Trains" in unterschiedlichen Farben, die übrigen fünf unlackiert.

Neben ihrer S-Bahn-Linie betreibt *Shizutetsu* die 1,1 km lange Nihondaira-Seilbahn, welche das Nihondaira-Plateau mit dem Toshogu-Schrein auf dem Mount Kuno (216 m), hoch über der Bucht von Suruga, verbindet. Die Seilbahn hat zwei Kabinen mit einer Kapazität von 55 Passagieren und überwindet einen Höhenunterschied von 120 m.

Shizutetsu verfügt über eine eigene IC Card, „LuLuCa", die nur auf ihrer S-Bahn-Linie sowie in den Bussen ihrer Tochtergesellschaft *Shizuoka Justline* genutzt werden kann. Allerdings werden auch die zehn landesweit wichtigsten IC Cards im LuLuCa-Gebiet akzeptiert. Ein „Shizutetsu Electric Train/Bus 1-Day Free Ticket" ist für 1.200 Yen erhältlich; für die S-Bahn allein gibt es keine Tageskarte.

stop services and short-workings boost the number of trains serving Shin-Shizuoka up to 15tph. The limited-stop trains run 'Express' westbound and 'Commuter Express' eastbound with different stopping patterns; the short-workings call at all stations between Shin-Shizuoka and Ken-Sogo-Undojo.

For the last 30 years, services have been operated by a standardised fleet of twelve 1000-series 2-car sets manufactured for Shizutetsu by Tokyu Car between 1973 and 1986. These sets have unpainted stainless steel bodies (some with overall advertisement wrapping), longitudinal seating and are equipped for driver-only operation. Fleet replacement commenced in March 2016 with the debut of the first A3000-series 2-car set built by J-TREC (Tokyu Car's successor) based on its 'Sustina' family of stainless steel bodied trains. Twelve trains are on order for delivery over eight years; seven of these will be in different colours, marketed as 'Shizuoka Rainbow Trains', and five will be unpainted.

In addition to its rail line, the company operates the 1.1 km Nihondaira Ropeway connecting Nihondaira Plateau with the Toshogu Shrine on Mt Kuno (216 m), an area of high land facing Suruga Bay within the city. The ropeway has two cabins with a capacity of 55 passengers and covers a vertical distance of 120 m.

Shizutetsu has its own LuLuCa IC card which can only be used on its rail service and on buses operated by its Shizuoka Justline subsidiary. However, the ten 'major IC cards' within the nationwide inter-operability scheme are accepted in the LuLuCa area. A Shizutetsu Electric Train/Bus 1-Day Free Ticket costs 1,200 Yen; there is no rail-only version.

A3000-series

Naganuma – Shizutetsu 1000-series ▶ Shin-Shimizu

JR CENTRAL

Auf der Tokaido Main Line (1067 mm, 1500 V DC) betreibt *JR Central* auch Vorortverkehr im Bereich Shizuoka und zu anderen Städten entlang der Pazifikküste. Tagsüber verkehren sich überlappende Linien mit Halt an allen Stationen, so dass durch die Stadt Shizuoka typischerweise sechs Züge pro Stunde angeboten werden. Richtung Westen enden diese meist in Shimada (27,6 km) oder Hamamatsu (76,9 km), gelegentlich in Toyohashi (113,4 km); Richtung Osten in Okitsu (15,9 km), Mishima (59,5 km) oder Atami (75,6 km). Als „Home Liner" bezeichnete Express-Züge fahren abends nach Hamamatsu und Numazu. Im Einsatz sind Elektrotriebwagen der Baureihen 211/311/313/373.

JR Central's Tokaido Main Line (1067 mm gauge, 1500Vdc) serves suburban stations within the Shizuoka built-up area and provides connections to towns and cities along the Pacific coast. The standard daytime service pattern is made up of overlapping all-stations services which combine to give a 6tph cross-city service through Shizuoka. Westbound services usually terminate at Shimada (27.6 km) or Hamamatsu (76.9 km) with occasional trains reaching Toyohashi (113.4 km); eastbound services run to Okitsu (15.9 km), Mishima (59.5 km) or Atami (75.6 km). Limited-stop Home Liner services run to Hamamatsu and Numazu in the evenings. Services are operated by 211/311/313/373-series EMU sets.

Shizuoka - JR Central Tokaido Main Line 211-series ▶ Okitsu

(Fahrerwechsel | *crew changeover*)

Takamatsu-Chikko – Kotoden Kotohira Line 1100-series (ex-Keio) – Ichinomiya

TAKAMATSU

Takamatsu (419.000 Einw.; 375 km^2) ist die Hauptstadt der Präfektur Kagawa auf Japans viertgrößter Insel Shikoku. Der Fährhafen der Stadt war lange das Tor zu Shikoku, bis im Jahr 1988 die 13,1 km lange Seto-Ohashi-Brücke (Eisenbahn/Straße) eröffnet wurde, wodurch eine feste Verbindung zur Hauptinsel Honshu geschaffen war. Fähren erschließen weiterhin nahe Inseln im Seto-Binnenmeer, doch große Gebiete am Hafen und um den JR-Bahnhof Takamatsu wurden städtebaulich umgestaltet als „Sunport Takamatsu" mit einer Promenade sowie einem Einkaufszentrum und Bürogebäuden, darunter der 30-stöckige „Symbol Tower". In der Stadt findet man den „Ritsurin-Koen", einen der drei berühmtesten japanischen Landschaftsgärten.

JR Shikoku betreibt Limited Express-Züge zwischen Takamatsu und den anderen Hauptzentren der Insel (Kochi, Tokushima und Matsuyama) und gemeinsam mit JR West den halbstündlichen „Marine Liner" über die Seto-Ohashi-Brücke nach Okayama (71,8 km, ca. 55 Min.). Im Gebiet um Takamatsu fahren Vorortzüge der privaten Takamatsu-Kotohira Electric Railway auf drei Linien sowie, wenn auch weniger häufig, von JR Shikoku auf der elektrifizierten Yosan Line und der diesel-betriebenen Kotoku Line.

Takamatsu (population 419,000; 375 km^2) is the capital of Kagawa Prefecture on Japan's fourth largest island, Shikoku. The city's ferry port was the main entry point for Shikoku until the opening of the 13.1 km road/rail Seto-Ohashi Bridge in 1988, which created a fixed link to the main island of Honshu. Ferries continue to serve nearby islands in the Seto Inland Sea but much of the area around the port and JR Takamatsu station has been redeveloped as Sunport Takamatsu, a pedestrian promenade, office and shopping complex including the 30-storey Symbol Tower. The city is home to Ritsurin Park, one of Japan's three most-famous landscape gardens.

JR Shikoku operates limited-express services between Takamatsu and the other main cities on the island (Kochi, Tokushima and Matsuyama) and, jointly with JR West, half-hourly Marine Liner rapid services across the Seto-Ohashi Bridge to Okayama (71.8 km, around 55 minutes). Local rail services in the Takamatsu area are provided by the privately-owned Takamatsu-Kotohira Electric Railway on its three-line network and, less frequently, by JR Shikoku on its electrified Yosan Line and diesel-operated Kotoku Line.

Busshozan Depot - ex-Keihin-Kyuko & ex-Keio stock

Takamatsu-Chikko > Kataharamachi
– Nagao Line 1200-series (ex-Keihin-Kyuko) ► Nagao

Kawaramachi
– Shido Line 600-series (ex-Nagoya Subway) ► Kotoden-Shido

TAKAMATSU-KOTOHIRA ELECTRIC RAILWAY   Takamatsu-Kotohira Denki Tetsudo - 'Kotoden'

Kotoden betreibt in erster Linie eine S-Bahn, die vorstädtische und halbländliche Gebiete rund um Takamatsu einschließlich des Pilgerorts Kotohira, wo der Kotohira Grand Shrine steht, erschließt. Die drei Linien des heutigen Unternehmens wurden durch verschiedene Gesellschaften gebaut, die 1943 vereint wurden. Zunächst hatten alle drei Linien getrennte Endbahnhöfe, die sich südlich des Stadtzentrums befanden: Die Endstation der Shido Line bei Koen-mae (am Ritsurin Park) war mit dem Hafen durch eine 2,2 km lange Straßenbahn verbunden, während die beiden anderen Linien in der Nähe der heutigen Station Kawaramachi endeten.

Im Anschluss an die Fusion von 1943 wurde die Nagao Line von 1067 mm auf 1435 mm umgespurt und alle Linien wurden in einem einzigen Endbahnhof Kawaramachi zusammengeführt; der Abschnitt Kawaramachi – Koen-mae der Shido Line und die Straßenbahn wurden 1945 nach einem Bombenangriff, der einen Großteil der Stadt zerstörte, aufgegeben. Im Rahmen des Wiederaufbaus nach dem Krieg wurde eine Verlängerung von Kawaramachi bis zu einer neuen Endstation Takamatsu-Chikko errichtet, um den Zugang zur Innenstadt, zum Hafen und zum JR-Bahnhof (etwa 200 m westlich) zu verbessern. Diese zweigleisige Strecke wurde zunächst als zwei eingleisige Strecken betrieben, das westliche Gleis mit 1500 V DC für die Kotohira Line und das östliche mit 600 V DC für die Shido Line, wobei letztere in der Station Kawaramachi Kopf machen musste; der regelmäßige zweigleisige Betrieb begann 1967, nachdem die Spannung auf der Shido Line angehoben worden war. Abgesehen vom 2,9 km langen Abschnitt Takamatsu-Chikko – Ritsurin-Koen auf der Kotohira Line ist das Netz eingleisig.

Im Jahr 1994 wurde die Shido Line vom Rest des Netzes getrennt, um den Bau des Sogo-Kaufhauses über dem Bahnhof Kawaramachi zu ermöglichen. Kawaramachi besteht heute also eigentlich aus zwei Stationen, die durch Fahrsteige verbunden sind; die Shido Line liegt mit zwei Bahnsteiggleisen rechtwinkelig zu den Nord-Süd-Bahnsteigen der Kotohira Line (zwei Gleise) und der Nagao Line (ein Gleis für beide Richtungen). Durch diesen Umbau wird heute die Nagao Line anstelle der Shido Line von Kawaramachi bis Takamatsu-Chikko durchgebunden.

Das Kaufhaus wurde 1997 eröffnet, doch der finanzielle Zusammenbruch des Investors Sogo Group im Jahr 2000

Kotoden is primarily a commuter railway serving suburban and semi-rural communities around Takamatsu including an interurban link to the pilgrimage town of Kotohira, home of the Kotohira Grand Shrine. The present company's three lines were built by separate concerns which were merged in 1943. Initially all three lines had separate termini located to the south of the city centre; the Shido Line's terminus at Koen-mae (serving Ritsurin Park) was linked to the port by a 2.2 km street tramway and the other two lines terminated close to present-day Kawaramachi station.

Following the 1943 merger, the Nagao Line was re-gauged from 1067 mm to 1435 mm and all lines were concentrated on a single terminus at Kawaramachi; the Kawaramachi – Koen-mae section of the Shido Line and the street tramway closed in 1945 following a wartime fire-bombing attack which destroyed much of the city. As part of the re-building effort after the war, an extension was built from Kawaramachi to a new terminus at Takamatsu-Chikko, providing better access to the city centre, port and JR station (about 200 m to the west). This double-track line was initially operated as two single-track lines, the western track electrified at 1500Vdc for Kotohira Line services and the eastern track at 600Vdc for Shido Line services, the latter reversing direction at Kawaramachi; regular double-track operation commenced in 1967 following an increase in the Shido Line voltage. Apart from the 2.9 km Takamatsu-Chikko – Ritsurin-Koen section of the Kotohira Line, the remainder of the network is single-track.

In 1994, the Shido Line was severed from the rest of the network to facilitate the construction of a Sogo department store above Kawaramachi station. Thus, today, Kawaramachi is effectively two stations connected by a pedestrian link with moving walkways; the Shido Line has a two-track platform which sits at right angles to the north-south platforms used by the Kotohira Line (two tracks) and Nagao Line (one bi-directional track). This change also saw Nagao Line services extended from Kawaramachi to Takamatsu-Chikko in place of the former Shido Line through service.

The department store opened in 1997 but the financial collapse of development partner, Sogo Group, in 2000 also forced the railway company into bankruptcy.

Takinomiya — 'Retro Train' #300 (1926) & #500 (1928) ▶ Kotoden-Kotohira

führte auch die Eisenbahngesellschaft in den Bankrott. Zur Rettung von *Kotoden* kam es zu einem Eigentümerwechsel, seither wurden verschiedene Verbesserungen eingeführt, etwa die IC Card „IruCa" (2005), Stationsnummerierung (2013), farbcodierte Linien und Fahrzeuge, neue Stationen (Kukodori und Ayagawa) sowie eine bessere Verknüpfung mit den *Kotoden*-Bussen.

Die Züge verkehren alle 15 Minuten auf der Kotohira Line zwischen Takamatsu-Chikko (K00) und Ichinomiya (K08) bzw. Takinomiya (K15), wobei jeder zweite Zug weiter nach Kotoden-Kotohira (K21, 60 Min.) fährt. Ein 20-Minuten-Takt herrscht auf der Nagao Line von Takamatsu-Chikko (N00) bis Nagao (N17, 37 Min.) sowie auf der Shido Line zwischen Kawaramachi (S00) und Kotoden-Shido (S15, 35 Min.). Alle Züge halten an allen Stationen, einzelne Kurzläufer gibt es auf der Nagao

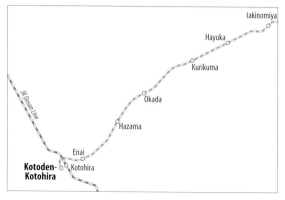

Takamatsu-Kotohira Electric Railway
3 Linien | *lines*; 60 km, 52 Bahnhöfe | *stations*; 1435 mm; 1500Vdc ⬆

Shido Line: Kawaramachi (S00) – Kotoden-Shido (S15)
12.5 km, 16 Bahnhöfe | *stations*

18-11-1911: Imabashi – Kotoden-Shido (11.9 km)
15-10-1913: Imabashi – Dehare (x) (0.5 km)
22-04-1915: Dehare (x) – Kawaramachi (0.1 km)

Nagao Line: Kawaramachi (N02) – Nagao (N17)
14.6 km, 16 Bahnhöfe | *stations*

30-04-1912: Hanazono – Nagao (13.7 km)
01-08-1954: Hanazono – Kawaramachi (0.9 km)

Kotohira Line: Takamatsu-Chikko (K00) – Kotoden-Kotohira (K21)
32.9 km, 22 Bahnhöfe | *stations*

21-12-1926: Ritsurin-Koen – Takinomiya (17.8 km)
15-03-1927: Takinomiya – Kotoden-Kotohira (12.2 km)
22-04-1927: Ritsurin-Koen – Kawaramachi (1.2 km)
18-02-1948: Kawaramachi – Kataharamachi (0.8 km)
26-12-1948: Kataharamachi – Chikko (x) (0.7 km)
10-09-1955: Chikko (x) – Takamatsu-Chikko (0.2 km)

(x) Bahnhof geschlossen | *station closed*

The financial rehabilitation plan for Kotoden saw a change of ownership, since when various improvements have been introduced including an IC card 'IruCa' (2005), station numbering (2013), colour-coded lines and rolling stock, new stations (Kukodori and Ayagawa) and better coordination with Kotoden bus services.

Trains run every 15 minutes on the Kotohira Line between Takamatsu-Chikko (K00) and Ichinomiya (K08) or Takinomiya (K15) with every other train continuing to Kotoden-Kotohira (K21), a journey of 60 minutes. The Nagao Line runs every 20 minutes from Takamatsu-Chikko (N00) to Nagao (N17) taking 37 minutes and the Shido Line also runs every 20 minutes between Kawaramachi (S00) and Kotoden-Shido (S15) taking 35 minutes. All trains call at all stations and there are a limited number of short workings on the Nagao and Shido lines. Most services are operated by 2 or 3-car trains with some 4-car trains at peak times.

Rolling stock comprises 80 EMU cars (ex-Nagoya Municipal Subway, Keihin-Kyuko and Keio Corporation) mainly in 2-car sets but with a few single cars. Cars are

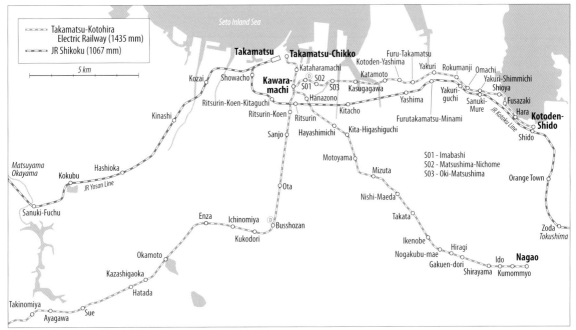

Takamatsu-Kotohira Electric Railway (1435 mm)
JR Shikoku (1067 mm)

5 km

Seto Inland Sea

Takamatsu · Takamatsu-Chikko · Furu-Takamatsu · Kotoden-Yashima · Yakuri · Rokumanji · Omachi · Yakuri-Shimmichi · Shioya · Fusazaki · Hara · Kotoden-Shido · Shido

Kozai · Showacho · Kawaramachi · Kataharamachi · Katamoto · Katsugagawa · Yashima · Yakuri-guchi · Sanuki-Mure

S02 · S03 · S01 · Hanazono · Kitacho · Furutakamatsu-Minami

Kinashi · Ritsurin-Koen-Kitaguchi · Ritsurin-Koen · Ritsurin · Kita-Higashiguchi

Sanjo · Hayashimichi · Motoyama · Mizuta

S01 - Imabashi
S02 - Matsushima-Nichome
S03 - Oki-Matsushima

Orange Town

Matsuyama Okayama · Hashioka · Kokubu · JR Yosan Line · Nishi-Maeda · Takata · Zoda Tokushima

Sanuki-Fuchu · Enza · Ichinomiya · Busshozan · Kukodori · Ikenobe · Hiragi · Nogakubu-mae · Ido · Nagao · Gakuen-dori · Shirayama · Kumommyo

Okamoto · Kazashigaoka · Hatada

Takinomiya · Sue · Ayagawa

Kawaramachi – Nagao Line 600-series (ex-Nagoya Subway)

und Shido Line. Die meisten Fahrten werden mit 2- oder 3-Wagen-Zügen durchgeführt, einige zu Spitzenzeiten auch mit 4-Wagen-Zügen.

Die Fahrzeugflotte umfasst 80 Elektrotriebwagen (ex *Nagoya Municipal Subway*, *Keihin-Kyuko* und *Keio Corporation*), vorwiegend als 2-Wagen-Einheiten, aber auch einige Einzelwagen. Die Wagen sind in der Linienfarbe gestrichen: 40 gelbe für die Kotohira Line, 20 grüne für die Nagao Line und 20 pinkfarbene für die Shido Line. Dazu kommen vier „Retro"-Wagen aus der Anfangszeit der Kotohira Line in den 1920er Jahren, die an ausgewählten Tagen im Einsatz sind.

Im Bahnhofsgebäude von Kawaramachi, in dem jetzt das Flag-Kaufhaus untergebracht ist, wurde die Etagenhöhe so gewählt, dass die Bahn durch das Obergeschoss geführt werden könnte. Dies war einst zur Beseitigung von Bahnübergängen im zentralen Bereich von Takamatsu geplant. Vom Bürgermeister 2007 gemachte Vorschläge, einen Teil der Bahn innerhalb der Stadt in eine Stadtbahn umzubauen, um so das Stadtzentrum sowie den JR-Bahnhof besser anzuschließen, werden auch nicht weiter verfolgt.

Ein „Kotoden 1-Day Free Ticket" (nur Bahn, inkl. „Retro Train") kostet 1.230 Yen. Die „IruCa" IC Card des Unternehmens gilt in allen Bussen und Bahnen von *Kotoden*, andere IC Cards werden jedoch nicht akzeptiert.

liveried by line of operation: Kotohira Line (40 yellow cars), Nagao Line (20 green cars) and Shido Line (20 rose pink cars). The fleet also includes four 'retro' cars dating from the opening of the Kotohira Line in the 1920s which are scheduled for operation on selected dates.

A feature of the Kawaramachi station building, now occupied by the Flag department store, is that it was built with floor heights suitable to accommodate future elevated railway tracks as part of a plan to eliminate road crossings in central Takamatsu. However, this project appears to have been abandoned, as do proposals put forward by the Mayor of Takamatsu in 2007 for conversion of part of the railway within the city to light rail operation with possible extensions into the heart of the city centre and to the JR station.

A Kotoden 1-Day Free Ticket (rail only, including 'Retro Train') costs 1,230 Yen; the company's IruCa IC card is valid on the company's bus and rail services but other IC cards are not accepted.

Imabashi
– Shido Line 800-series (ex-Nagoya Subway) ▶ Kawaramachi

Kokubu River – Tosaden Kotsu #804 (1959) ► Ino (mit Ino-Fronttafel | *displaying Ino headboard*)

KOCHI

Die Hauptstadt der Präfektur Kochi ist eine Hafen- und Industriestadt (337.989 Einw., 309 km²) an der Pazifikküste von Shikoku. Das Stadtzentrum liegt etwa 7 km landeinwärts auf einer Fluss-Ebene an der Spitze der Urado-Bucht; im Norden ist die Stadt durch Berge begrenzt. Bevor die Dosan Line durch die zentrale Bergkette der Insel 1935 fertiggestellt wurde, waren Küstenschiffe das wichtigste Verkehrsmittel, um Kochi zu erreichen. Heute verbinden Dieseltriebwagen von *JR Shikoku* als *Limited Express* „Nanpu" Kochi mit Okayama (179,3 km, 2½ Std.) auf der Hauptinsel Honshu, von wo der *Sanyo Shinkansen* Verbindungen in andere Regionen Japans herstellt.

Ende des Zweiten Weltkriegs stark zerstört, wurde der zentrale Bereich mit breiten Straßen wiederaufgebaut, mit Straßenbahn und vier bis sechs Fahrspuren. Das Tram-

Kochi (population 337,989; 309 km²), capital of Kochi Prefecture, is a port and industrial city located on the Pacific coast of Shikoku. The city centre lies around 7 km inland on a river plain at the head of Urado Bay, bounded by mountains to the north. Coastal shipping provided the main means of access to Kochi until the Dosan Line was completed across the mountainous spine of the island in 1935. Today, JR Shikoku's DMU-operated limited-express 'Nanpu' service links Kochi with Okayama (179.3 km, 2h 30m) on the main island of Honshu from where the Sanyo Shinkansen provides connections to other parts of Japan.

As with many Japanese cities a large proportion of the built-up area was destroyed by bombing in 1945, the central area being re-built with wide roads accommodating tram tracks and four to six lanes of general traffic.

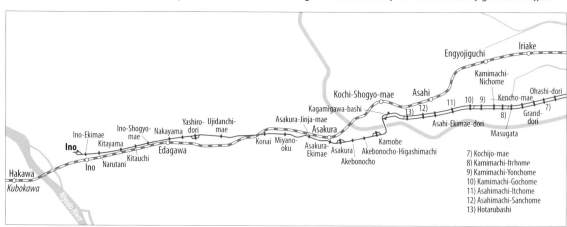

7) Kochijo-mae
8) Kamimachi-Itchome
9) Kamimachi-Yonchome
10) Kamimachi-Gochome
11) Asahimachi-Itchome
12) Asahimachi-Sanchome
13) Hotarubashi

Tosaden Kotsu
25.3 km, 76 Haltestellen | *stops*; 1067 mm, 600Vdc ⬆

Ino Line: 11.2 km
02-05-1904: Horizume – Grand-dori (0.9 km)
09-10-1906: Grand-dori – Asahimachi-Sanchome (2.2 km)
16-09-1907: Asahimachi-Sanchome – Konai (3.8 km)
07-11-1907: Edagawa – Ino (2.0 km)
20-02-1908: Konai – Edagawa (2.0 km)
31-10-1908: Horizume – Harimayabashi (0.3 km)

Gomen Line: 10.9 km
31-10-1908: Harimayabashi – Hoeicho (1.0 km)
30-10-1909: Hoeicho – Chiyoricho-Sanchome (1.4 km)
15-10-1910: Chiyoricho-Sanchome – Kako (3.1 km)
04-12-1910: Kako – Otsu [geschlossen | *closed*] (1.7 km)
27-01-1911: Otsu [geschlossen | *closed*] – Gomen-Nakamachi (3.2 km)
14-05-1911: Gomen-Nakamachi – Gomen-Higashimachi (0.2 km)
21-02-1925: Gomen-Higashimachi – Gomen-Machi (0.3 km)

Sambashi Line: 3.2 km
02-05-1904: Umenotsuji – Sambashi-Shako-mae (1.6 km)
07-04-1905: Sambashi-Shako-mae – Sambashidori-Gochome (0.2 km)
16-02-1928: Umenotsuji – Kochi-Ekimae (1.4 km)

Kochi-Ekimae – Tosaden #630 (neuer Anstrich & Logo – *new livery & logo*) ► Sambashidori-Gochome
(Oben | *Above*) JR Shikoku Dosan Line DMU

Netz besteht aus einer Nord-Süd- und einer Ost-West-Strecke, die äußeren Abschnitte der letzteren erstrecken sich bis in die Nachbarstädte Gomen und Ino. An den Vorortbahnhöfen an der nicht elektrifizierten, eingleisigen JR Dosan Line halten Regionalbahnen von *JR Shikoku* sowie von der *Tosa-Kuroshio Railway*. Die JR-Strecke verläuft im Zentrum von Kochi aufgeständert, einschließlich des JR-Bahnhofs Kochi, der im Jahr 2008 viergleisig ausgebaut und mit einem auffallenden Dach, dem „Whale Dome", versehen wurde.

The city is served by north-south and east-west tram routes, the outer sections of the latter extending into neighbouring communities of Gomen and Ino. Suburban stations on the un-electrified single-track JR Dosan Line are served by local services operated by JR Shikoku and by the third-sector Tosa-Kuroshio Railway. The JR line is elevated in central Kochi, as is JR Kochi station which was rebuilt in 2008 with four tracks covered by a distinctively designed overall roof nicknamed the 'Whale Dome'.

TOSADEN TRANSPORTATION   Tosaden Kotsu

Tosaden Kotsu ist ein öffentliches Unternehmen (50% Präfektur, 35% Stadt Kochi, 15% andere Kommunen), das im Jahr 2014 durch die Fusion des privaten Tram- und Busbetriebs *Tosa Electric Railway* (*Tosa Denki Tetsudo*) mit zwei privaten Busunternehmen entstand. Alle drei Unternehmen hatten nach anhaltend rückläufigen Fahrgastzahlen Insolvenz angemeldet. Das neue Unternehmen

Tosaden Kotsu is a publicly-owned company (Kochi Prefecture 50%, Kochi City 35% and other local authorities 15%) which was formed in 2014 by merging privately-owned tram and bus operator Tosa Electric Railway (Tosa Denki Tetsudo) with two private bus companies. All three companies were financially insolvent following a prolonged period of declining ridership. The new com-

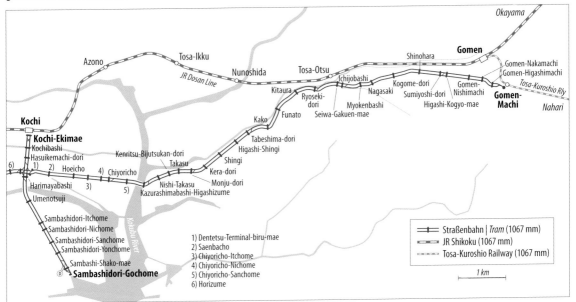

1) Dentetsu-Terminal-biru-mae
2) Saenbacho
3) Chiyoricho-Itchome
4) Chiyoricho-Nichome
5) Chiyoricho-Sanchome
6) Horizume

▬▬ Straßenbahn | *Tram* (1067 mm)
▬ ▬ JR Shikoku (1067 mm)
▭ ▭ Tosa-Kuroshio Railway (1067 mm)

1 km

Horizume – 'Heartram' 100-series ▶ Ryoseki-dori

wählte Grün und Orange als Firmenfarben, die für einen Neuanstrich einiger übernommener Straßenbahnwagen und Busse verwendet wurden. „Tosa" ist der ehemalige Name der Präfektur Kochi.

Straßenbahn
Das Netz umfasst eine 3,2 km lange Nord-Süd-Linie (**Sambashi Line**), die den JR-Bahnhof Kochi mit dem Hafen und dem nahegelegenen Straßenbahndepot verbindet. In der Innenstadt kreuzt am Knoten Harimayabashi die 22,1 km lange Ost-West-Linie (**Gomen & Ino Line**). Die Harimayabashi-Kreuzung hat zwar eine zweigleisige Verbindungskurve zwischen Nord- und Westast, aber die anderen Kurven verfügen jeweils nur über das linke Gleis, weshalb die Bahnen auf manchen Kursen, bei denen sie von einer Strecke auf die andere übergehen, über Gleiswechsel umsetzen müssen.

Bei der Nord-Süd-Linie handelt es sich um eine normale städtische Straßenbahn, zweigleisig abmarkiert in Straßenmittellage, teilweise heute aber auch mit Rasengleis. Die südliche Endstelle liegt eingleisig am Straßenrand, während sich die nördliche zweigleisig auf dem südlichen Vorplatz des JR-Bahnhofs Kochi befindet. Die übrigen Haltestellen haben in der Regel an Straßenkreuzungen versetzt angeordnete Bahnsteiginseln. Die Strecke überquert zwei Flussläufe.

Der zentrale Abschnitt der langen Ost-West-Linie ist auch zweigleisig in Straßenmittellage, doch das Bild ändert sich auf den äußeren Abschnitten. Im Westen sind die letzten 7 km zwischen Kagamigawa-bashi und Ino eingleisig mit vier Ausweichen (einschließlich der an der Endstelle). Die Trasse liegt teils in engen Straßen, aber meist in Randlage im Stil traditioneller Überlandbahnen. Das Token-System, mit dem die Einfahrt in die eingleisigen Abschnitte überwacht wird, verstärkt das altmodische Flair, genauso wie der Einstieg von der Straße an einigen Haltestellen. Im Osten ist die Strecke zweigleisig bis auf die eingleisige Endstelle Gomen-Machi. Die Straßenmittellage erstreckt sich bis Chiyoricho-Sanchome, danach wird der Kokubu-Fluss auf einer eigenen Brücke überquert. Der Rest der Trasse liegt am Straßenrand bis hin zu den Außenbereichen von Gomen – innerhalb dieser Stadt gibt es einen kurzen straßenbündigen Abschnitt, doch schließlich erreicht die Tram auf eigenem Gleiskörper die Endstation, die sich etwa 50 m vom Bahnhof Gomen-Machi der *Tosa-Kuroshio Railway* befindet.

pany has adopted a green and orange corporate identity which has been applied to some trams and buses of the former operators. Tosa is the former name of Kochi Prefecture.

Tramway
The company's tramway comprises a 3.2 km north-south line (**Sambashi Line**) connecting JR Kochi station with the port (and nearby tramway depot) and a 22.1 km east-west line (**Gomen/Ino Lines**) which intersect at Harimayabashi in the city centre. Harimayabashi junction has double-track curves between its north and west arms but its other three quadrants only have single-track left-hand curves, thus trams on some workings change direction via crossovers when switching between the two lines.

The north-south line is a standard urban tramway with double tracks running centrally along a wide street, mainly separated from other traffic by white lines but partly converted to grassed reservation. The southern terminus is a single-track roadside stub and the northern terminus is a modern double-track facility situated within the southern forecourt of JR Kochi station; intermediate stops generally have island platforms staggered either side of road junctions. The line passes over two river bridges.

The central section of the long east-west line also has centre-running double tracks on wide streets but the picture changes on the outer sections. To the west, the outer 7 km between Kagamigawa-bashi and the town of Ino is single-track with four passing loops (including the one at Ino terminus), partly on narrow streets but mainly at the roadside in traditional interurban fashion. The token system used to control access to the single-track sections reinforces the old-style feel of this line, as does the street-level boarding at some stops. To the east, the line is double-track throughout, apart from the single-track stub terminus at Gomen-Machi. Centre-running extends as far as Chiyoricho-Sanchome after which there is a reserved-track bridge across the Kokubu River followed by roadside running all the way to the outskirts of Gomen – within the town there is a short section of street-running followed by a section of private right-of-way leading to the terminus, which is located about 50m from Gomen-Machi station on the Tosa-Kuroshio Railway.

Kagamigawa-bashi – #2002
(1955, umgebaut | re-built 2004)
▶ Ryoseki-dori

Die Straßenbahnlinien sind nicht nummeriert. Normaler-weise herrscht auf der Nord-Süd-Linie ein 7-Minuten-Takt bei 16 Minuten Fahrzeit. Auf der Ost-West-Linie gibt es eine Reihe von sich überlappenden „Linien", wobei keine Bahn von einem Ende zum anderen durchfährt. Die Trams von Ino im Westen verkehren nur bis Monju-dori und die von Gomen-Machi nur bis Kagamigawa-bashi. Dazu kommen in Spitzenzeiten gelegentliche „ums Eck"-Fahrten zwischen Kochi-Ekimae und Masugata auf der Ino Line sowie Fahr-ten vom Depot zu verschiedenen Zielen auf der Ost-West-Linie und umgekehrt, was in manchen Fällen ein Umsetz-manöver an der Harimayabashi-Kreuzung erfordert.

Auf dem zentralen Abschnitt der Ost-West-Linie (Kaga-migawa-bashi – Monju-dori) fährt mindestens alle 5 Minu-ten eine Bahn, in der Morgenspitze bis zu alle 2½ Minuten. Die äußeren Endstellen Ino und Gomen-Machi erreichen tagsüber drei Bahnen pro Stunde, in Spitzenzeiten mehr. Bis ans Streckenende bzw. Asakura durchfahrende Wagen erkennt man an vorne angebrachten Fahrtzieltafeln.

Im engeren Stadtgebiet (gesamte Nord-Süd-Linie sowie im Abschnitt von Akebonocho-Higashimachi bis Kera-dori der Ost-West-Linie) gilt ein Einheitstarif von 200 Yen. Tageskarten gibt es für das Stadtgebiet (500 Yen) oder das gesamte Netz (1.000 Yen). Die regionale „DESUCA" IC Card kann in Straßenbahnen und lokalen Bussen verwendet werden, ist jedoch nicht mit anderen IC Cards kompatibel.

Der Fuhrpark besteht aus 62 Fahrzeugen, davon 52 Drehgestellwagen aus den Jahren 1950-59, die meist für die Straßenbahn Kochi gebaut wurden, einige in eigener Werkstatt, aber auch einige, die aus Shimonoseki oder Gifu übernommen wurden. Neuere Wagen sind hingegen eher selten: zwei Wagen von 1981; drei aus den 1950er Jahren, die 2000-04 neue Wagenkästen bekamen; und schließlich ein einzelner dreiteiliger Niederflurwagen „Heartram" von Alna Koki (17,9 m). Seit den 1990er Jahren hat das Unternehmen mehrere Straßenbahnen aus dem Ausland importiert und umgespurt, um so mehr Fahrgäste anzulocken – im Einsatz sind derzeit ein Wagen aus Oslo (Baujahr 1939), einer aus Lissabon (1947) und einer aus Graz (1949). Dazu kommt ein Nachbau von 1984 eines Wagens aus dem Jahr 1904, der wie die Importwagen im regelmäßigen Fahrbetrieb sowie bei besonderen Veran-staltungen zu sehen ist. Weitere ausländische Wagen sind abgestellt oder wurden weitergegeben – z. B. der ex-Stuttgart GT4 von 1964, der nun in Fukui zu Hause ist.

Asakura (Ausweiche | *passing loop*) – #617 ▶ Monju-dori

Tram routes are not numbered. The standard service pattern comprises a 7-minute frequency service over the full length of the north-south line taking 16 minutes from end-to-end and a series of overlapping services on the east-west line. There is no through service over the entire east-west line, trams from Ino in the west only run as far as Monju-dori and those from Gomen-Machi only as far as Kagamigawa-bashi. In addition, there is an occasional peak 'around the corner' service between Kochi-Ekimae and Masugata on the Ino Line together with depot workings to/from various destinations on the east-west line, some of which involve reversal at Harimayabashi.

On the core urban section of the east-west line (Kagamigawa-bashi – Monju-dori) the minimum headway is every 5 minutes for most of the day, increasing to every 2.5 minutes through Harimayabashi at the height of the morning peak. Frequencies are lower on the outer sections with a base service of 3tph to Ino and Gomen-Machi with some peak enhancement and short workings. Trams running to outer destinations (Gomen-Machi, Ino or Asakura) carry dash-mounted destination headboards.

A 200 Yen flat fare applies within the urban area (entire north-south line and Akebonocho-Higashimachi – Kera-dori section of east-west line) with stage fares beyond. Day tickets are available for the urban area (500 Yen) or the entire network (1,000 Yen). The com-pany's DESUCA IC card can be used on trams and local buses but is not compatible with other IC cards.

Rolling stock comprises 62 cars, 52 of which are bogie cars dating from 1950-59, mostly built for Kochi, some in the company's own workshops, but also including a few ex-Shimonoseki and Gifu cars. More modern stock is limited to two 1981-built cars, three 1950s cars re-bodied in 2000-04 and a single 17.9 m long three-section low-floor Alna Koki articulated tram branded 'Heartram'. Commencing in the 1990s, the company imported and re-gauged foreign trams to attract more business – those currently in the operational fleet are ex-Oslo (built 1939), ex-Lisbon (1947) and ex-Graz (1949) which together with a 1904-style historical replica car (built 1984) are used in regular service and for special events. Other foreign cars remain in store or have been disposed of – such as ex-Stuttgart GT4 from 1964 which is now in Fukui.

Depot – #208 (1952) neben | *alongside* ex-Graz (vorne | *front*) & ex-Lisboa (hinten | *rear*)

Teppocho – Iyotetsu #54 (1953) & Niederflur-Tw. | *low-floor* #2108 (2005) auf den Ringlinien 1 & 2 | *on circular routes 1 & 2*

MATSUYAMA

Matsuyama (516.459 Einw., 428,86 km²) ist die Hauptstadt der Präfektur Ehime und Shikokus größte Stadt. Sie liegt auf der Dogo-Ebene im Nordwesten der Insel mit Blick auf das Seto-Binnenmeer. Die Stadt ist ein wichtiges Handels- und Industriezentrum mit Hafenanlagen für Gütertransport und Passagierfähren. Zu den Touristenattraktionen gehören die Burg aus dem Jahr 1603 (umgebaut 1854) und Dogo-Onsen, eines der ältesten Thermalbäder Japans.

Die private *Iyo Railway* betreibt neben der städtischen Straßenbahn auch drei S-Bahn-Linien sowie Busse und eine Seilbahn. Die ersten lokalen Bahnstrecken wurden zwar bereits im späten 19. Jahrhundert gebaut, aber bis 1927 war Matsuyama nicht ans nationale Schienennetz angebunden und bis zur Eröffnung der Seto-Ohashi-Brücke 1988 gab es keinen direkten Schienenverkehr zur Hauptinsel Honshu. Trotz verbesserter Straßen-, Bahn- und Flugverbindungen ist Matsuyama weiterhin mit Fähren erreichbar, vor allem ab Hiroshima – in 70-80 Minuten mit dem Tragflügelboot (stündlich) bzw. in 2½ Stunden mit der Fähre (10 Mal pro Tag). *Limited Express* „Shiokaze"-Züge von *JR Shikoku* verbinden Matsuyama und Okayama (214 km) über die größtenteils eingleisige Yosan Line und die Seto-Ohashi Line in 2 Stunden 40 Minuten.

Matsuyama (population 516,459; 428.86 km²) is capital of Ehime Prefecture and Shikoku's largest city. It is situated on the Dogo plain in the north-west of the island facing the Seto Inland Sea. The city is an important commercial and industrial centre with port facilities handling cargo and passenger ferries; tourist attractions include the city's hilltop castle dating from 1603 (re-built 1854) and Dogo-Onsen, one of Japan's oldest hot spring resorts.

The privately-owned Iyo Railway operates urban trams and three suburban rail lines as well as buses and an aerial ropeway. The first local rail lines were built in the late 19th century but Matsuyama was not connected to the national rail network until 1927 and there was no direct rail service to the main island of Honshu until the Seto-Ohashi Bridge opened in 1988. Today, improved road, rail and air links have reduced the role of sea transport but Matsuyama is still served by various ferry services, notably to/from Hiroshima – 70-80 minutes by hydrofoil (hourly) and 2h 30min by ferry (10 per day). JR Shikoku's 'Shiokaze' limited express services link Matsuyama and Okayama (214 km) via the mainly single-track Yosan Line and the Seto-Ohashi Line in 2h 40min.

郊外電車運賃表 Fare Table

460		360	300	260	210	210	160	160	●	160		160	210	210	260	300	360	460	520	520	520

160 / 松山市

高浜線 *Takahama Line*
横河原線 *Yokogawara Line*
郡中線 *Gunchu Line*

小児運賃〈小学生の方〉
●大人運賃の半額とし、10円未満は切り上げます。
●松山観光港までは230円です。

IYOTETSU

Iyotetsu Tram
9.0 km, 27 Haltestellen | *stops*; 1067mm, 600Vdc ↑

22-08-1895: Komachi – Kiyacho (1.1 km)
01-09-1911: Dogo-Onsen – Hommachi-San (4.1 km)
03-04-1927: Kami-Ichiman – Kiyacho (1.7 km)
01-05-1936: Nishi-Horibata – Komachi (1.4 km)
25-03-1947: Minami-Horibata – Matsuyama-shi-Eki (0.4 km)
01-07-1948: Hommachi-San – Hommachi-Yon (0.3 km)
01-02-1962: Hommachi-Yon – Hommachi-Roku (0.6 km)

Matsuyama-shi-Eki > Minami-Horibata – Iyotetsu-Niederflur-Tw. | *low-floor cars* ▶ Ring

Okaido – #61 (1957) Line 5 ▶ JR Matsuyama-Ekimae

IYO RAILWAY   Iyo Tetsudo – 'Iyotetsu'

Die *Iyo Railway*, benannt nach der ehemaligen Provinz Iyo, ist ein traditionsreiches Unternehmen, das bereits 1888 die erste Eisenbahnlinie auf der Insel Shikoku zwischen Matsuyama und Mitsu eröffnete und später nach Übernahme anderer Firmen zum wichtigsten Verkehrsbetrieb mit Straßenbahn, Bus und Vorortbahn in und um Matsuyama wurde. *Iyo Railway* gehört zur *Iyo Group*, die auch in den Bereichen Einzelhandel, Immobilien, Anlagenmanagement, Schifffahrt und Tourismus tätig ist. Ein neues Corporate Image wurde 2015 eingeführt, einige Fahrzeuge verkehren seither in Orange mit weißem *Iyotetsu*-Logo.

Die IC Card des Unternehmens gilt in den eigenen Straßenbahnen, S-Bahnen und Bussen, ist aber nicht Teil des landesweiten Kartensystems. Zur Erkundung des Netzes empfiehlt sich ein „City Tram Day Ticket" (1 Tag - 500 Yen; 2 Tage - 800 Yen) oder ein „All Iyotetsu Ticket" (Straßenbahn/S-Bahn/Bus: 1 Tag - 1.500 Yen, 2 Tage - 2.000 Yen).

Straßenbahn

Matsuyamas erste Lokalbahnen waren dampfbetriebene Strecken mit 762-mm-Spurweite, die zwischen 1888 und 1899 errichtet wurden und heute größtenteils Bestandteil des S-Bahn-Netzes von *Iyotetsu* sind. Elektrische Straßenbahnen tauchten 1911 auf, als *Iyotetsu* zwei ehemalige Strecken der *Dogo Railway* zwischen Matsuyama und dem nahe gelegenen Kurort Dogo-Onsen elektrifizierte und auf 1067 mm umspurte. Noch im selben Jahr nahm

Iyo Railway, named after the former Iyo Province, is a long-established company which opened Shikoku's first railway between Matsuyama and Mitsu in 1888, subsequently merging with other companies to become the main provider of public transport services (tram, bus and local rail) in and around Matsuyama. It lies at the centre of the Iyo Group which has extensive commercial interests including retailing, real estate, facilities management, shipping and tourism. A new corporate image was adopted in 2015, since when some trams, trains and buses have appeared in all-over orange livery with white Iyotetsu logos.

The company's IC card is valid on its tram, rail and bus services but is not part of the nationwide interoperability scheme. Ride-at-will tickets are available: City Tram Day Ticket (1-day - 500 Yen; 2-days - 800 Yen); All Iyotetsu Ticket (tram/rail/local bus: 1-day - 1,500 Yen; 2-days - 2,000 Yen).

Tramway

Matsuyama's first local railways were steam-operated 762 mm gauge lines built between 1888 and 1899 which are now mostly incorporated into Iyotetsu's suburban network. Electric trams appeared in 1911 when Iyotetsu electrified, and re-gauged to 1067 mm, two ex-Dogo Railway lines linking Matsuyama and the nearby hot spring resort of Dogo-Onsen. Later the same year, Matsuyama Electric Tramway (Matsuyama Denki Kido) opened a

Sekijuji-Byoin-mae (Red Cross Hospital)

Dogo-Onsen – 2100-series - Lines 3 & 6

die *Matsuyama Electric Tramway* (*Matsuyama Denki Kido*) eine Strecke mit 1435-mm-Spurweite zwischen Matsuyama und Dogo-Onsen in Betrieb; beide Bahnen konkurrierten bis zur Fusion (als *Iyotetsu*) im Jahr 1921. Ein Großteil des ehemaligen *Dogo Railway*-Netzes wurde geschlossen (der historische Bahnhof in Dogo-Onsen von 1895 wird noch heute als Straßenbahnendstelle genutzt) und die 1435-mm-Strecke von Matsuyama nach Dogo-Onsen wurde auf 1067 mm umgebaut. Eine Ringlinie wurde bis 1936 fertiggestellt und mit zwei kurzen Nachkriegserweiterungen, bis Matsuyama-shi-Eki (Bahnhof Matsuyama City) und Hommachi-Roku, war das gegenwärtige Netz 1962 vollständig.

Auf dem heutigen Straßenbahnnetz verkehren offiziell zwar fünf Linien, die Gesamtstreckenlänge beträgt jedoch lediglich 9,6 km; das Netz liegt innerhalb eines überschaubaren Gebiets von 3 km (Ost-West) mal 2 km (Nord-Süd). Es gibt 27 nummerierte Haltestellen. Der Abschnitt zwischen JR Matsuyama-Ekimae und Dogo-Onsen ist zweigleisig, ebenso der Abzweig zum Bahnhof Matsuyama City, dem Knoten des Iyotetsu-S-Bahn-Netzes. Der westliche und nördliche Abschnitt der Ringlinie sowie der Abzweig bis Hommachi-Roku sind hingegen eingleisig. Der Großteil

1435 mm gauge tramway between Matsuyama and Dogo-Onsen and competition ensued until the two companies merged (as Iyotetsu) in 1921. A period of rationalisation followed; most of the ex-Dogo Railway network was closed (though the historic 1895-built Dogo-Onsen station is still used as a tramway terminus today) and the 1435 mm Matsuyama — Dogo-Onsen line was re-gauged to 1067 mm. A new loop line was completed by 1936 and two short post-war extensions, to Matsuyama-shi-Eki (Matsuyama City Station) and Hommachi-Roku, completed the current network by 1962.

The present-day tramway officially comprises five separate lines but is a very compact system, 9.6 km in length and contained within an area only 3 km (east-west) by 2 km (north-south). There are 27 numbered stops. The section between JR Matsuyama-Ekimae and Dogo-Onsen is double-tracked as is the spur to Matsuyama City Station, the hub of Iyotetsu's suburban network; the western and northern sides of the loop line and the branch to Hommachi-Roku are single-tracked. Most of the network is conventional on-street tramway centrally placed on wide streets but the northern section of the loop, serving inner suburbs and the university

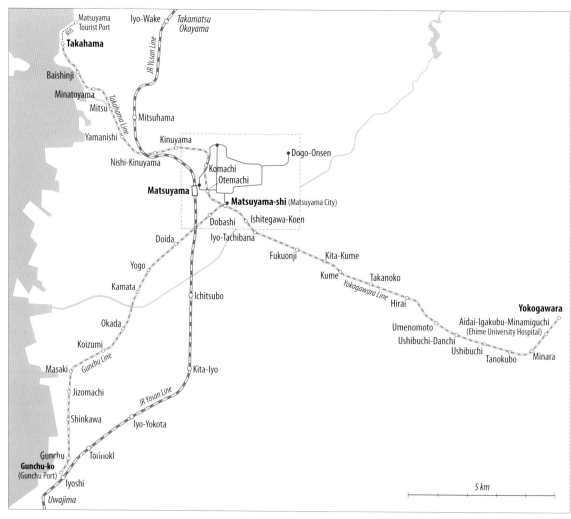

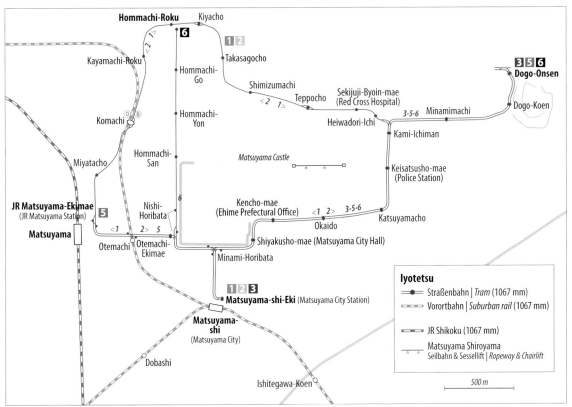

Hommachi-Roku
Kiyacho
Kayamachi-Roku
Hommachi-Go
Takasagocho
Shimizumachi
Teppocho
Sekijuji-Byoin-mae
(Red Cross Hospital)
Dogo-Onsen
Dogo-Koen
Minamimachi
Heiwadori-Ichi
Kami-Ichiman
Komachi
Hommachi-Yon
Miyatacho
Hommachi-San
Matsuyama Castle
Keisatsusho-mae
(Police Station)
JR Matsuyama-Ekimae
(JR Matsuyama Station)
Nishi-Horibata
Kencho-mae
(Ehime Prefectural Office)
Okaido
Katsuyamacho
Matsuyama
Otemachi
Otemachi-Ekimae
Shiyakusho-mae (Matsuyama City Hall)
Minami-Horibata
Matsuyama-shi-Eki (Matsuyama City Station)
Matsuyama-shi
(Matsuyama City)
Dobashi
Ishitegawa-Koen

Iyotetsu

- ●━━● Straßenbahn | *Tram* (1067 mm)
- ▭┄┄▭ Vorortbahn | *Suburban rail* (1067 mm)
- ▭━━▭ JR Shikoku (1067 mm)
- Matsuyama Shiroyama
  Seilbahn & Sessellift | *Ropeway & Chairlift*

500 m

Matsuyama-shi-Eki – Niederflur-Tw. | *low-floor car* #2109 (Alna Koki - Little Dancer Type 'S') ▶ Dogo-Onsen

Matsuyama-shi-Eki > Minami-Horibata – 'Botchan Ressha' ▶ Matsuyama-shi-Eki

des Netzes ist straßenbündig in Mittellage breiter Straßen, nur der nördliche Teil der Ringlinie, der innere Vorstädte sowie das Universitätsviertel nördlich der Burg erschließt, verläuft auf schmalem eigenem Gleiskörper quer durch die Bebauung. Ein kurzer Abschnitt auf eigenem Gleiskörper ist auch am Endpunkt Dogo-Onsen vorhanden. An zwei Stellen kreuzt die Straßenbahn die Takahama Line der S-Bahn niveaugleich – bei Otemachi an einem konventionellen Bahnübergang und bei Komachi, wo die Straßenbahn die Eisenbahngleise diagonal überquert. Am gemeinsamen Bahnhof Komachi befindet sich sowohl das Tram- als auch das Bahndepot von *Iyotetsu*. Zwischen der Hommachi Line und der Ringlinie gibt es im Bereich Hommachi-Roku keine Gleisverbindung.

Die fünf Routen werden durch Nummern gekennzeichnet. Die Linien 1 (im Uhrzeigersinn) und 2 (gegen den Uhrzeigersinn) verkehren ab/bis Matsuyama City Station und benötigen für die 7 km lange Ringstrecke 35 Minuten. Die Linien 3, 5 und 6 beginnen in Dogo-Onsen und teilen sich den Weg bis Minami-Horibata, wo die Linie 3 zur Matsuyama City Station abzweigt, während die Linien 5 und 6 weiter zum JR-Bahnhof Matsuyama bzw. bis Hommachi-Roku führen. Die Linien 1, 2, 3 und 5 verkehren alle 10 Minuten und die Linie 6 alle 30 Minuten.

Die Tram-Flotte besteht aus 38 Fahrzeugen: 23 Moha-Drehgestellwagen der Serie 50 von 1951-63, fünf Moha-Wagen der Serie 2000 (Baujahr 1964, ex Kyoto) sowie 10 niederflurigen Moha-Drehgestellwagen der Serie 2100 aus den Jahren 2002-07. Letztere fallen durch ihr Design und ihre geringe Kapazität auf, nur 47 Passagiere mit 20 Sitzplätzen – ältere Wagen befördern rund 80 Personen. Es wird hinten eingestiegen und vorne ausgestiegen. Der Einzelfahrpreis beträgt 160 Yen.

Zusätzliche Abwechslung bereiten die zwei „Botchan Ressha"-Züge mit nachgebauten Dampflokomotiven (mit Dieselantrieb und Dampfeffekten) und offenen Waggons, die regelmäßig zwischen Matsuyama (JR- oder City-Bahnhof) und Dogo-Onsen verkehren; die originalen Vorbilder der Loks wurden für die ursprüngliche 762-mm-Bahn aus Deutschland importiert.

district to the north of the castle, is on narrow private right-of-way squeezed between adjoining buildings. There is also a short section of private right-of-way at Dogo-Onsen terminus and there are two instances where the tramway crosses the suburban Takahama Line at grade – at Otemachi, where there is a road/rail level crossing, and at Komachi, where the reserved-track tramway crosses the railway alignment. Trams and suburban trains share Komachi station, which is also the location of the company's tram and rail depots. There is no track connection between the Hommachi Line and the loop line at Hommachi-Roku.

Five numbered routes are operated - routes 1 (clockwise) and 2 (anti-clockwise) run to/from Matsuyama City Station around the loop line taking 35 minutes for the 7.0 km round trip. Routes 3, 5 and 6 commence at Dogo-Onsen and provide a combined service to Minami-Horibata, with route 3 terminating at Matsuyama City Station and routes 5 and 6 continuing to JR Matsuyama-Ekimae and Hommachi-Roku respectively. Routes 1, 2, 3 and 5 run every 10 minutes and route 6 every 30 minutes.

The regular tramway fleet comprises 38 cars: Moha 50-series bogie cars dating from 1951-63 (23 cars), Moha 2000-series 1964 ex-Kyoto (5 cars) and Moha 2100-series low-floor bogie cars (10 cars) dating from 2002-07. The latter are notable for their distinctive design and low capacity — only 47 passengers including 20 seated — which compares with an overall capacity of around 80 for the older cars. Trams are rear entrance/front exit with a 160 Yen flat fare.

Additional variety comes in the form of two 'Botchan Ressha' tourist trains with replica steam locomotives (diesel-powered) and balcony carriages; the design of the locomotives is based on those imported from Germany to operate Matsuyama's original 762 mm gauge lines. The trains, which come complete with steam engine sound effects, operate on the tram network between Matsuyama (either JR or City stations) and Dogo-Onsen.

Matsuyama-shi-Eki – 'Botchan Ressha'
- Umsetzen mit Muskelkraft | *manual shunting*

Minami-Horibata – #74 - Line 2 ▶ Matsuyama-shi-Eki

Dogo-Onsen – #2105 Line 5 ▶ JR Matsuyama-Ekimae

Matsuyama-shi-Eki – #2006 (ex-Kyoto) - Line 3

#61 (1957)

Matsuyama-shi – Iyotetsu 3000-series (ex-Keio) ▶ Takahama

S-Bahn

Alle drei *Iyotetsu*-S-Bahn-Linien entstanden ursprünglich als eingleisige 762-mm-Dampfeisenbahnen, die in den 1930er Jahren auf 1067 mm umgespurt wurden. Die Takahama Line wurde zwischen Matsuyama-shi (Matsuyama City) und Baishinji (8,2 km) zweigleisig ausgebaut und 1931 elektrifiziert. Die beiden anderen Linien, die weiterhin durchweg eingleisig sind, wurden zwar auch in den 1930er Jahren umgespurt, aber erst 1950 (Gunchu Line) bzw. 1967 (Yokgawara Line) elektrifiziert. Die Takahama Line hat wie die städtische Straßenbahn eine Spannung von 600 V DC, da sie diese zweimal niveaugleich kreuzt. Die beiden anderen Linien verwenden 750 V DC.

Matsuyama City ist die Drehscheibe des S-Bahn-, Tram- und Busverkehrs von *Iyotetsu*; das Bahnhofsgebäude umfasst ein Kaufhaus und eine unterirdische Einkaufspassage. Zwei Durchgangsgleise werden von der Takahama und Yokogawara Line verwendet, die seit 1981 fahrplanmäßig miteinander verknüpft sind; der Gunchu Line steht ein Stumpfgleis zur Verfügung. Die S-Bahn fährt auf allen Linien alle 15 Minuten mit Halt an allen Stationen.

Die S-Bahn erschließt das einst ländliche Hinterland von Matsuyama, wohin sich die Vorstädte immer weiter ausdehnen. Die Takahama Line endet 0,75 km vor dem Fährhafen (für Fähren nach Hiroshima), weshalb eine Anschluss-Buslinie eingerichtet wurde.

Suburban Rail

All three of Iyotetsu's suburban rail lines started life as single-track 762 mm gauge steam railways which were re-gauged to 1067 mm in the 1930s. The Takahama Line was double-tracked between Matsuyama-shi (Matsuyama City) and Baishinji (8.2 km) and electrified in 1931; the other two lines, which remain single-track throughout, were also re-gauged in the 1930s but were not electrified until 1950 (Gunchu Line) and 1967 (Yokgawara Line). The Takahama Line has the same 600Vdc voltage as the urban tramway which it crosses at grade at two locations; the other lines use 750Vdc.

Matsuyama City is the hub of the rail network and a tram/bus interchange; the station building incorporates a department store and underground shopping arcade. Two through tracks are used by Takahama/Yokogawara Line services which, since 1981, have been linked and run through from one line to the other; Gunchu Line services use a single terminating track. Trains run every 15 minutes on each line and call at all stations.

The network serves Matsuyama's formerly rural hinterland which is now increasingly suburbanised. The Takahama Line terminus is 0.75 km from Matsuyama Tourist Port (for ferries to Hiroshima), sufficiently distant to require a connecting bus service.

Iyotetsu Vorortbahn | *Suburban rail*
3 Linien | *lines*, 33.9 km, 35 Bahnhöfe | *stations*

Takahama Line
Takahama (IY01) – Matsuyama-shi (IY10)
9.4 km, 10 Bahnhöfe | *stations*; 1067 mm, 600Vdc ⊕
+ Bus Takahama (IY01) – Matsuyama Tourist Port (IY00)

28-10-1888: Matsuyama-shi – Mitsu (6.4 km)
01-05-1892: Mitsu – Takahama (2.6 km)
10-01-1905: Takahama verschoben | *relocated* (0.4 km)

Yokogawara Line
Matsuyama-shi (IY10) – Yokogawara (IY24)
13.2 km, 15 Bahnhöfe | *stations*; 1067 mm, 750Vdc ⊕

07-05-1893: Matsuyama-shi – Hirai (6.9 km)
04-10-1899: Hirai – Yokogawara (6.3 km)

Gunchu Line
Matsuyama-shi (IY10) – Gunchu-ko (IY35)
11.3 km, 12 Bahnhöfe | *stations*; 1067 mm, 750Vdc ⊕

04-07-1896: Matsuyama-shi – Gunchu-ko (11.3 km)

Komachi - 700-series (ex-Keio) ▶ Yokogawara
(Rechts | *Right*) Wagen der Linie 1 wartet darauf, die Eisenbahngleise kreuzen zu können | *Route 1 tram waiting to cross railway tracks.*

Die *Iyotetsu*-S-Bahn hat insgesamt 53 Elektrotrieb-wagen, vorwiegend als 3-Wagen-Einheiten, jedoch auch vier als 2-Wagen-Einheiten. Eine 2-Wagen-Einheit (Baureihe 610) wurde 1995 für *Iyotetsu* neu gebaut, alle anderen stammen von *Keio* (Tokyo) aus den 1960ern.

Rolling stock comprises 53 EMU cars mainly in 3-car formation but including four 2-car sets. One 2-car set (610-series) was built new for Iyotetsu in 1995 but all others are ex-Keio (Tokyo) dating from the 1960s.

Ropeway (Seilbahn | *Aerial Cable Car*)

Iyotetsu betreibt im Auftrag der Stadt Matsuyama die Seilbahn *Matsuyama Shiroyama Ropeway* sowie den parallelen Sessellift. Die Luftseilbahn von 1955 führt zur Burg von Matsuyama. Auf einer Länge von 327 m überwindet sie 62 m. Die beiden Gondeln haben jeweils eine Kapazität von 51 Passagieren. Die Fahrkarten sind entweder für die Seilbahn oder für den Sessellift, der 1966 eröffnet wurde, gültig. Die Fahrtzeit beträgt 3 Minuten mit der Seilbahn oder 6 Minuten mit dem Sessellift.

Iyotetsu operates the Matsuyama Shiroyama Ropeway and parallel chairlift on behalf of the City of Matsuyama. The two-station aerial ropeway, built in 1955, provides access to Matsuyama Castle. It has an overall length of 327 m and height difference of 62 m. The two gondolas each have a capacity of 51 passengers. Tickets are valid for either the ropeway or the chairlift, which opened in 1966. Journey time is 3 minutes by ropeway or 6 minutes by chairlift.

Sessellift | *Chairlift*

Seilbahn | *Ropeway*

Oroku – Yui Rail ▶ Shuri   RS

NAHA

Naha (321.467 Einw., 39,57 km²) ist die Hauptstadt von Okinawa, der südlichsten Präfektur Japans, etwa 650 km südlich der Insel Kyushu gelegen. Die Präfektur umfasst den südlichen Teil der Ryukyu-Inselkette, die sich Richtung Taiwan erstreckt. Das tropische Klima, die Strände und Korallenriffe machen die Inselgruppe zu einem vor allem bei Japanern beliebten Reiseziel. Naha liegt mit Blick auf das Ostchinesische Meer an der Südspitze der Insel Okinawa, der größten der Kette. Es ist das wirtschaftliche Zentrum der Präfektur und rund 800.000 der 1,4 Mio. Einwohner leben im Ballungsraum von Naha. Es ist auch der regionale Verkehrsknotenpunkt mit Flügen und Fähren in andere Teile von Okinawa, Japan und Asien. Die häufig durchgeführten Flüge nach Tokyo dauern etwa 2 Stunden 35 Minuten (1.560 km), direkte Flüge gibt es auch zu den meisten anderen großen japanischen Städten. Von 1945 bis zur Rückgabe an Japan 1972 stand Okinawa unter US-Verwaltung; auch heute werden noch rund 20% der Landfläche der Insel Okinawa von US-Militärbasen genutzt. Die einzige Bahnlinie in der Präfektur ist die Einschienenbahn Yui Rail in Naha.

Naha (population 321,467; 39.57 km²) is the capital of Okinawa, the southernmost prefecture of Japan located about 650 km south of Kyushu, the southernmost of Japan's main islands. The prefecture encompasses the southern part of the Ryukyu chain of islands extending towards Taiwan, and its tropical climate, beaches and coral reefs make it a tourist destination, mainly attracting Japanese visitors. Naha is situated at the southern end of Okinawa Island, the largest in the chain, facing the East China Sea; it is the main economic centre of the prefecture with around 800,000 of its 1.4 million population living in the city region. It is also the regional transportation hub with flights and ferries to other parts of Okinawa, Japan and Asia. Frequent Tokyo flights take around 2h 35m (1,560 km) and direct flights are available to most other large Japanese cities. Okinawa was governed by the U.S.A. from 1945 until returned to Japan in 1972; however, around 20% of the land area of Okinawa Island remains occupied by U.S. military bases. The only rail line in the prefecture is the Yui Rail monorail in Naha.

Yui Rail
Naha-Kuko (Airport) (1) — Shuri (15)
12.9 km, 15 Bahnhöfe | *stations*; 1500Vdc; Einschienenbahn | *straddle monorail*

10-08-2003: Naha-Kuko (Airport) – Shuri (12.9 km)

Tsubogawa – Yui Rail ▶ Shuri   *RS*

YUI RAIL   Okinawa Toshi Monorail – Okinawa Urban Monorail

Vor dem Zweiten Weltkrieg gab es in Naha kurzzeitig eine elektrische Straßenbahn (*Okinawa Denki Kido*, 1914-33), außerdem drei Bahnstrecken mit 762-mm-Spurweite in andere Teile der Insel, die von der *Okinawa Prefectural Railway* mit Dampf bzw. Diesel betrieben wurden. Jedoch wurde Naha während der Schlacht von Okinawa (1945) weitgehend zerstört und das Bahnnetz nach dem Krieg nicht wiederhergestellt, denn die US-Behörden gaben dem Straßenbau größere Priorität. Nach der Rückgabe der Insel an Japan im Jahr 1972 wurden bald Pläne für eine Monorail

Prior to World War II Naha was served by a short-lived electric tramway (Okinawa Denki Kido, 1914-33) and linked to other parts of the island by three 762 mm gauge steam/diesel operated lines run by the Okinawa Prefectural Railway. However, Naha was largely destroyed during the Battle of Okinawa (1945) and its rail network was not reinstated after the war, greater priority being given to road construction by the U.S. authorities. Following the resumption of Japanese control in 1972, plans for a monorail were soon

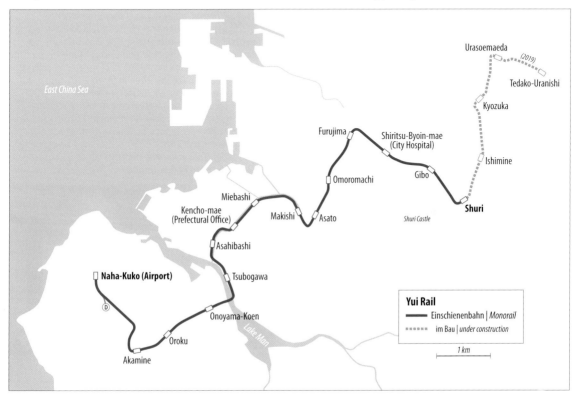

Omoromachi – Yui Rail ▶ Shuri

RS

Kencho-mae (Prefectural Office)

RS

vorangetrieben, um dem zunehmenden Straßenverkehr in Naha entgegenzuwirken. Das Unternehmen *Okinawa Urban Monorail* (ca. 80% im Besitz von der Präfektur Okinawa, Naha City und Okinawa Development Finance Corporation) wurde 1982 gegründet, aber der Bau begann erst 1996, so dass die Strecke erst 2003 eröffnet werden konnte.

Die als „Yui Rail" bekannte Einschienenbahn („Yui" bedeutet „Zusammenarbeit" im Dialekt von Okinawa) verbindet auf einer Länge von 12,9 km den Flughafen von Naha im Westen mit dem Stadtzentrum und den Vororten im Osten der Stadt. Die doppelspurige Trasse verläuft zwischen 8 und 20 Metern über dem Boden, meist getragen von einzelnen Betonpfeilern. Der Großteil der Strecke folgt breiten Straßen, doch im Stadtzentrum schwebt die Bahn entlang von Kanälen, wodurch die Kokusai-dori [Internationale Straße], die eher schmale Haupteinkaufsstraße, umfahren wird; an beiden Enden liegen jedoch Monorail-Stationen, nämlich Kencho-mae (Prefectural Office) und Makishi. Die steigungsreiche Strecke bietet eine gute Aussicht und einen langen Anstieg bis zur östlichen Endstation Shuri. In deren Nähe liegt die Burg Shuri, der rekonstruierte Königspalast des ehemaligen Ryukyu-Reichs aus dem 14. Jahrhundert.

2013 begann der Bau einer 4,1 km langen Verlängerung mit vier Stationen in den nordöstlichen Vororten bis Tedako-Uranishi in der benachbarten Stadt Urasoe, wo eine Park-&-Ride-Anlage eingerichtet wird, um Autofahrer vom nahen Okinawa Expressway zum Umsteigen einzuladen. Die Verlängerung soll 2019 eröffnet werden.

developed to address increasing road congestion in Naha. Third-sector company, Okinawa Urban Monorail (approximately 80% owned by Okinawa Prefecture, Naha City and Okinawa Development Finance Corporation), was established in 1982 but it was not until 1996 that construction eventually commenced, and 2003 by the time the line opened.

Known as Yui Rail (meaning 'mutual cooperation' in Okinawan dialect), the 12.9 km straddle-type monorail links Naha Airport in the west with the city centre and suburban areas to the east of the city. The dual beam line is entirely elevated between 8 and 20 metres above ground and is mainly supported on single concrete pillars. Most of the line runs above dual-carriageway roads but within the city centre the line runs alongside a series of canals, avoiding Kokusai-dori (International Street), the rather narrow main shopping street, but with stations at either end, namely Kencho-mae (Prefectural Office) and Makishi. The line offers good views and an undulating ride and a long climb up to the eastern terminus at Shuri, which is close to the tourist attraction of Shuri Castle, the restored 14th century royal palace of the former Ryukyu Kingdom.

In 2013 construction started on a 4.1 km extension with four stations which will serve north-eastern suburbs beyond Shuri and terminate at Tedako-Uranishi in neighbouring Urasoe City. This station is designed to attract park-and-ride users from the nearby Okinawa Expressway. The extension is due to open in 2019.

Asato

RS

Yui Rail 1000-series

RS

Kencho-mae (Prefectural Office) – Yui Rail ▶ Shuri

Alle Stationen befinden sich in Hochlage und haben entweder Seiten- oder Mittelbahnsteige, die lang genug für vier Wagen sind; alle Bahnsteige sind mit halbhohen Bahnsteigtüren ausgestattet. Die Stationen sind nummeriert und die Farbschattierung der Schilder geht von Blau (Naha-Kuko) über Grün und Orange bis Rot (Shuri), jeweils ergänzt durch ein traditionelles Muster aus Okinawa. Die wichtigsten Stationen sind Naha-Kuko [Flughafen], Kencho-mae [Präfekturamt] im Stadtzentrum und Omoromachi, wo auf dem Gelände einer ehemaligen Siedlung des US-Militärs ein modernes Einkaufszentrum sowie ein Museumskomplex entstanden sind.

Die 14 eingesetzten Zwei-Wagen-Einheiten der Serie 1000 wurden von Hitachi geliefert, 13 im Jahr 2003 und eine 2016, wobei jeder Doppelwagen eine Kapazität von 165 Passagieren (65 Sitzplätze) aufweist. Die Züge werden von einem Fahrer mit LZB- und ATC-Unterstützung manuell gesteuert. Die Höchstgeschwindigkeit beträgt 65 km/h.

Für Einzelfahrten gilt ein Entfernungstarif, aber auch Tageskarten werden angeboten (1 Tag - 700 Yen; 2 Tage - 1.200 Yen). Es handelt sich um Papiertickets mit einem QR-Code, der an den Zugangssperren gescannt werden muss. Die IC Card „OKICA" kann man bei Yui Rail und in den lokalen Bussen nutzen, sie gehört aber nicht zum landesweiten Kartensystem.

Tagsüber herrscht ein 10-Minuten-Takt mit zusätzlichen Fahrten in den Spitzenzeiten. Die Züge fahren stets auf der Gesamtstrecke und benötigen dafür 27 Minuten. Das Depot befindet sich in der Nähe des Flughafens.

All stations are elevated with either side or island platforms which are long enough for eventual 4-car operation; platforms have half-height safety gates. There is a station numbering system and station nameboards progress from blue (Naha Airport) through shades of green and orange to red (Shuri), each decorated with a distinctive Okinawan pattern. The busiest stations are Naha-Kuko (Airport), Kencho-mae (Prefectural Office) in the city centre and Omoromachi which serves a modern commercial, shopping and museum complex built on a former U.S. military housing site.

Rolling stock comprises 14 two-car 1000-series sets built by Hitachi, 13 sets dating from 2003 and 1 set from 2016, each set having an overall capacity of 165 passengers (65 seated). Trains are one-person operated, manually driven with cab signalling and ATC. Maximum speed is 65 km/h.

Stage fares apply with 1 and 2-day tickets (700/1200 Yen) available. Paper tickets carry QR codes which have to be scanned to pass through ticket gates. The OKICA IC card is valid on Yui Rail and local buses but is not part of the nationwide inter-operability scheme.

A 10-minute frequency service is operated with some peak enhancement. All trains run the full length of line calling at all stations with a journey time of 27 minutes. The depot is situated near to Naha-Kuko (Airport) station.

⑤ Tsubogawa
壺川
つぼがわ

■ METROS & TRAMS IN JAPAN

Sapporo Transport Museum – *Diesel tram #D1041 (Tokyu Car, 1964)* & 4. U-Bahn-Testwagen | *4th experimental rapid transit car*

QUELLEN UND VERWEISE

Bei der Vorbereitung dieser Buchreihe haben wir zahlreiche japanisch- und englischsprachige Bücher, Zeitschriften, Netzpläne, Fahrpläne und Websites konsultiert sowie persönlich vor Ort recherchiert. Eine Liste englisch- und deutschsprachiger Quellen und Verweise haben wir bereits in Band 1 veröffentlicht. Zusätzlich möchten wir noch zwei Publikationen erwähnen, die vor allem für diejenigen interessant sein könnten, die mehr über die in diesem Band behandelten Betriebe wissen wollen:

SOURCES AND REFERENCES

In preparing this series of books we have consulted a wide range of Japanese and English language books, magazines, maps, timetables and websites as well as undertaking personal research. A list of English and German language sources and references appears in Volume 1. In addition, the following two publications are recommended for those who may wish to study the systems covered in this volume in more depth:

- *Demery, Forty, DeGroote & Higgins:* **Electric Railways of Japan Vol 2 Central Japan**
    – *1985, Light Rail Transit Association, ISBN 0-948106-02-6*

- *Demery, Forty, DeGroote & Higgins:* **Electric Railways of Japan Vol 3 Western Japan**
    – *1997, Light Rail Transit Association, ISBN 0-948106-20-4*

Die meisten in diesem Buch enthaltenen Verkehrsbetriebe haben Websites (siehe nächste Seite), auf denen man meist auch Informationen in englischer Sprache findet. Für Fahrpläne und Bahnverbindungen empfehlen wir
www.hyperdia.com/en

Most operators covered in this book maintain websites (see next page) which usually contain at least some information in English. Timetable and journey planning information can be obtained in English at
www.hyperdia.com/en

Die in diesem Buch angegebenen Fahrgastzahlen beziehen sich auf das Jahr 2015 und stammen von der „Japan Subway Association" (www.jametro.or.jp).

The ridership figures quoted are for 2015 and are sourced from the Japan Subway Association (www.jametro.or.jp).

Nagoya City Science Museum (ex-Nagoya #1401 von | *from* 1936)

Meiji-Mura #1 (ex-Kyoto – Bj. 1911, rekonstruiert im Stil von 1895
    - *built in 1911, restored to 1895-appearance*)

Photo Oliver Mayer   Photo Bernhard Kußmagk

WEBSITES

Verkehrsbetriebe | *Transport Operators*

Aichi Loop Railway – www.aikanrailway.co.jp
Aonami Line – www.aonamiline.co.jp
Echizen Railway – www.echizen-tetudo.co.jp
Fukui Railway – www.fukutetsu.jp
Hakodate City Transportation Department –
    www.city.hakodate.hokkaido.jp/bunya/hakodateshiden
Hokuriku Railway – www.hokutetsu.co.jp
Iyo Railway – www.iyotetsu.co.jp
JR Central – english.jr-central.co.jp
JR East – www.jreast.co.jp/e
JR Hokkaido – www2.jrhokkaido.co.jp/global
JR Shikoku – www.jr-shikoku.co.jp/global/en
Kintetsu Railway – www.kintetsu.co.jp/foreign/english
Linimo – www.linimo.jp/en
Manyosen – www.manyosen.co.jp

Nagano Electric Railway – www.nagaden-net.co.jp
Nagoya City Transportation Bureau – www.kotsu.city.nagoya.jp
Nagoya Railway (Meitetsu) – www.meitetsu.co.jp/eng
Okinawa Urban Monorail - www.yui-rail.co.jp/en
Sapporo City Transportation Bureau – www.city.sapporo.jp/st
Sendai Airport Transit – www.senat.co.jp
Sendai City Transportation Bureau – www.kotsu.city.sendai.jp
Shizuoka Railway - www.shizutetsu.co.jp
Takamatsu-Kotohira Electric Railway – www.kotoden.co.jp
Tokai Transport Service Company (Johoku Line) – www.tkj-i.co.jp
Tosaden Kotsu – www.tosaden.co.jp
Toyama Chiho Railway – www.chitetsu.co.jp
Toyama Light Rail (Portram) – www.t-lr.co.jp
Toyohashi Railway – www.toyotetsu.com
Utsunomiya Light Rail – www.miyarail.co.jp
Yutorito Line – www.guideway.co.jp

Weitere Links unter | *For further websites see* - www.urbanrail.net

Eisenbahnmuseen in Nord- und Zentraljapan | *Railway Museums in North and Central Japan*

Sapporo City Transportation Museum
www.stsp.or.jp
Sapporo Subway Namboku Line – Jieitai-mae Station

Sendai Municipal Tramway Museum
www.kotsu.city.sendai.jp/shiden
Sendai Subway Namboku Line – Tomizawa Station

Nagoya City Tram and Subway Museum
http://www.kotsu.city.nagoya.jp/jp/pc/ENJOY/TRP0000498.htm
Nagoya Municipal Subway Tsurumai Line – Akaike Station

SCMAGLEV and Railway Park
www.museum.jr-central.co.jp
Aonami Line – Kinjo-Futo Station

Meiji-Mura (Open-air museum with tramway)
www.meijimura.com
Meitetsu – Inuyama Station + Bus ► Meiji-Mura

Robert Schwandl Verlag

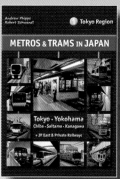

Andrew Phipps & Robert Schwandl:

Metros & Trams in Japan
Band 1 | Vol. 1: Tokyo Region

160 Seiten | pages
Detaillierte Netzpläne | Detailed network maps
250 Farbfotos | colour photos
Text deutsch & English

06/2016
ISBN 978 3 936573 47 3
19,50 EUR

Feat. Tokyo Metro & Toei Subway, Yokohama Subway, Arakawa Line,
Peoplemover & Monorail Systems, JR East, Private Railways, etc.

Band 3: West- & Südjapan | Vol. 3: West & South Japan (ISBN 978 3 936573 54 1) > 2018/19!

SUBWAYS & LIGHT RAIL IN THE U.S.A. Vol. 1 & 2
URBAN RAIL DOWN UNDER

Robert Schwandl:

TRAM ATLAS MITTELEUROPA | CENTRAL EUROPE
Tschechien, Slowakei & Ungarn | Czechia, Slovakia & Hungary

160 Seiten | pages
ca. 300 Fotos | photos
Detaillierte Netzpläne | Detailed network maps
Text deutsch & English

03/2017
ISBN 978 3 936573 48 0
19,50 EUR

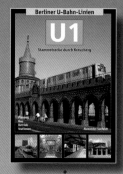

Berlin U2 (2017), U5, U6, U7, U8 & U9

Robert Schwandl:

TRAM ATLAS POLEN | POLAND

144 Seiten | pages
ca. 300 Fotos | photos
Detaillierte Netzpläne | Detailed network maps
Text deutsch & English

~11/2017
ISBN 978 3 936573 50 3
19,50 EUR

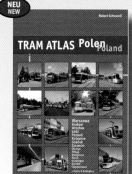

TRAM ATLAS Spanien | Spain, Frankreich | France, etc.
+
METROS IN ... Italien | Italy, Frankreich/France, Holland,
Belgien/Belgium, Portugal

Robert Schwandl:

TRAM ATLAS DEUTSCHLAND / Germany

160 Seiten | pages
Detaillierte Netzpläne | Detailed network maps
200 Farbfotos | colour photos
Text deutsch & English

4. Auflage | 4th edition
06/2016
ISBN 978 3 936573 49 7
19,50 EUR

Frankfurt, Köln/Bonn, Rhein-Ruhr 1,
Rhein-Ruhr 2, Hannover, München,
Nürnberg, Wuppertal

Robert Schwandl Verlag, Hektorstraße 3, 10711 Berlin
Tel. 030 - 3759 1284, Fax 030 - 3759 1285
books@robert-schwandl.de - www.robert-schwandl.de